AF565096

PowerPoint® for Windows® 95 Essentials Revised Edition

Linda Bird

QUE E&T

PowerPoint® for Windows® 95 Essentials Revised Edition

Copyright© 1998 by Que® Education & Training

All rights reserved. Printed in the United States of America. No part of this book may be used or reproduced in any form or by any means, or stored in a database or retrieval system, without prior written permission of the publisher except in the case of brief quotations embodied in critical articles and reviews. Making copies of any part of this book for any purpose other than your own personal use is a violation of United States copyright laws. For information, address Que Education and Training, Macmillan Computer Publishing, 201 W. 103rd Street, Indianapolis, IN 46290.

Library of Congress Catalog No.: 95-71653

ISBN: 1-58076-029-5

This book is sold *as is*, without warranty of any kind, either express or implied, respecting the contents of this book, including but not limited to implied warranties for the book's quality, performance, merchantability, or fitness for any particular purpose. Neither Que Education and Training nor its dealers or distributors shall be liable to the purchaser or any other person or entity with respect to any liability, loss, or damage caused or alleged to be caused directly or indirectly by this book.

99 98 4 3 2 1

Interpretation of the printing code: the rightmost double-digit number is the year of the book's printing; the rightmost single-digit number, the number of the book's printing. For example, a printing code of 96-1 shows that the first printing of the book occurred in 1996.

Screens reproduced in this book were created using Collage Plus from Inner Media, Inc., Hollis, NH.

Publisher: Robert Linsky

Executive Editor: Charles O. Stewart III

Acquisitions Editor: Rob Tidrow

Managing Editor: Caroline Roop

Cover Designer: Ann Jones

Book Designer: Paula A. Carroll

Production Editor: Sally A. Yuska

Production Team: Mary Ann Abramson, Michael Brumitt, Louisa Klucznik, Kevin Laseau, Donna Martin, Nancy C. Price, Brian-Kent Proffitt, SA Springer, Mark Walchle

Developed by Tracy Cramer

Technical review by Liz Reding

Composed in *Stone Serif* and *MCPdigital* by Que Corporation

This book was produced digitally by Macmillan Computer Publishing and manufactured using computer-to-plate technology (a film-less process) by GAC/Shepard Poorman, Indianapolis, Indiana.

About the Author

Linda Bird specializes in corporate and end-user training and support through Software Solutions, her own company. She has successfully trained users representing more than 75 businesses, including several Fortune 500 companies. Her clients include Appalachian Electric Power Co., Borg Warner Automotive, Goodyear, Pillsbury, and Shell Chemical. Her background also includes teaching at Averett College and serving as computer trainer coordinator for Adult Services. She is currently associated with the University of Rio Grande.

Linda has contributed to several books on PowerPoint, Lotus 1-2-3, and Windows 95. She also writes customized training manuals for client businesses.

Linda, a graduate of the University of Wisconsin, lives in Gallipolis, Ohio with her husband, Lonnie, and daughter, Rebecca.

Acknowledgments

Que Education and Training would like to thank the following people: Linda Bird, for creating first-rate instructional material on a tight schedule; Liz Reding, for an outstanding technical review of the manuscript; Rob Tidrow, for the acquisitions efforts on this project in the midst of his own own many writing and development projects; Tracy Cramer, for helping ensure that this book would meet the needs of adults and students learning PowerPoint for Windows 95; Jenny Watson, for managing the production schedule and making sure the project ran smoothly; and Sally Yuska, for editing the text superbly and shepherding the book through production.

Trademark Acknowledgments

All terms mentioned in this book that are known to be trademarks or service marks have been appropriately capitalized. Que cannot attest to the accuracy of this information. Use of a term in this book should not be regarded as affecting the validity of any trademark or service mark.

Microsoft and Windows are registered trademarks of Microsoft Corporation.

Preface

Que Education and Training is the educational publishing imprint of Macmillan Computer Publishing, the world's leading computer book publisher. Macmillan Computer Publishing books have taught more than 20 million people how to be productive with their computers.

This expertise in producing high-quality computer tutorial and reference books is evident in every Que Education and Training title we publish. The same tried-and-true authoring and product development process that makes Macmillan Computer Publishing books best-sellers is used to ensure that training materials from Que Education and Training contain the most accurate and most up-to-date information. Experienced and respected software trainers write and review every manuscript to provide class-tested pedagogy. Quality-assurance editors check every keystroke and command in Que Education and Training books to ensure that instructions are clear and precise.

Above all, Macmillan Computer Publishing and, in turn, Que Education and Training have years of experience in meeting the learning demands of adult users in business and at home. We offer tiered courseware that:

- provides broad-based, flexible training for novices through expert users
- is anchored in the practical and professional needs of adult learners
- includes trainer support in fully annotated *Instructor's Manuals*

The "Essentials" of Hands-On Learning

The *Essentials* series of applications tutorials are appropriate for use in both corporate training and college classroom settings. The *Essentials* are ideal for short courses from a few hours to a full day or more, and meet the needs of adult learners. They can also be used effectively as computer lab applications modules to accompany Que Education and Training's computer concepts text, *Computers in Your Future*, by Marilyn Meyer and Roberta Baber both of Fresno City College, and *Using Computers and Information* by Jack Rochester of Plymouth State College. The *Essentials* enable users to become self-sufficient quickly, encourage self-learning after instruction, maximize learning through clear, complete explanations, and serve as future references. Each Essentials module is two-color throughout and sized at 8-1/2 X 11 inches for maximum screen shot visibility. Each text contains a disk with the data files needed to complete the tutorials and end of chapter exercises.

Project Objectives list what learners will do and learn from the project.

"Why Would I Do This?" shows learners why this material is essential.

Step-by-Step Tutorials simplify the procedures with large screen shots, captions, and annotations.

If There's a Problem... anticipates common pitfalls and advises learners accordingly.

Inside Stuff provides tips and shortcuts for more effective applications.

Key Terms are highlighted in the text and defined in the margin when they first appear.

Jargon Watch offers a layperson's view of "technobabble" in easily understandable terms.

Applying Your Skills contains directed, hands-on exercises to check comprehension and reinforce learning.

Checking Your Skills provides True/False, Multiple Choice, and Screen Labeling exercises.

Data Disks contain files for the text's step-by-step tutorials.

Instructor's Manual

If you have adopted this text for use in a college classroom, you will receive, upon request, an Instructor's Manual on disk at no additional charge. The manual contains suggested curriculum guides for courses of varying lengths, teaching tips, answers to exercises in the "Checking Your Skills" and "Applying Your Skills" sections, test questions and answers, and the data files needed to complete each exercise, along with solution files. Please contact your local representative or write to us on school letterhead at Macmillan Computer Publishing, 201 West 103rd Street, Indianapolis, IN 46290-1097, Attn: S. Dollman.

Also available is a printed *Instructor's Manual*, which is an ideal companion guide to workbooks in the *Essentials* series. It includes teaching concepts and procedures, strategies for structuring content and organizing the class, ideas for adapting the material for various audiences, pre-training assessment and post-class evaluation tools, and much more. The backbone of the *Instructor's Manual* is a heavily annotated student workbook that serves as an indispensable resource for trainers. New instructors will appreciate the tips that help them teach a topic successfully for the first time. Experienced instructors will appreciate fresh approaches to teaching familiar topics.

Contents at a Glance

Table of Contents

Note to the Learner

Welcome to the *PowerPoint for Windows 95 Essentials* workbook! The *Essentials* series consists of student workbooks and instructor manuals for use in instructor-led classes.

If this is your first experience with instructor-led training, you're in for a real treat. Instructor-led, hands-on training is the fastest and most efficient means of teaching software applications. Your instructor is an expert in this application, so he/she can answer your questions and pass on valuable advice about using the software.

What all this means is that with the use of these materials, you'll be up and running in the shortest amount of time possible.

Who Should Use This Book?

The *Essentials* workbooks are designed to be used in the classroom and corporate training environment. The projects in the *Essentials* workbooks are designed to teach only the "bare essentials"—just enough for you to get the job done.

To ensure your success with PowerPoint for Windows 95, you should have a basic understanding of the computer. This workbook assumes that you are familiar with the keyboard, monitor, floppy drives, and mouse. You should also be familiar with the basics of Windows 95. For a quick review, consult the appendix titled "Working with Windows 95." This workbook *does not* assume any prior knowledge of the PowerPoint for Windows 95 program.

How To Use This Book

Because an instructor will be present in the classroom, the *Essentials* workbooks contain a minimum of explanation and the maximum of step-by-step directions. As you begin each project, you are told what you want to accomplish and why. Realistic examples are given so that you can quickly relate to the task and see the value of completing the project.

Each project is a series of separate lessons with detailed instructions to guide you through the completion of a task. After each numbered step, a brief explanation of the action is given to help you really understand "why you just did that." At the end of each lesson, tips and shortcuts are given to satisfy the more curious reader. A Project Summary table is included at the end of each project to give you a quick reference you can use when you need a quick refresher.

To make your learning experience as enjoyable as possible, the projects are task-oriented, and they use real-world, business examples.

Task-Oriented Lessons

The workbook lessons are *task-oriented*, which means you will actually accomplish a task as you work through the lesson. For example, rather than merely *reading* about moving and copying text, you learn how to rearrange your text by actually moving and copying sentences in a paragraph. Likewise, you learn how to format documents by changing the margins, changing the line spacing, setting justification, changing the font and font size, adding page numbers and a header.

Once you get past the first two projects, the remaining projects are independent of the others, so they can be completed in any order. If your time is limited, you can pick and choose your projects, depending on which concepts you need to learn right away.

Real-World Examples

Concepts are illustrated with realistic situations that you would encounter in a workplace. The more realistic the examples are, the easier it is for the reader to relate to the situation. For example, in the lesson in which you complete a newsletter, the sample file contains information that you would find in a typical corporate newsletter. You work with letters to conference attendees, status reports, annual reports, and job descriptions, rather than letters to book clubs, and public domain documents, such as the Declaration of Independence.

Conventions Used in This Book

The *Essentials* series use the following conventions to make it easier for you to understand the material:

- Text that you are to type appears in **color and boldface**.
- Underlined letters in menu names, menu commands, and dialog box options appear in a different color. Examples are the **F**ile menu, the **O**pen command, and the File **n**ame list box.
- Important words or phrases appear in *italic* the first time they are discussed.
- *Key terms* are defined in the margin as soon as they are introduced.
- On-screen text and messages appear in a `special font`.
- *If you have problems...* boxes contain troubleshooting tips that anticipate common pitfalls. These are designed to help you solve your own problems so you can keep up with the rest of the class.
- Jargon Watch boxes are used to define a group of key terms used in the project.
- Inside Stuff boxes contain tips and shortcuts to help you use the application more effectively.

Project 1

Getting Started with PowerPoint

Objectives

In this project, you learn how to

- Launch PowerPoint
- Create a New Presentation
- Change the View
- Move among Slides in the Outline View
- Move among Slides in the Slide View
- Move among Slides in Slide Show
- Save a Presentation
- Get Help
- Close the Presentation and Exit PowerPoint

Why Would I Do This?

Presentation Graphics Program
A software application that helps you structure, design, and present information.

PowerPoint is a powerful *presentation graphics program*. Its primary purpose is to help computer users create professional-looking handouts, signs, overheads, organization charts, and so on, effectively and efficiently. Whether you are creating a marketing plan, reporting progress on a project, or simply conducting a meeting, PowerPoint will help you to quickly create great presentations. You can add text, clip art, sounds, movie clips, and tables to strengthen your arguments. You can also change the colors of the text, as well as the design and layout of the background for a stronger visual effect.

You can deliver PowerPoint presentations in various ways—using printed handouts, 35mm slides, or overhead transparencies. One of the most popular ways to use PowerPoint is to create an *electronic slide show*. The show can be run on a computer monitor or using an LCD panel to project the image from your computer onto a large screen.

Lesson 1: Launching PowerPoint

Launch
The process of starting a program in Windows 95.

You can start PowerPoint in a number of ways. The easiest method is to use the Start button on the Windows 95 Taskbar, and then choose PowerPoint from the **P**rograms menu. In this lesson, you start PowerPoint using this method.

To Launch PowerPoint

1. **Move the mouse pointer to the Start button at the left edge of the Taskbar and click the left mouse button.**

   A pop-up menu appears above the Start button.

2. **Move the mouse pointer to the Programs item.**

   A listing of available programs appears (see Figure 1.1).

3. **Move the mouse pointer to Microsoft PowerPoint and click the left mouse button.**

   PowerPoint is loaded into the computer's working area (commonly called memory or *Random Access Memory)*. Unless the feature has been turned off, a Tip of the Day dialog box appears in the opening screen (see Figure 1.2).

Random Access Memory (RAM)
The temporary storage space that the computer uses for programs it's currently working with.

If You Have Problems...

If you don't see Microsoft PowerPoint as a program listing, look for the Microsoft Office folder. Move the mouse pointer to the PowerPoint listing in the folder and click to start the program.

Figure 1.1
The Programs menu and associated file folders.

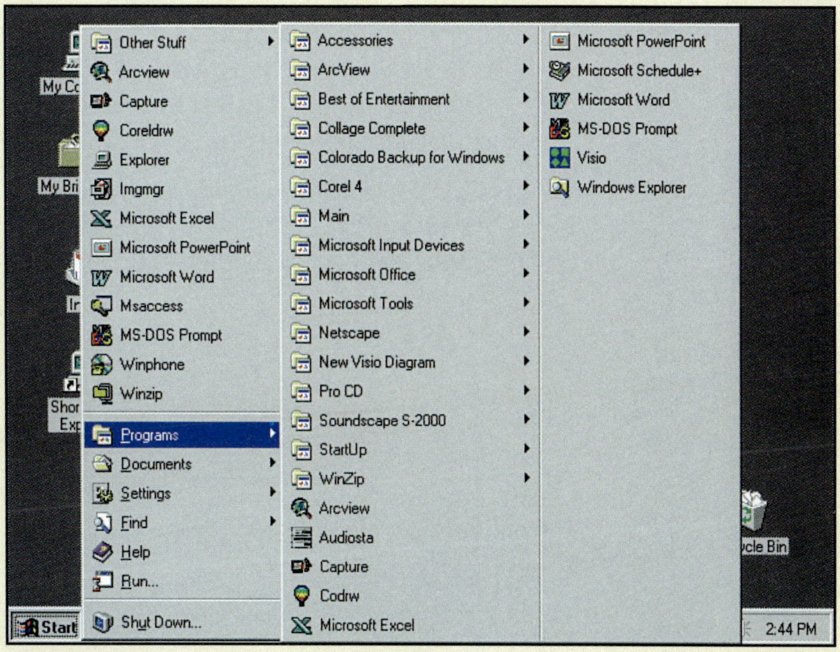

Figure 1.2
The PowerPoint opening screen with the Tip of the Day dialog box.

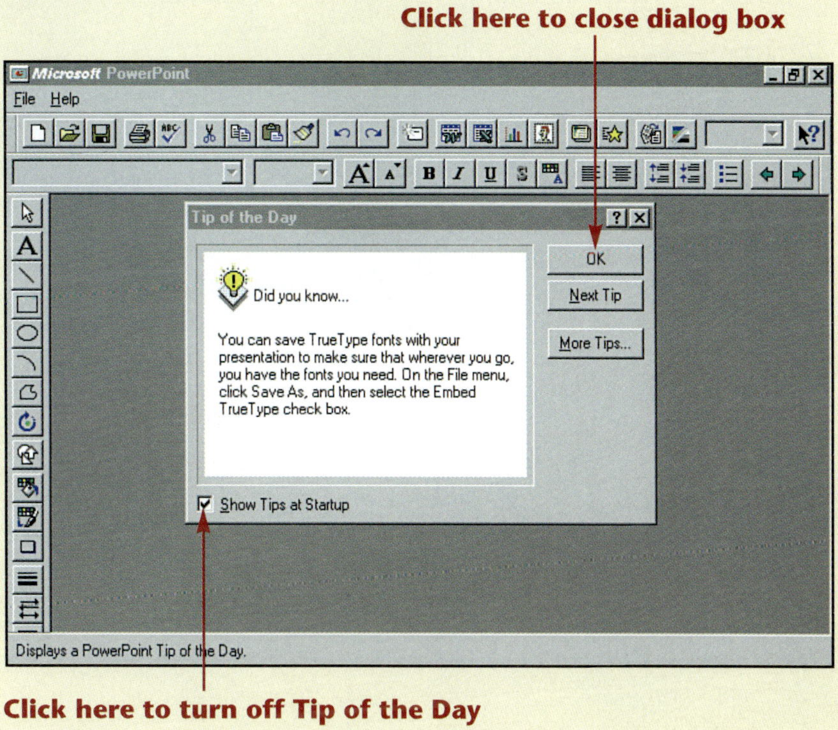

continues

To Launch PowerPoint (continued)

4 Click the Next Tip button if you would like to view more helpful hints on using PowerPoint effectively. When you are finished viewing tips, click OK.

The PowerPoint start-up dialog box appears, giving you the choice of either creating a new presentation, or opening one that was created and saved earlier—an existing presentation (see Figure 1.3).

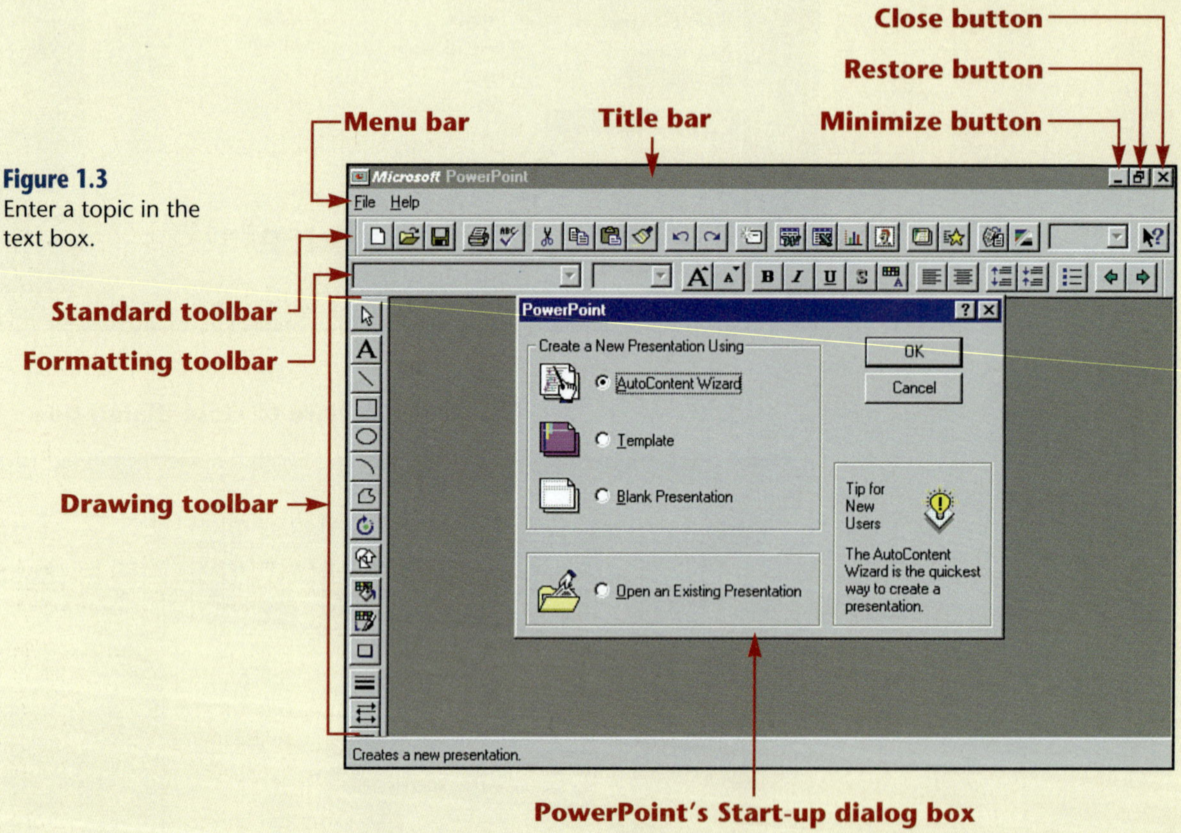

Figure 1.3
Enter a topic in the text box.

5 Note the parts of the PowerPoint screen, which are similar to other Windows programs.

Leave the PowerPoint screen open for the next lesson, where you create a new presentation.

INSIDE Stuff

You can also start PowerPoint by double-clicking the PowerPoint Shortcut icon on the Windows 95 desktop. Alternatively, click the right mouse button while resting the mouse pointer over the icon, and then choose Open from the short-cut menu that appears.

Jargon Watch

PowerPoint for Windows 95 is a type of software known as **presentation graphics software**. Programs of this type help you quickly create presentations that can include text, pictures, graphs, and other objects. Each of the screens of information in PowerPoint are referred to as a **slide**.

Once created, the presentation can be used in several ways. You can **output**, or produce the slides on your printer, just like any other document. But PowerPoint also gives you the ability to create **electronic slide shows**. Electronic slide shows, like the name implies, are similar to slide shows created with a camera and film, but are created and displayed on the computer instead. PowerPoint's electronic slide shows can be viewed directly on the computer's monitor. They can also be shown on a large screen using an **LCD Panel** and overhead projector hooked up to the computer.

Lesson 2: Creating a New Presentation

AutoContent Wizard
A tool that guides you through the steps of a proposed presentation and includes suggestions for content.

Template
In a program, a document that includes the text needed to create standardized documents. The template can be used to automate the creation of these documents in the future.

PowerPoint's built-in presentations and *templates* help you create slides quickly. PowerPoint's *AutoContent Wizard,* a built-in tool that contains sample content for creating presentations, such as recommending a strategy, conducting training, or reporting progress. The AutoContent Wizard guides you through the steps of planning a presentation by suggesting slide types, formats, and contents. Table 1.1 lists the available options in the PowerPoint start-up dialog box.

Table 1.1 Creating and Opening Presentations

Use	To
AutoContent Wizard	Create a presentation with sample content already included. The Wizard is a tutorial program that helps you create a presentation by answering a series of questions.
Template	Create a presentation based on one of 32 professionally designed slide layouts.
Blank Presentation	Create a presentation from scratch using a blank slide and default font settings.
Open an Existing Presentation	Open a presentation that has previously been created and saved.

In the following exercise, you use the AutoContent Wizard to create a presentation to recommend that your organization upgrade to PowerPoint for Windows 95.

To Use the AutoContent Wizard to Create a New Presentation

1 In the PowerPoint start-up dialog box open from Lesson 1, click the AutoContent Wizard option button (if it's not already selected), and then choose OK.

The first AutoContent Wizard dialog box appears, as shown in Figure 1.4.

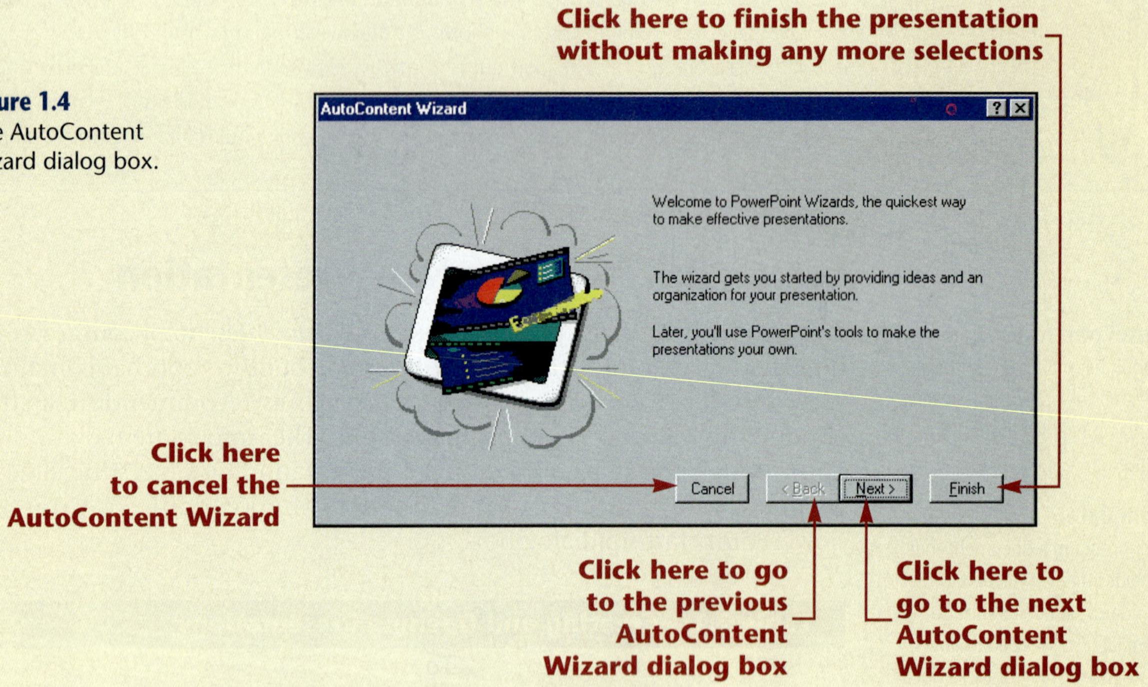

Figure 1.4
The AutoContent Wizard dialog box.

2 Click the Next Button.

The next AutoContent Wizard dialog box appears.

3 In the What is your name? text box, type your name and press Tab.

If your computer is set up specifically for you, your name will already appear in the What is your name? text box. Pressing Tab moves the insertion point to the What are you going to talk about? text box.

4 Type Upgrading to PowerPoint 95 in the What are you going to talk about? text box, then press Tab.

This enters the title of your presentation and moves you to the Other information you'd like to display text box. For this example, enter the name of your company or the name of your school (see Figure 1.5).

Figure 1.5
The AutoContent Wizard dialog box.

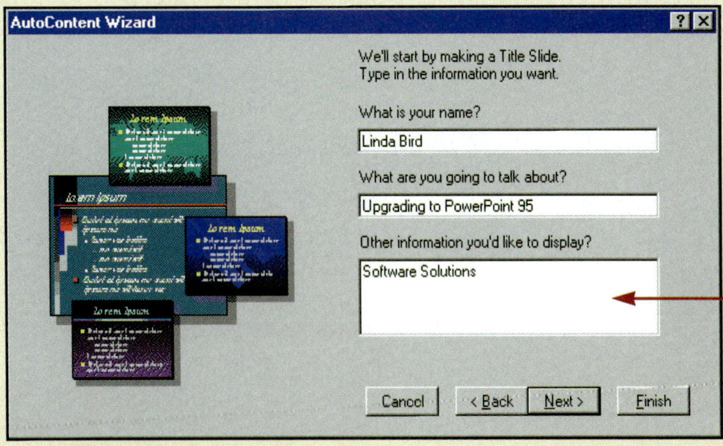

Type additional information for the first slide here

5 Click the Next button.

The next AutoContent Wizard dialog box appears, where you can select the type of presentation you want to give (see Figure 1.6).

Figure 1.6
Select the type of presentation you want to give in this dialog box.

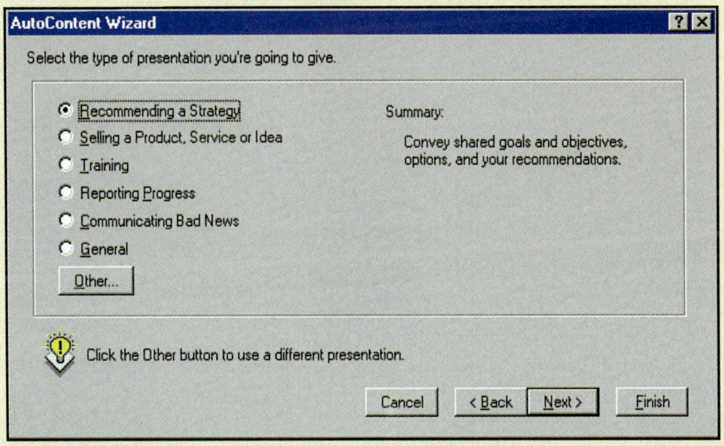

6 Select the Recommending a Strategy option button, then click the Next button.

The next dialog box appears, where you can select options relating to the look and length of the presentation. In this lesson, you want a presentation with a professional look and less than 30 minutes in length.

7 Click the option buttons for Professional and 30 minutes or less; then click the Next button.

The next AutoContent dialog box appears, where you can decide what type of output will be used and whether you want to print handouts. For this example, you want to create an on-screen presentation but don't need handouts.

continues

To Use the AutoContent Wizard to Create a New Presentation (continued)

8 Choose the options for an on-screen presentation and no handouts; then choose Next.

The final AutoContent Wizard dialog box appears, indicated by a finish flag.

9 Read the information displayed, then click the Finish button.

PowerPoint creates the presentation and shows the presentation window on-screen in the Slide View (see Figure 1.7). The information you typed in the AutoContent Wizard dialog box is inserted in the first slide in the presentation. The rest of the presentation is created as a series of slides with major topics and sub points. These suggested topics serve as a guideline for your presentation.

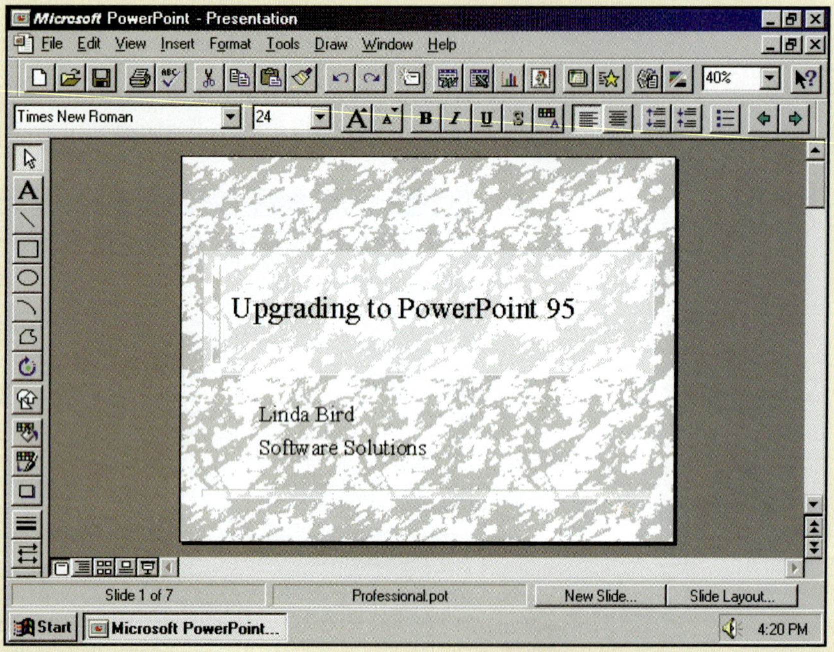

Figure 1.7
The presentation window in Slide View.

Keep this presentation open for the next lesson, where you learn how to use different views.

You can also create a new presentation by clicking the New button on the Standard toolbar or choosing **F**ile, **N**ew from the menu bar. Once **F**ile, **N**ew is chosen, you can click the Presentations tab to find the AutoContent Wizard button.

Lesson 3: Changing the View

Once you have created a presentation, you can view it in a number of different ways: Slide View, Outline View, Slide Sorter View, Notes Pages View, or Slide Show. Table 1.2 describes the purpose of each of these views.

Table 1.2 PowerPoint's Presentation Views

Use	To
Slide View	Work with one slide at a time, add or change text and graphics, or draw shapes.
Outline View	Work with only the slide title and text in traditional outline form.
Slide Sorter View	Display miniature versions of all slides, including texts and graphics. Use this view to change the order of slides, add transitions, and set timings for electronic slide shows.
Notes Pages View	Create speaker's notes for each slide.
Slide Show	Display your presentation as an on-screen electronic slide show.

The two most commonly used screen views, especially as you develop the presentation, are Outline View and Slide View. Outline View displays only text, enabling you to make quick and easy changes to the presentation's text content. Outline View is also handy for making text changes because several slides are shown at one time.

In contrast to Outline View, Slide View displays only one slide at a time, but includes graphics and charts as well as text. This makes it a good choice to use when you want to modify those elements on a slide.

The sample presentation should currently be in Slide View. Now try changing the view of the presentation.

To Change the View

1. **In the presentation you created in Lesson 2, move the mouse pointer to any of the view buttons on the left-hand side of the status bar.**

   In a second or two, a ToolTip appears, containing the name of the button (see Figure 1.8).

continues

To Change the View (continued)

Figure 1.8
The View buttons with an active ToolTip.

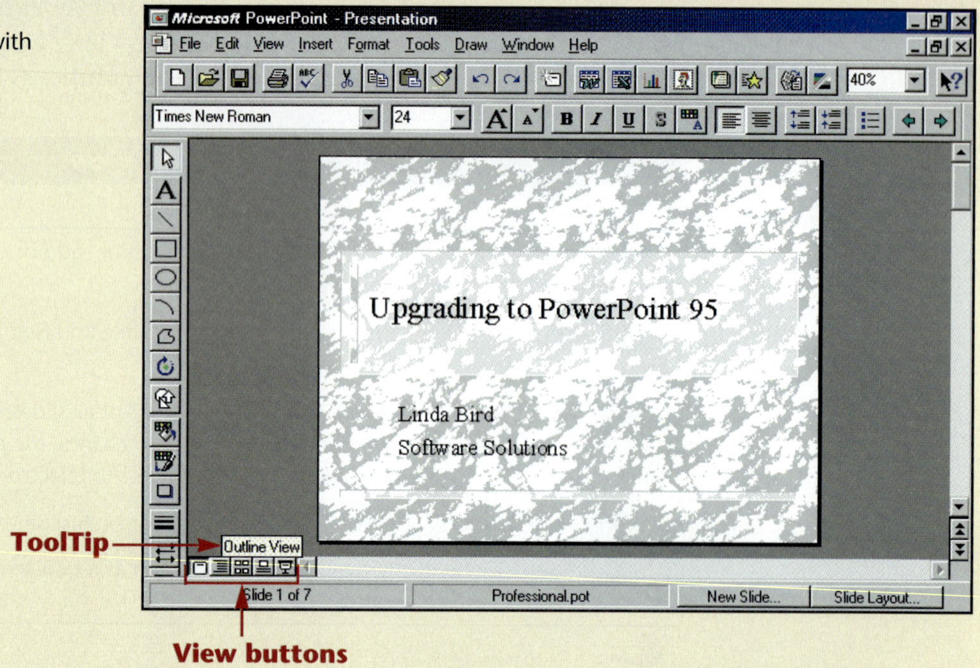

If you have problems...

If the ToolTips don't appear, choose **V**iew, **T**oolbars. In the Toolbars dialog box, click the **S**how ToolTips check box, then choose OK.

2 Move the mouse pointer to each of the five view buttons.

A ToolTip shows you the name of each button. In addition, a more complete explanation of the button's function is displayed on the status bar.

3 Click the Slide View button.

Only the current slide is shown on-screen, including the colors, text, and graphics.

4 Click the Outline View button.

The Outline View of the sample presentation is displayed. This view is the best for getting an overview of the presentation's contents. Notice that this view has its own toolbar on the left edge of the screen (see Figure 1.9).

Figure 1.9
The sample presentation in the Outline View.

Outlining toolbar

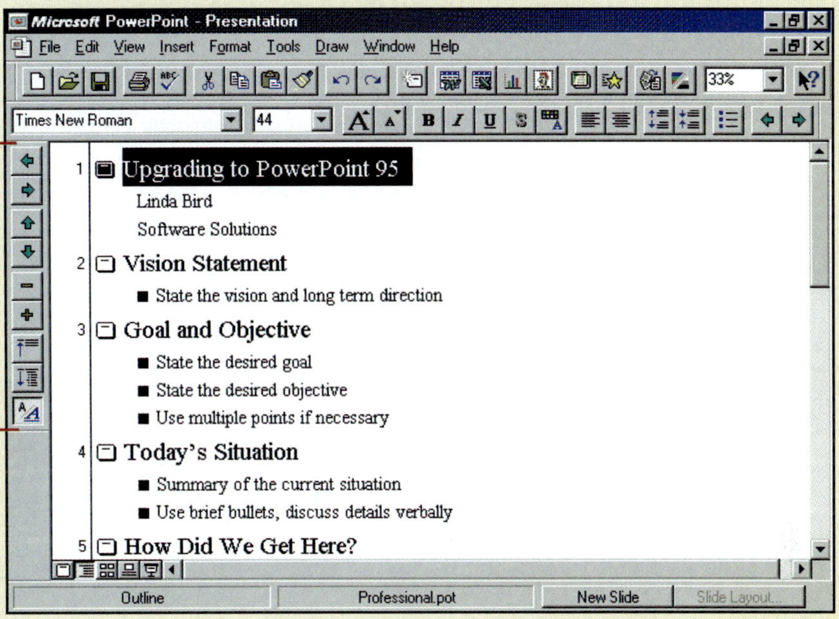

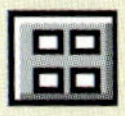

❺ **Click the Slide Sorter View button.**

You can now see the first six slides of the presentation on-screen (see Figure 1.10). The Slide Sorter View has its own toolbar.

Figure 1.10
The Slide Sorter View.

Slide Sorter toolbar

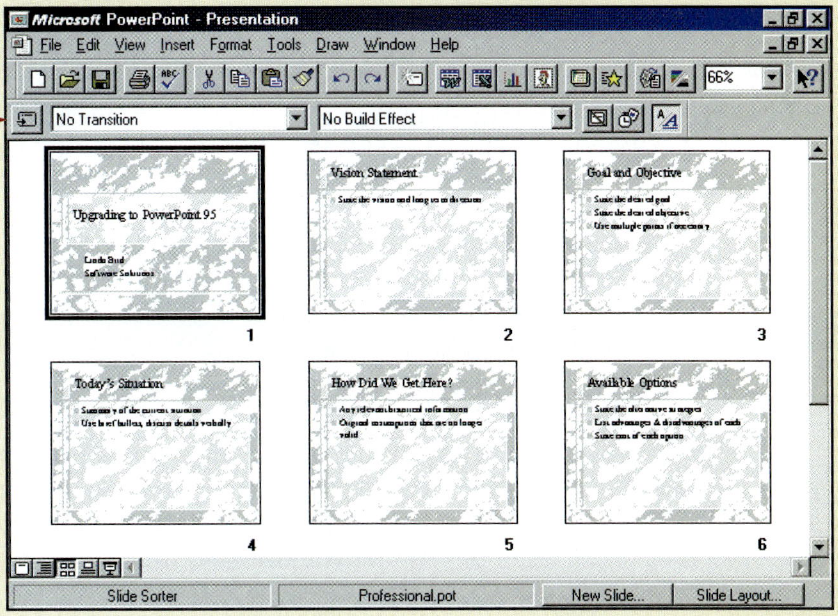

continues

To Change the View (continued)

6 Click the Notes Pages View button.

The slide displays the notes page, which includes a miniature version of the slide, along with space for speaker notes you write. You can print these notes and then use them to remember key points while giving your presentation.

7 Click the Slide Show button.

The electronic slide show version of the presentation begins.

8 Click the left mouse button to advance through the slides.

Once you have viewed each slide, PowerPoint returns you to the Notes Pages View—the last view you used before starting the slide show. Keep this sample presentation open for the next lesson, where you learn how to move among slides in the Outline View.

When you are running a slide show, you can end a slide show before you have viewed all the slides. To do this, press Esc.

Lesson 4: Moving among Slides in the Outline View

The Outline View is the most convenient way to enter text and modify information created by one of the Wizards. Because many presentations are developed in this view, it is important to know efficient methods of getting around.

Try to move among slides in the sample presentation now.

To Move among Slides in the Outline View

1 Click the Outline View button.

The outline for the sample presentation appears. Notice that not all the text can be displayed on-screen at once. Also note that PowerPoint provides a vertical scroll bar on the right side of the screen that you use to move among the slides. (see Figure 1.11).

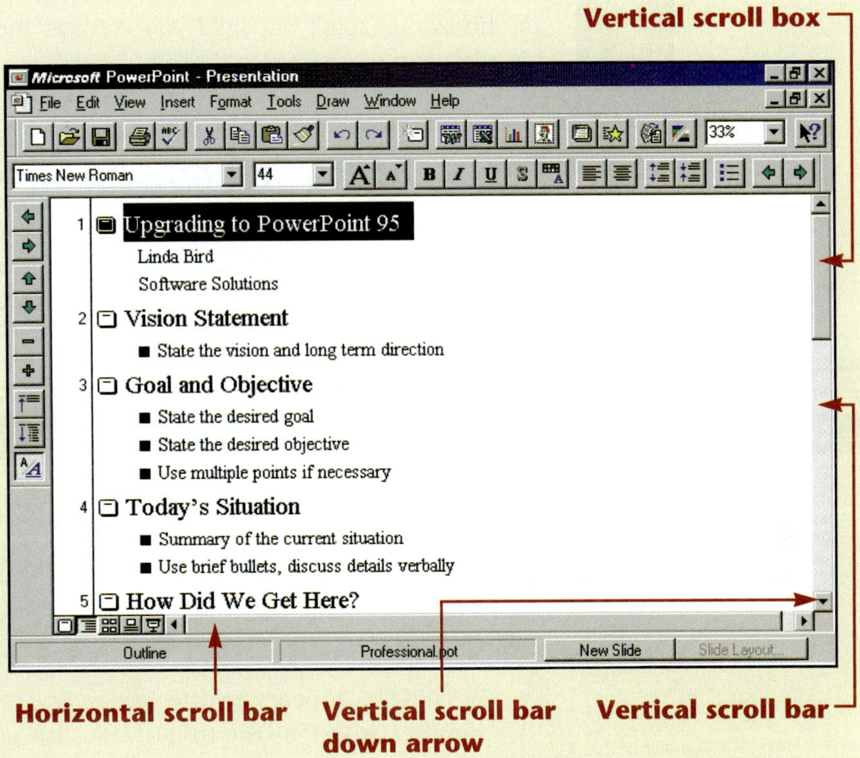

Figure 1.11
The presentation in the Outline View and the scroll bars.

❷ **Click the down arrow located at the bottom of the vertical scroll bar.**

The text on the screen scrolls up, moving your viewpoint downward. Technically, clicking the down arrow advances the presentation forward one line at a time. However, if you press and hold down the left mouse button while pointing to the arrow, rather than just clicking it, the presentation scrolls continually.

❸ **Press and hold down the mouse button while pointing to the up arrow.**

The scroll box moves to the top of the scroll bar, indicating that you have moved to the top of the presentation.

❹ **Click the vertical scroll bar below the vertical scroll box. The presentation scrolls down one screen (rather than one line) at a time.**

❺ **Click in the vertical scroll bar area above the vertical scroll box. The presentation scrolls up one screen at a time.**

❻ **Press ↓.**

The cursor advances one line at a time through the presentation. In the same manner, pressing ↑ moves the cursor backwards through the presentation.

Make sure that you have moved to the beginning of the sample presentation, and leave it open for the next lesson.

Inside Stuff

If the text extends beyond the right side of the screen, click the right arrow in the horizontal scroll bar until you can see the text. Click the horizontal scroll bar's left arrow to move to the left.

Lesson 5: Moving among Slides in the Slide View

In the Slide View, you design and modify one slide at a time. In this lesson, you learn how to move among the slides in a presentation. You can use either the mouse or the keyboard to move around the presentation in the Slide View. Use whichever method is most efficient for you.

To Move among Slides in the Slide View

1. **In the open sample presentation, click the Slide View button.**

   The presentation is shown in the Slide View, with the first slide displayed.

2. **Click the vertical scroll box, and drag it up and down slowly.**

   A ToolTip appears to the left of the scroll bar. It shows the slide number as well as the title of the slide (see Figure 1.12).

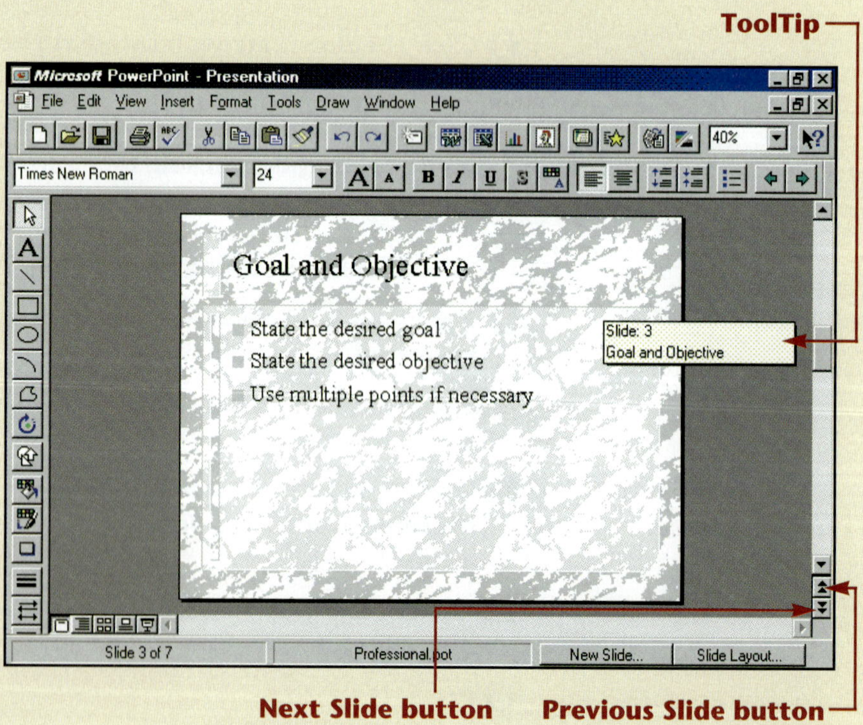

Figure 1.12
The ToolTip displaying the slide number and title of the slide.

3. **Stop at Slide 3, Goal and Objective, then release the mouse button.**

   Whatever slide is shown in the ToolTip becomes the active slide, shown in the Slide View.

4. **Drag the vertical scroll box to the first slide in the presentation, Upgrading to PowerPoint 95.**

   Slide 1 becomes active.

5. **Move the mouse pointer to the double up and down arrows at the bottom of the vertical scroll bar.**

   A ToolTip appears, indicating that these buttons will move the presentation to the next slide or to the previous slide.

6. **Click the Next Slide button.**

   The second slide is shown in Slide View.

7. **Click the Previous Slide button.**

   The first slide is now displayed. Leave this presentation open for the next lesson, where you learn to move among slides in Slide Show.

INSIDE Stuff

If you prefer to use the keyboard rather than the mouse to move around in the Slide View, press PgUp and PgDn to move forward and back one slide at a time. Press Ctrl+Home to return to the first slide; press Ctrl+End to move to the last slide.

Table 1.3 lists the different mouse and keyboard commands to move around a presentation in the Slide View.

Table 1.3 Commands Used to Move around in the Slide View

To Move to	Use This Keyboard Command	Use This Mouse Command
First Slide	Ctrl+Home	Drag the vertical scroll bar box to the top of the scroll bar.
Last Slide	Ctrl+End	Drag the vertical scroll bar box to the bottom of the scroll bar.
Next Slide	PgDn	Click the Next Slide button at the bottom of the vertical scroll bar.
Previous Slide	PgUp	Click the Previous Slide button at the bottom of the vertical scroll bar.

Lesson 6: Moving among Slides in Slide Show

Shortcut menu
A context-sensitive menu that is activated by right-clicking the mouse on an object or area of the screen.

In Lesson 3, you learned how to activate an electronic slide show using the Slide Show button. In this lesson, you learn special commands to move around in Slide Show. These commands are especially useful when you are running PowerPoint's slide show on an LCD display. An efficient way to control a running slide show is to use the slide show *shortcut menu*.

Now try moving among slides in Slide Show.

To Move among Slides in Slide Show

1 Make sure that the active slide is Slide 1 (the title slide) in the sample presentation.

2 Click the Slide Show button.

The slide show begins. Notice that the first slide shown is Slide 1 (the slide that was active when you selected the Slide Show button). If Slide 4 had been active when you clicked the Slide Show button, the slide show would have started from that point.

3 Click the left mouse button.

The slide show advances to the next slide.

4 Click the right mouse button.

A pop-up menu is shown, with choices related to running a slide show (see Figure 1.13). Any time you click the right mouse button, a shortcut menu is activated. Shortcut menus contain several common commands from which you can quickly choose. Although shortcut menus are activated by pressing the right mouse button, choices are made from the resulting menu with the left mouse button.

Figure 1.13
The Slide Show shortcut menu.

5 From the shortcut menu, use the left mouse button to choose Previous.

The presentation moves back to Slide 1.

6 Click the right mouse button to display the shortcut menu, choose Go To, then choose Slide Navigator from the submenu.

The Slide Navigator dialog box appears, as shown in Figure 1.14. This dialog box shows all the slide numbers and titles in the presentation. If all the slides don't fit in the dialog box, a vertical scroll bar appears on the right side.

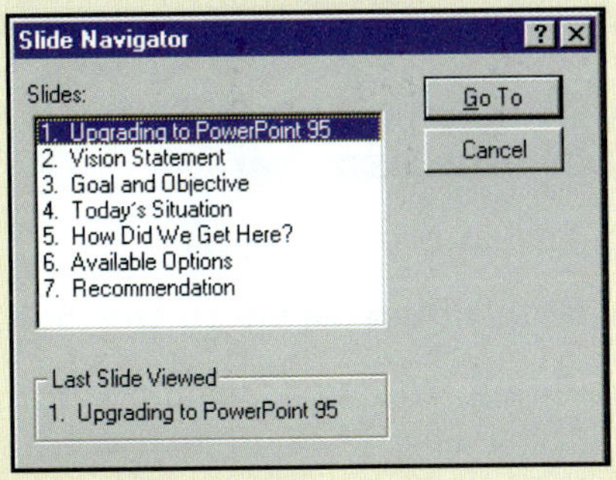

Figure 1.14
The Slide Navigator dialog box.

7 Double-click Slide 5, How Did We Get Here?.

The presentation jumps to Slide 5.

8 Right-click the mouse to activate the shortcut menu, then choose End Show.

PowerPoint returns you to Slide View. Keep this sample presentation open for the next lesson.

If you have problems...

If a shortcut menu doesn't appear when you right-click the mouse, choose **T**ools, **O**ptions from the menu bar. Click the View tab and click Popup Menu on Right Mouse Click check box to activate it.

Lesson 7: Saving a Presentation

So far, the presentation you have developed and worked with exists only in memory—the working area of the computer. If the power was interrupted to your computer, you would lose the presentation because everything in memory would disappear. However, if you save the presentation to one of the computer's permanent storage areas (the floppy disk, the hard drive, or a network drive), you will have a stored copy. This saved file can be opened, used, and revised at a later time. When you first save a file, you must tell PowerPoint the name and the storage location for the presentation, just as you would label a file before placing it in a filing cabinet.

To save a presentation, you can choose the **F**ile, **S**ave or **F**ile, Save **A**s command. Use the **F**ile, Save **A**s command when you save a presentation for the first time or when you change the name, drive, or directory of a saved presentation. Use the **F**ile, **S**ave command to save a previously saved presentation with the same name, drive, and directory.

In this lesson, you save the sample presentation to your floppy disk drive. Before starting the tutorial, make sure that you have a formatted disk in drive A.

To Save a Presentation

1 Make sure the sample presentation is open, then choose File, Save As from the menu bar.

The File Save dialog box appears.

2 Click the drop-down arrow to the right of the Save in list box.

A list (including icons) of available locations on your computer is shown.

3 Click the icon that represents drive A.

Drive A is selected as the storage location for your presentation (see Figure 1.15).

Click here to select where to save your file

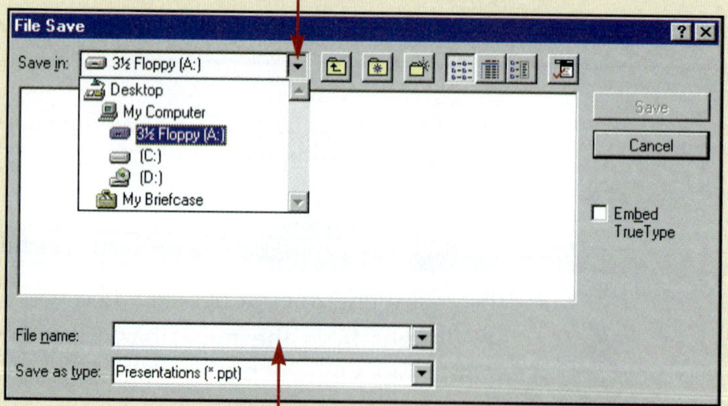

Enter the file name here

Figure 1.15 The File Save dialog box.

4 Move the mouse pointer to the File name text box.

The cursor changes to an I-beam, indicating that this is an area that can accept text.

5 Click in the text box with the left mouse button.

This changes the I-beam to an insertion point so that you can enter text.

6 Type Upgrade and click the Save button.

This saves the presentation as a file named Upgrade to the floppy disk drive. You now have a permanent copy stored for later use.

You can type any name you want using Windows 95 file-naming rules. You can include spaces as well as upper- and lowercase letters. PowerPoint automatically adds the PPT file extension, so you don't need to type it.

If you make changes to the presentation (either now or later), you can update the stored file simply by choosing **F**ile, **S**ave from the menu or clicking the Save button. The file is then updated with the same name and location. The existing file is replaced, rather than a second copy made. Keep this presentation open for the next lesson.

INSIDE Stuff

In previous versions of PowerPoint, file names are limited to eight characters or less. In PowerPoint for Windows 95, you can use up to 255 characters to name your presentations, making it easier to find files. Examples of descriptive file names include "Business Plan" and "Sales Projections."

Lesson 8: Getting Help

To find a quick solution to a problem, you can use PowerPoint's on-line Help. The Help feature is useful when you can't remember how to complete a task or you simply want to learn more about the software.

PowerPoint has two main ways of providing you with help: the **H**elp menu and *context-sensitive* help.

In this lesson, you use the **H**elp menu to get help.

To Get Help

1 Click Help on the menu bar, then choose Microsoft PowerPoint Help Topics.

The Help Topics: Microsoft PowerPoint dialog box appears, as shown in Figure 1.16). Notice the tabs representing the different categories of help available: Contents, Index, Find, and Answer Wizard.

continues

To Get Help (continued)

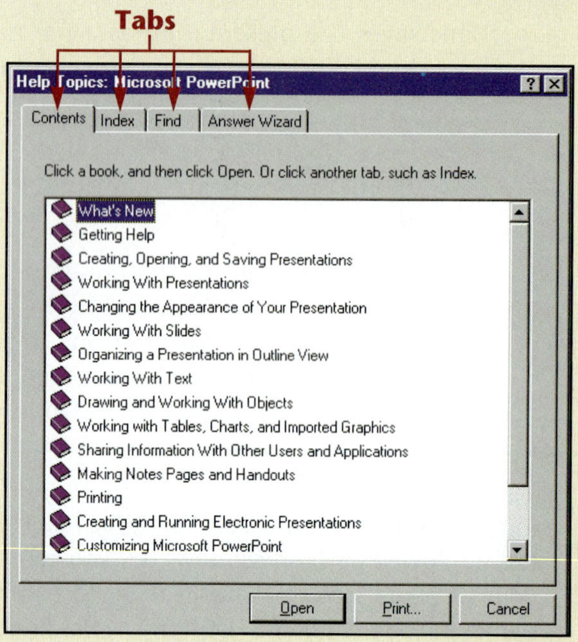

Figure 1.16
The Help Topics: Microsoft PowerPoint dialog box.

2 Click the Index tab.

The Index page is moved to the front. Notice that the blinking insertion point is already in the **T**ype the first few letters of the word you're looking for text box. In the **C**lick the index entry you want, and then click Display list box is an alphabetical listing of help topics.

3 In the Type the first few letters of the word you're looking for text box, type Creating Presentations.

The topic creating presentations is highlighted, as shown in Figure 1.17.

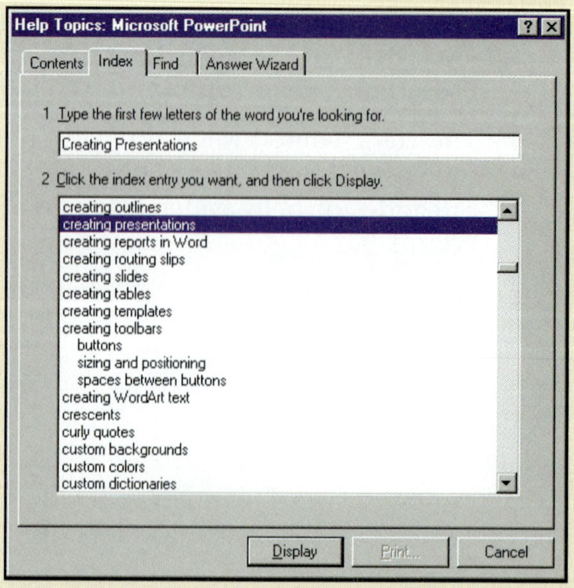

Figure 1.17
The Index page of the Help Topics dialog box.

4 Click the Display button.

A Topics Found dialog box appears, with a list of topics related to creating presentations. Note that the first item on the list, Create a new presentation (Microsoft PowerPoint), is already highlighted.

5 Click the Display button.

This displays an information dialog box on the selected topic.

6 Click the Help Topics button.

This returns you to the Microsoft PowerPoint: Help Topics dialog box.

7 Click the Contents tab.

A list of categories is shown on the Contents page, each indicated by a "book" icon (see Figure 1.18).

8 Double-click the Getting Help book icon.

Subtopics are listed, as shown in Figure 1.18.

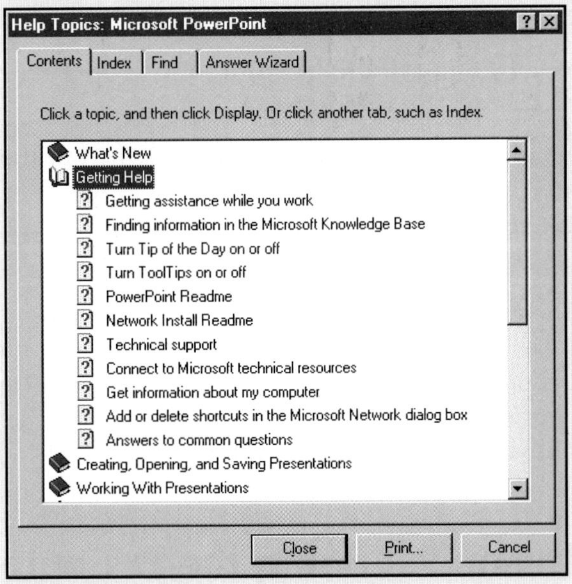

Figure 1.18
The Contents page of the Help Topics dialog box.

9 Double-click the first subtopic, Getting assistance while you work.

A Microsoft PowerPoint for Windows 95 dialog box appears, as shown in Figure 1.19.

continues

To Get Help (continued)

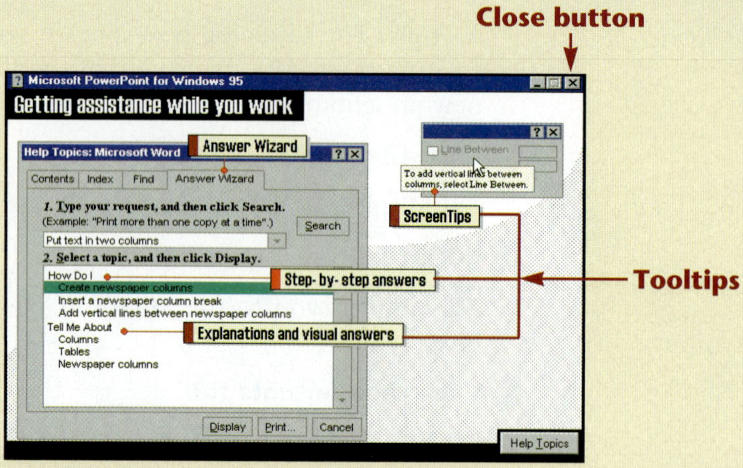

Figure 1.19
The Getting assistance while you work dialog box.

10. **Move the mouse pointer to any of the yellow ToolTip boxes until you see the mouse pointer change to a helping hand; then click the left mouse button.**

    Information related to that topic is shown.

11. **Click the Help Topics Close button in the upper right corner of the dialog box.**

    Help closes and you are returned to the presentation. Leave the presentation open for the next lesson.

The Answer Wizard is an interactive tutorial program that leads you through a series of steps when you type in the name of the command you are trying to perform. Access the Answer Wizard from the **H**elp menu, type the command you want to learn about (such as saving a file), then choose **D**isplay. The Answer Wizard will lead you through the steps to performing the action.

Lesson 9: Closing the Presentation and Exiting PowerPoint

When you have finished working on your presentation, you will want to close it—just as you clear your desk at work to make room for another project. PowerPoint will prompt you to save the presentation if you haven't already done so (or have made changes since the last time it was saved). Choosing to save (or update) the presentation is similar to putting an updated copy of a project in a filing cabinet. Closing a presentation without saving it is the same as throwing away papers on your desk that you don't need anymore.

Exiting the entire program is like leaving your office. In PowerPoint, exiting the program clears it from memory and returns you to the Windows 95 desktop.

Now close the presentation you have worked on in this project, and exit PowerPoint.

To Close a Presentation and Exit PowerPoint

1. **With the presentation open from the previous lesson, choose File, Close.**

   If you have not made any changes to the Upgrade presentation file since you saved it, the file closes and the blank working area in the opening PowerPoint window appears. If you have made changes since you saved the file, the Microsoft PowerPoint dialog box appears, asking if you would like to save changes to your presentation (see Figure 1.20).

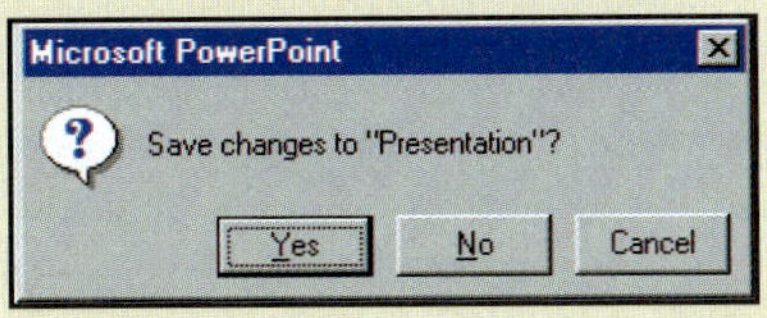

Figure 1.20
The Microsoft PowerPoint save changes dialog box.

2. **Choose No.**

   The Upgrade presentation closes, without saving any changes you may have made.

3. **From the menu bar, choose File, Exit.**

   PowerPoint is cleared from memory and you are returned to the Windows 95 desktop.

INSIDE Stuff

Two close buttons are located in the upper right corner of the screen. Clicking the lower Close button closes the presentation, while clicking the upper Close button exits you from PowerPoint.

Project Summary

To Do This	Use This Command
Start PowerPoint	Click the Start button, then click **P**rograms and choose PowerPoint from the list.
Create a new presentation	Choose **F**ile, **N**ew.
Use different views	Click the View buttons located on the status bar.
Move to the first slide	Drag the vertical scroll box to the top of the vertical scroll bar.
Move to the last slide	Drag the scroll box to the bottom of the vertical scroll bar.

To Do This	Use This Command
Move to the next slide	Click the Next Slide button at the bottom of the vertical scroll bar.
Move to the previous slide	Click the Previous Slide button at the bottom of the vertical scroll bar.
End a running slide show	Choose End Show from the shortcut menu.
Save a presentation	Choose **S**ave or Save **A**s from the **F**ile menu.
Get Help	Choose **H**elp from the menu bar.
Close a Presentation	Choose **F**ile, **C**lose from the menu bar.
Exit PowerPoint	Choose **F**ile, E**x**it from the menu bar.

Applying Your Skills

At the end of each project in PowerPoint for Windows 95 Essentials, you can learn how to apply your PowerPoint skills to various business and collegiate situations. The following exercises enable you to practice the skills you have learned in this project. Take a few minutes to work through these exercises now.

Creating a Presentation

Because you have attended a PowerPoint class, everyone in your department now considers you a computer guru. As such, your co-workers want you to convince management to buy the latest and greatest computers for them. You decide to use PowerPoint to present your idea that purchasing new computers for your entire department would be cost-effective. Because you need to prepare the presentation by tomorrow, you decide to use the AutoContent Wizard. After creating the presentation, you can practice displaying the presentation in different views and running an electronic slide show.

To Create the Presentation

1. Start PowerPoint.
2. Use the AutoContent Wizard to create the presentation.
3. Use the title **Improving Productivity** when asked what you are going to talk about.
4. Choose the **S**elling a Product, Service or Idea type of presentation.
5. Select a presentation with the default look and less than 30 minutes in length. Finish creating the presentation.
6. Using the View buttons, observe the presentation in each of the five views.
7. Use the methods listed in Table 1.3 on page 15 to move among slides in the Slide View and the Outline View.

8. Run the slide show. Use the shortcut menu to move to the previous and next slides as well as to end the show.
9. Save the presentation as **Our Plan for Getting New Computers**.
10. Close the presentation.

Creating a Training Presentation

You need to create a presentation for a class on "How to Be Successful in Business." You decide to use the AutoContent Wizard to develop it because you know that the Wizard will help you to quickly create a presentation. After you create the presentation view the presentation in different views and run the Slide Show.

To Create the Training Presentation

1. Start PowerPoint and choose the **A**utoContent Wizard from the PowerPoint start-up dialog box.
2. Use the title **How to Be Successful in Business** when asked, What are you going to talk about?
3. Select Training as the type of presentation you are going to give; then click the **F**inish button.
4. Use the vertical scroll bar to move through the slides in the Slide View.
5. View the text contents of the presentation by clicking the Outline View button.
6. Run the electronic slide show. Use the shortcut menu to move to the previous and next slides.
7. End the slide show.
8. Save the presentation as **Success in Business**, then close it.

Creating a New Presentation Using the AutoContent Wizard

You are working for a company that deals in computer ergonomic products—products designed to help people work more effectively on the computer. You decide to create a presentation to promote your products for a sales meeting. You decide to use the AutoContent Wizard to create the basic framework and suggested slide context. Once created, you can enter text in the slides and view them in different ways.

To Create the New Presentation Using AutoContext Wizard

1. Start PowerPoint, if necessary, and choose the **A**utoContent Wizard from the PowerPoint start-up dialog box.
2. In the second AutoContent Wizard dialog box, enter your name. Enter **Ergonomic Products** as the topic you are going to talk about, and enter **ABC Ergonomic Products** in the Other information you'd like to display? text box.
3. Choose **S**elling a Product, Service or Idea as the type of presentation, then click the **F**inish button.

4. Enter the following in Slide 2:

   Objectives:

   To help workers become more productive

   To reduce stress and down-time from computer-related injuries

5. Display the presentation in each of the available views in PowerPoint.
6. Save the presentation as **ABC Ergonomic Corp**.
7. Close the presentation.

Creating a Presentation from Scratch

You are in charge of finding a new project manager for your organization. You create a presentation outlining the type of person you would like for the position. Because you have decided to create this presentation from scratch, you select the Blank Presentation option in the PowerPoint dialog box. You add slides as you need them and completely create the framework and contents of the presentation, rather than relying on the AutoContent Wizard

To Create a Presentation from Scratch

1. Start PowerPoint, if necessary, and choose **B**lank Presentation from the PowerPoint start-up dialog box.
2. Choose a Title Slide for the first slide in your presentation.
3. Add the title **Project Manager Recruitment** to your slide.
4. Add the subtitle **Our Search for Excellence**.
5. Save the presentation as **Project Manager**, then close it.

Checking Your Skills

True/False

For each of the following, check *T* or *F* to indicate whether the statement is true or false.

__T __F **1.** PowerPoint has Standard and Formatting toolbars.

__T __F **2.** Menu options that appear dimmed are not appropriate in the current situation.

__T __F **3.** PowerPoint can help you by creating speaker notes as part of your presentation.

__T __F **4.** The Slide Sorter button automatically sorts the slides alphabetically by title.

__T __F **5.** The Outline View, the Slide View, and Slide Show are different ways of viewing the same set of slides.

Multiple Choice

In the blank provided, write the letter of the correct answer for each of the following questions.

1. The best way to view only the text contained in a presentation is to use the ______.

   a. Slide View

   b. Slide Sorter View

   c. Notes Pages View

   d. Outline View

2. A quick way to create a presentation that already contains sample content is to use the ______.

   a. Template Wizard

   b. Outline View

   c. AutoContent Wizard

   d. Answer Wizard

3. An LCD panel is ______.

   a. a device used with an overhead projector to display images from the computer on a screen

   d. another name for the toolbar

   c. a list of special effects for transition from one slide to another

   d. the Learning Center Display panel that you get when you request help

4. To edit a single slide, you most probably will use the ______.

   a. Slide View

   b. Outline View

   c. Notes Pages View

   d. Slide Sorter View

5. One way to move between slides in the Slide View is to ______.

   a. choose the appropriate **H**elp menu command

   b. use the Search feature on the **H**elp menu

   c. click the status bar

   d. use the vertical scroll bar

Completion

In the blank provided, write the correct answer for each of the following statements.

1. Help that is related to the command you are performing is called ________________.
2. The temporary working area that the computer uses to run programs is called ________________.
3. You use the ________________ toolbar to select type fonts and sizes and to change the appearance of selected text.
4. The ________________ View shows six slides on-screen at one time.
5. A pop-up box that shows the name of a button is called a(n) ________________.

Project 2

Working with Text

Objectives

In this project, you learn how to

- Open an Existing Presentation
- Add and Delete Slides
- Work with Text
- Change Slide Order
- Change Text Characteristics
- Print an Outline
- Print a Slide

Why Would I Do This?

In Lesson 1, you created a presentation by using the AutoContent Wizard. However, the product of this Wizard is only a basis for your presentation. With PowerPoint, you can edit and enhance the existing presentation in various ways for more impact.

Any time you are presenting your ideas, you want to make a powerful impression. In this project, you develop a business plan for a small business you are starting that provides computer training. You need to present your business plan to a group of potential investors. To develop the presentation, you open an existing presentation, add and delete slides, and change text and slide order. You also change text appearance and print your presentation. Through this process, you customize the presentation so that it is truly your own and makes the greatest impression on your audience.

Lesson 1: Opening an Existing Presentation

If you want to work with a file in your office, you may get it from a file cabinet, make a copy, and put it on your desk so that you can work on it. In the same way, opening an existing presentation in PowerPoint simply creates a copy from one of the computer's storage areas and places it in memory so that you can work with it.

In PowerPoint you can open an existing presentation in a number of ways. The easiest way is to either click the Open an Existing Presentation button on the opening PowerPoint dialog box, or click the Open button on the Standard toolbar. To make it really easy to open a file, PowerPoint lists the four most recently opened presentations at the bottom of the File menu. Simply click the file that you want to open. This is useful if you use the same presentations frequently.

Now try opening an existing presentation using the PowerPoint start-up dialog box.

To Open an Existing Presentation

1. **Start PowerPoint and choose OK if the Tip of the Day dialog box is displayed.**

   The PowerPoint start-up dialog box appears (see Figure 2.1).

2. **Double-click the Open an Existing Presentation option button.**

   The File Open dialog box is displayed, as shown in Figure 2.2.

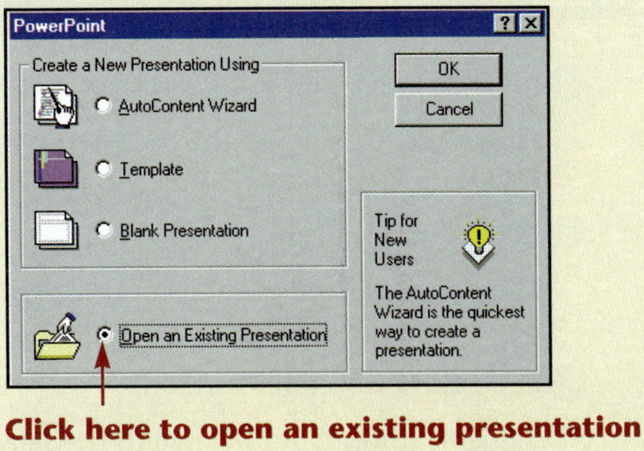

Figure 2.1
The PowerPoint start-up dialog box.

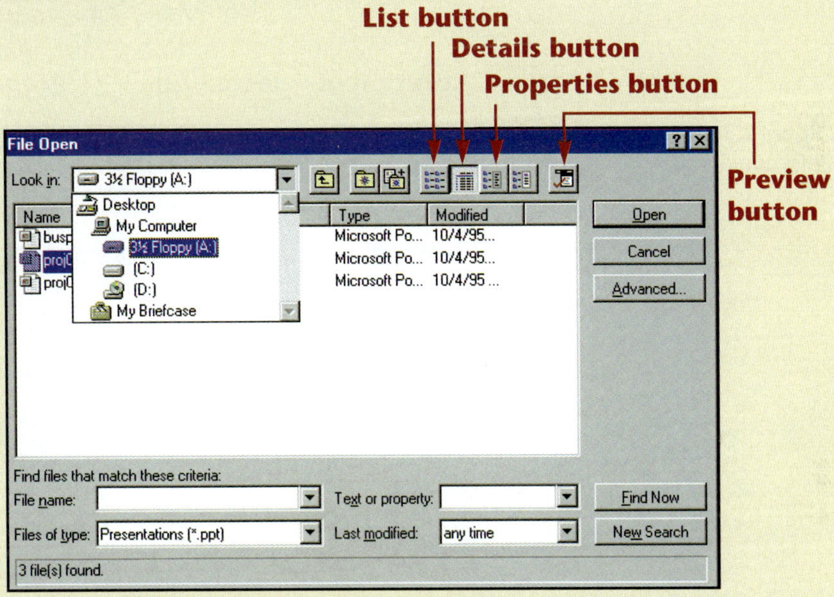

Figure 2.2
The File Open dialog box.

If you have problems...

If PowerPoint is already started, choose **F**ile, **O**pen to display the File Open dialog box.

3 **Insert the data file disk in the 3½-inch drive (usually drive A), click the Look in drop-down list arrow, and select the floppy disk drive.**

A list of files previously saved on the floppy disk is displayed. Before you actually open the file into memory, quite a bit of information can be learned about the file. This is especially helpful because it is easy to forget the name or contents of a presentation that was created some time ago. By default, the first presentation on the list is highlighted.

continues

To Open an Existing Presentation (continued)

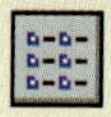

4 Click the List button, located at the top of the dialog box.

Only the file names of the presentations on the floppy disk drive are listed.

5 Click the Details button.

The size, type, and modification date of the files are shown in addition to the file name.

6 Click the Properties button.

Valuable information related to the selected file is shown, including its title, creator, number of slides, and last modification date (see Figure 2.3).

Figure 2.3 Information displayed as a result of selecting the Properties button.

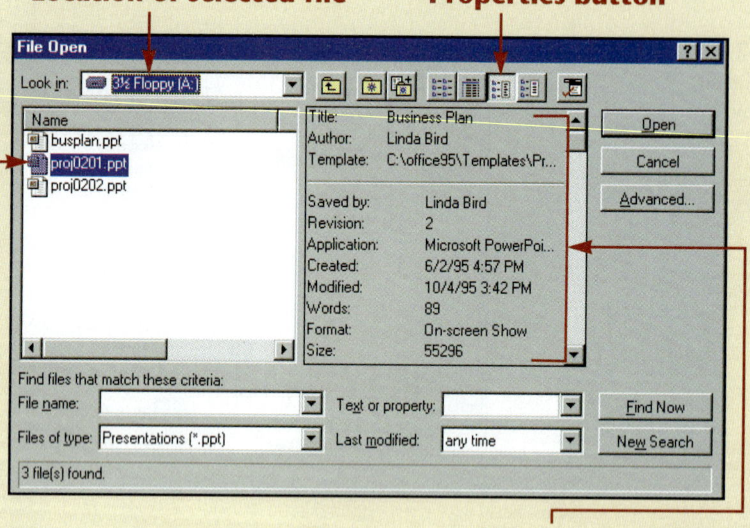

7 Click the Preview button.

The title slide for the selected presentation is shown in miniature.

8 Select the file Proj0201.ppt and click the Open button.

PowerPoint opens the selected file and the title slide is displayed in the Slide View. Another way to open the file from the File Open dialog box is to double-click the file name.

9 Choose File, Save As.

This opens the Save As dialog box.

10 In the File name text box, type Business Plan, then choose Save.

You have now named the presentation Business Plan. You work with this file throughout the rest of this project, so leave it open.

You can sort files in the File Open dialog box by categories such as Name, Size, Type, and Modified. Clicking the buttons bar at the top of the file list sorts the files by the category chosen. Clicking them a second time sorts that category list in reverse order.

Lesson 2: Adding and Deleting Slides

Whether you rely on the AutoContent Wizard to create your presentations or you create them from scratch, you will want the flexibility of adding and deleting slides. Table 2.1 lists the methods to add and delete slides.

Table 2.1 Summary of Adding and Deleting Slides

To Add a Slide
Choose **I**nsert, **N**ew Slide from the menu bar.
Click the New Slide button on the status bar.
Press Ctrl+M.
Click the New Slide button on the Standard toolbar.
To Delete a Slide
In Outline and Slide Sorter views, click to select the slide and press Del.
In the Slide View, choose **E**dit, **D**elete Slide.

In this lesson, you add and delete slides in the Outline View and the Slide Sorter View because there are the easiest ways to see what you are doing. Try adding and deleting slides now.

To Add and Delete Slides

1. **With the Business Plan presentation open on your screen, click the Outline View button.**

   This shows the presentation in the Outline View.

2. **Place the mouse pointer over the slide icon for Slide 2, Agenda.**

   The mouse pointer changes to a four-sided arrow.

3. **Click the Slide 2 slide icon.**

   The slide icon is selected, as displayed in Figure 2.4. If the selected slide contains bullet points, they will be selected as well.

continues

To Add and Delete Slides (continued)

Figure 2.4
Selecting a slide in the Outline View.

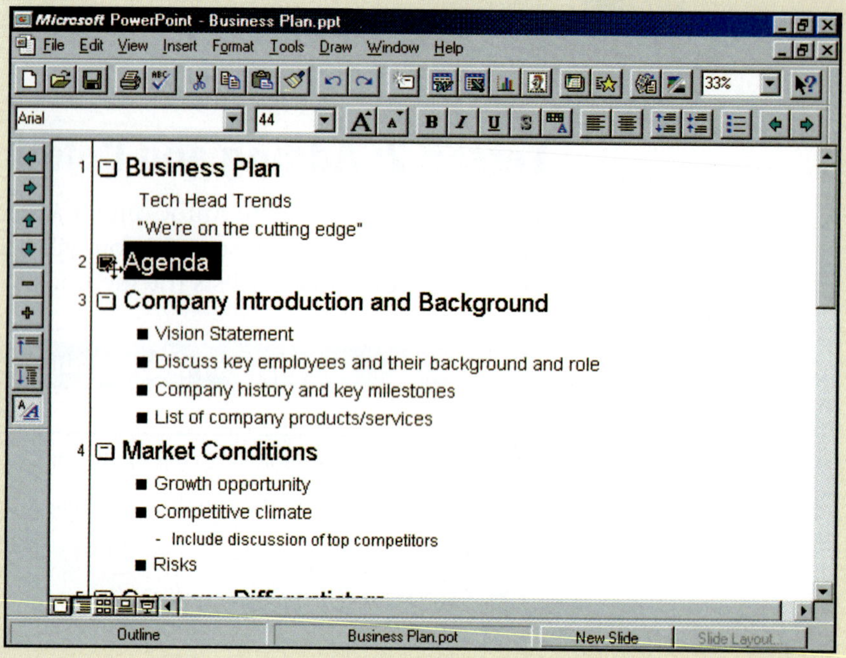

4 Press Del.

Slide 2 is deleted from the presentation.

5 Click the Slide Sorter View button and click to select Slide 2, Company Introduction and Background.

The presentation is shown in the Slide Sorter View with a darkened border surrounding Slide 2. This indicates that it is the selected slide.

6 Press Del.

The Company Introduction and Background slide is deleted. The black line between Slides 1 and 2 indicates that the cursor is between the two slides. This is where you want to add a new slide.

7 Click the Insert New Slide button on the Standard toolbar.

PowerPoint displays the New Slide dialog box (see Figure 2.5). This dialog box contains 24 predefined layout options, called AutoLayouts. Each one contains *placeholders* for text, graphics, charts, and media objects. Using the AutoLayouts greatly saves time over defining the format each time you add a slide. Notice that as you single click an AutoLayout, its name is displayed in the lower right corner of the dialog box.

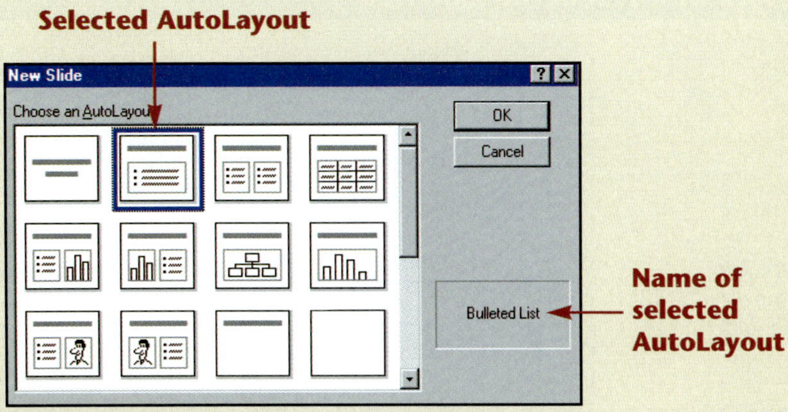

Figure 2.5
The New Slide dialog box with AutoLayout formats.

Placeholders
An area on a PowerPoint slide that can accept text, graphics, or objects (such as movie clips).

8 Double-click the AutoLayout for a Bulleted List, which is the second layout in the first row.

A slide containing placeholders for a bulleted list is inserted into your presentation between Slides 1 and 2.

9 Double-click the new slide (Slide 2).

Slide 2 is displayed in the Slide View with the placeholders for inserting text. You use this slide in the next lesson to enter and edit text. Save your changes and keep this presentation open for the next lesson.

You can also add a new slide to a presentation by clicking the Insert Slide button on the status bar. Alternately, choose **I**nsert, **N**ew Slide from the menu.

When you add a slide to a presentation, it is inserted after the slide where the cursor is currently located. You can add slides in any view except the Slide Show View.

In the Outline View, you can delete several slides at a time by selecting more than one. Click to select the first slide you wish to delete. Press and hold down Shift, then click the last slide you want to delete. You have selected all continuous slides from the first one clicked on to the last. Press Del to remove them all.

If you accidentally delete a slide, immediately choose **U**ndo from the **E**dit menu. The slide will be reinserted in your presentation.

Lesson 3: Working with Text

When you first create a presentation, you have only a framework for adding text and graphics. Once the framework is in place, there are numerous ways to enter and modify text so that the presentation becomes your own. Being able to manipulate text in a presentation is an important skill. This lesson focuses on ways to enter, edit, and move text in both the Slide View and the Outline View.

To Work with Text in the Slide View

1 Move to Slide 2 of the Business Plan presentation, if necessary, and display it in the Slide View.

The blank, new slide is shown with *placeholders* for adding a title and a bulleted list (see Figure 2.6).

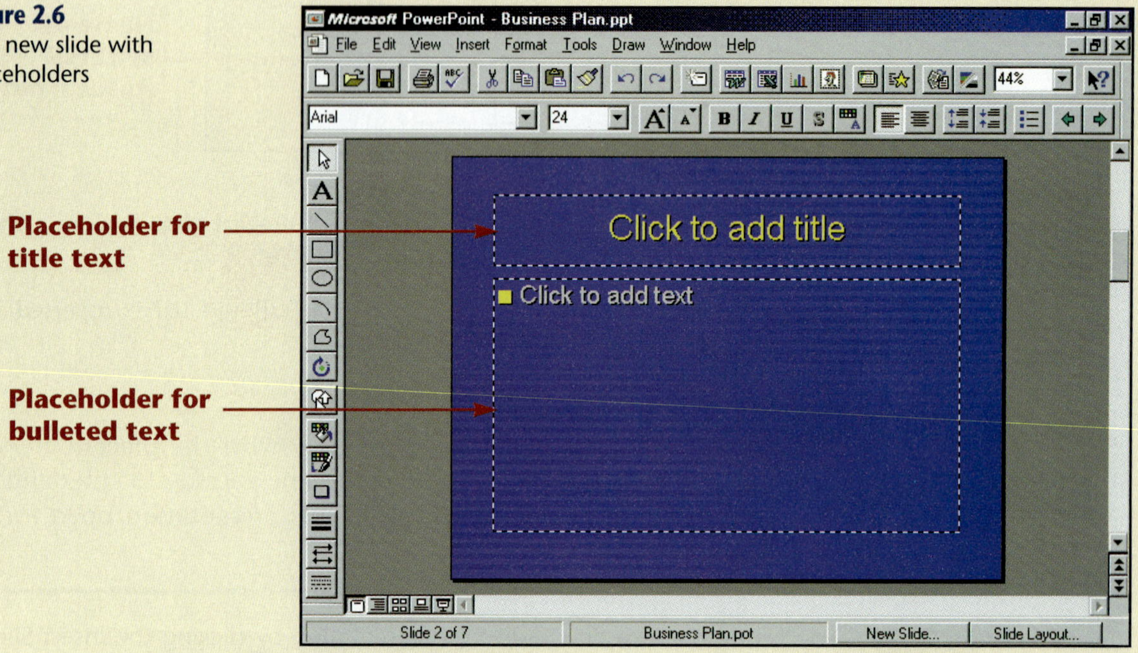

Figure 2.6
The new slide with placeholders

2 Click the top placeholder.

The placeholder words disappear and an insertion point is placed in the middle of the title box area.

3 Type Marketing Ideas and click the lower placeholder.

The title is fixed in the upper placeholder and the insertion point is moved to the bulleted list area.

4 Type Open House as the first bullet point and press Enter.

Open House is listed as the first bullet point and a second bullet is created.

5 Type Networking as the second bullet point and press Enter.

6 Press Tab, type Professional Groups, then press Enter.

Pressing Tab *demotes* this line, indenting it to show that it has less importance than the previous one.

Demote
To indent a line of text more than the previous one.

7 Type Chamber of Commerce and press Enter.

Your slide should now look similar to Figure 2.7.

Figure 2.7
The slide with demoted points.

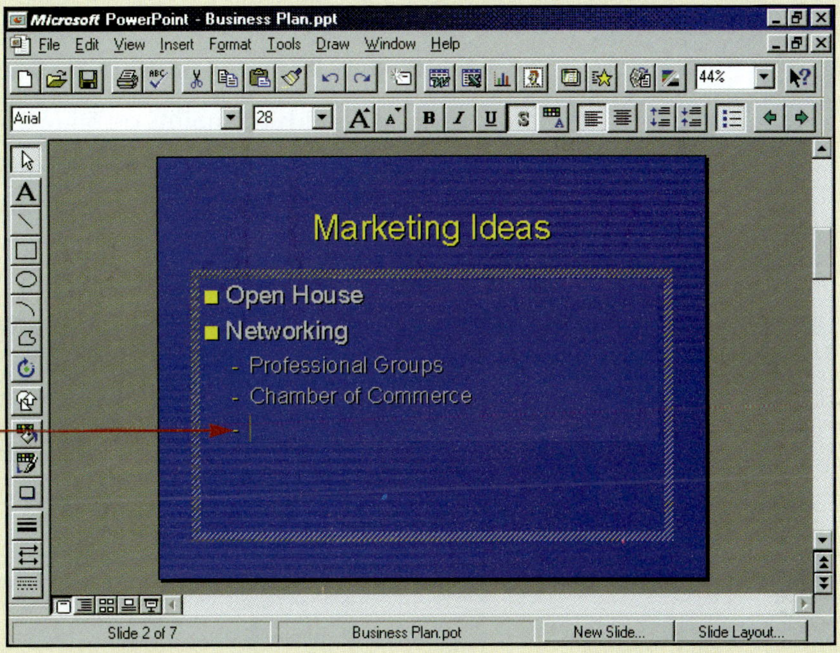

Promote
To indent a line of text less than the previous one, indicating a greater level of importance.

8 Press Shift+Tab to *promote* the bullet on the current line, and type Cold Calls.

Keep the Business Plan presentation open for the next lesson, in which you work with text in the Outline View.

If you don't want to use the keyboard method of promoting and demoting bullet points, you can use the Demote and Promote buttons on the Formatting toolbar.

To Work with Text in the Outline View

1 In Slide 2 of the Business Plan presentation, choose View, Outline from the menu bar.

The presentation is displayed in the Outline View.

2 Click to set the insertion point to immediately after Cold Calls, then press Enter.

A bullet point is inserted following the last item on Slide 2.

3 Type Advertising and press Enter.

Advertising is entered as text following the last bullet point.

4 Press Tab and type Newspaper.

Newspaper is listed as one of the demoted bullet subpoints.

continues

To Work with Text in the Outline View (continued)

5 Add Yellow Pages and Direct Mail as other demoted points.

PowerPoint adds the points on Slide 2.

6 Move the cursor over the bullet point for Cold Calls until it changes into a four-sided arrow; then click.

Cold Calls is highlighted, as shown in Figure 2.8.

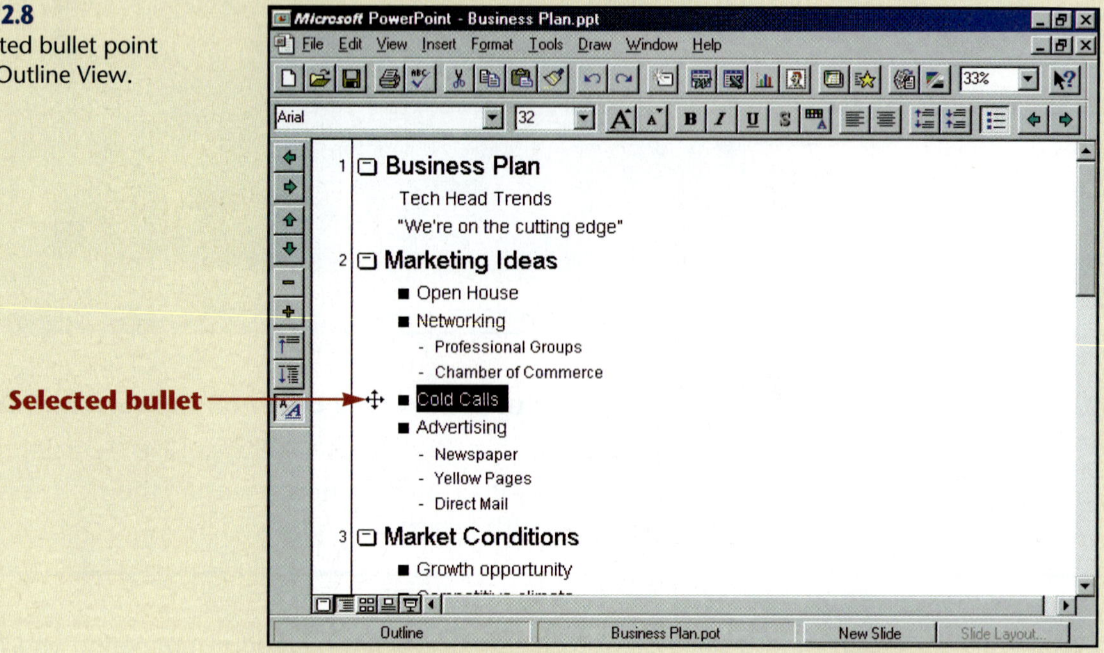

Figure 2.8
A selected bullet point in the Outline View.

7 Press Del.

The bullet and its text are removed from the slide.

8 Replace the suggested text on Slides 3 and 4 as follows:

Slide 3: **Market Conditions**

20% increase in new computer users/year

New software programs require training

Several new companies moving into area

Slide 4: **Company Differentiators**

Perform needs assessments prior to training

Personalized, customized training

Top-notch facilities

9 Save the changes to the Business Plan and leave it open for the next lesson.

INSIDE Stuff

You delete text in PowerPoint the same way as you do in a word processing program. Press Del or ←Backspace to erase one character at a time. You can also select larger sections of text with the mouse and then press Del.

If you accidentally delete too much text, click the Undo button on the Standard toolbar.

When you click a first level bullet, all the text associated with it is selected, including any demoted bullets. Clicking a demoted bullet selects only its text.

In addition to entering text, you can change the order of the presentation bullet points. The easiest way to move points is in the Outline View. Try moving bullet points now.

To Work with Text in the Outline View

1 Click to select the first bullet point in Slide 3, Market Conditions.

2 Position the mouse pointer over the selected bullet.

The pointer turns into a four-sided arrow.

3 Press and hold down the left mouse button and drag slowly downward.

The four-sided mouse pointer changes to a two-sided arrow. An indicator line shows the new location for the bullet point (see Figure 2.9).

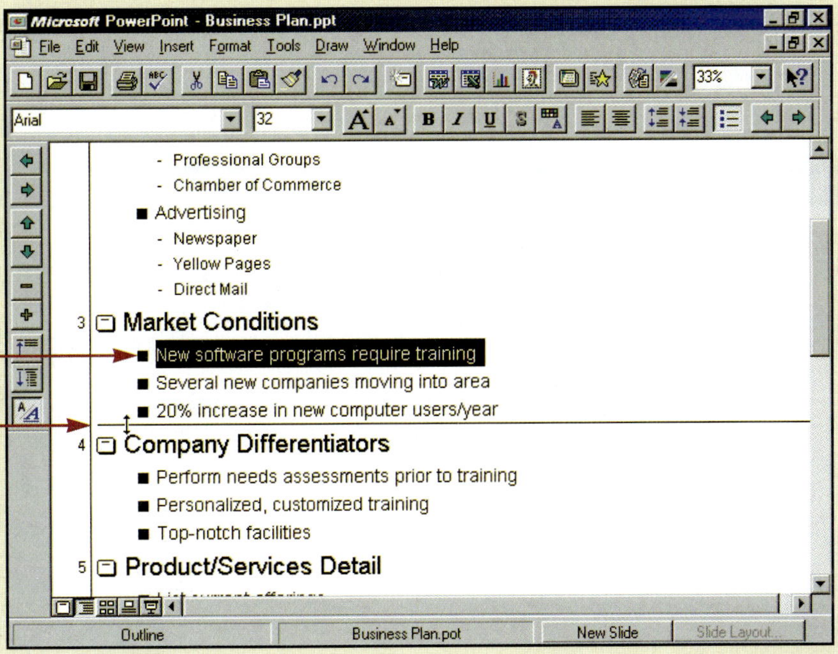

Figure 2.9
The indicator line shows the new location for the bullet point.

continues

To Work with Text in the Outline View (continued)

4. **Move the mouse pointer until the indicator line is below the last bullet point on slide, Several new companies moving into area.**

5. **Release the mouse button.**

   The bullet is moved to the new location. Bullet points can be moved in the same way using the Slide View. Keep the Business Plan presentation open for the next lesson.

If you have problems...

If you release the mouse button too soon when dragging text to a new location, it will be placed in the wrong location. Click the Undo button to reverse the action, then try again.

INSIDE Stuff

In addition to rearranging points on a slide, they may be moved to another slide. Using the Outline View, simply select and drag the bullet point to whichever slide (and location within that slide) that you want.

Lesson 4: Changing Slide Order

You will often find that you need to rearrange the slides in your presentation to create a more logical sequence. Using the Slide Sorter View and the Outline View enables you to immediately see the effect of the move on the entire presentation. Try moving slides now.

To Change Slide Order

1. **In the Business Plan presentation, click the slide icon for Slide 2, Marketing Ideas.**

   The entire slide contents, including all bullet points, are selected.

2. **Move the mouse pointer over the Slide 2 icon until the four-sided arrow is shown.**

3. **Drag the entire slide below Slide 3, Market Conditions.**

   The line indicator is displayed below the last bullet point in Slide 3 (see Figure 2.10).

Figure 2.10
Moving a slide using the Outline View.

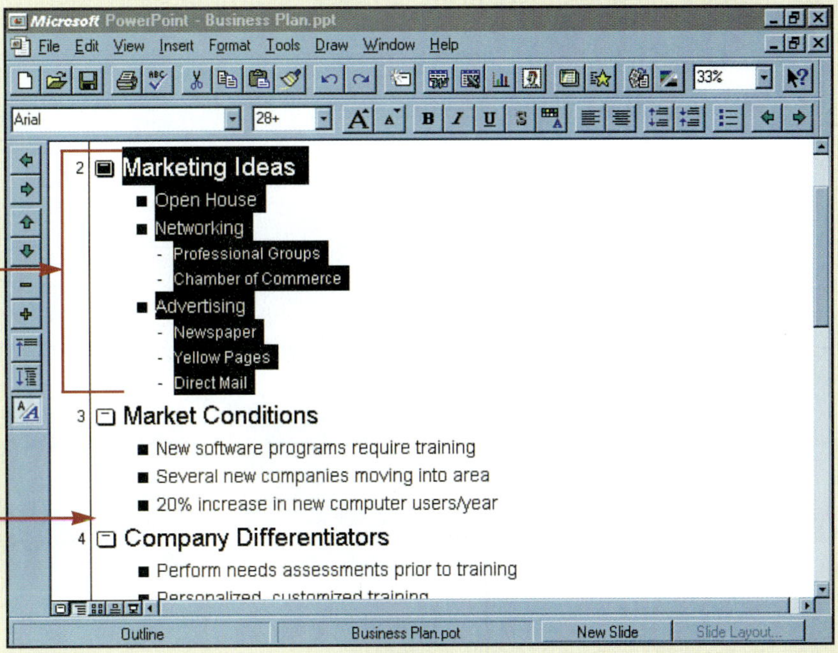

4 Release the mouse button.

The Marketing Ideas slide is moved so that it is now Slide 3.

5 Click the Slide Sorter View button.

This displays the presentation in the Slide Sorter View.

6 Select Slide 4, Company Differentiators.

7 Move the mouse pointer to the middle of the selected slide, and drag the white pointer to the space between Slide 1 and Slide 2.

The location for the slide is indicated by the inserted line between Slides 1 and 2 (see Figure 2.11).

8 Release the mouse button.

The Company Differentiators slide is moved to the position between Slide 1 and Slide 2. Keep the Business Plan presentation open for the next lesson.

continues

To Change Slide Order (continued)

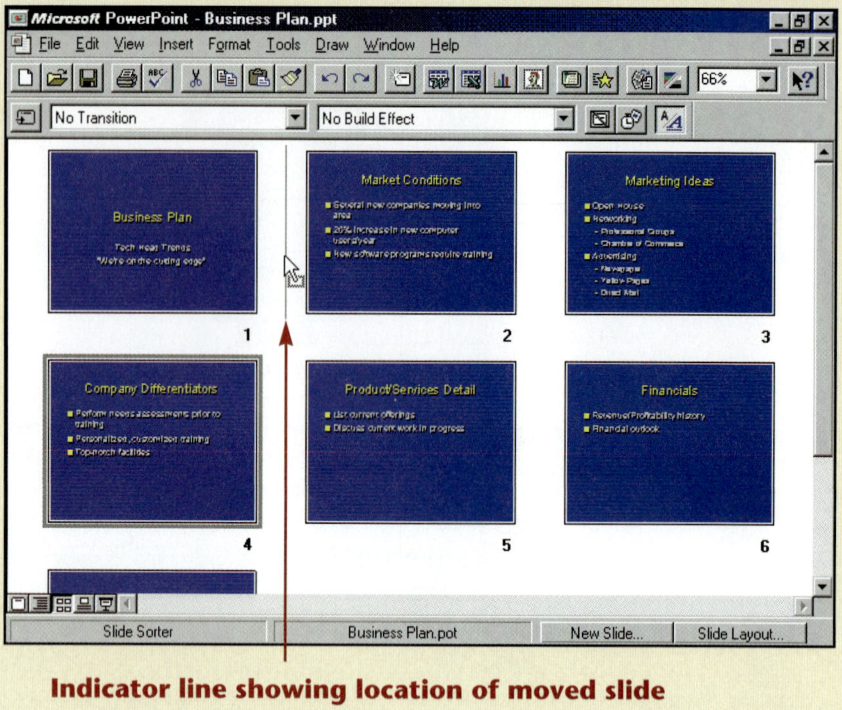

Figure 2.11
The move indicator in Slide Sorter View.

You can move more than one slide at a time in the Slide Sorter View. Press and hold down Shift as you click to select (or deselect) multiple slides. Release Shift and drag the group of slides to a new location in the same way you move one slide.

Lesson 5: Changing Text Characteristics

PowerPoint gives you the capability to change the look of your presentations. One way to customize a presentation is to add enhancements such as text color, size, and style. Other enhancements include changing the alignment and paragraph spacing of text. Finally, you can use the Format Painter to quickly apply your favorite formatting to other sections of text. PowerPoint provides most of the commonly used commands on the Formatting toolbar (see Figure 2.12).

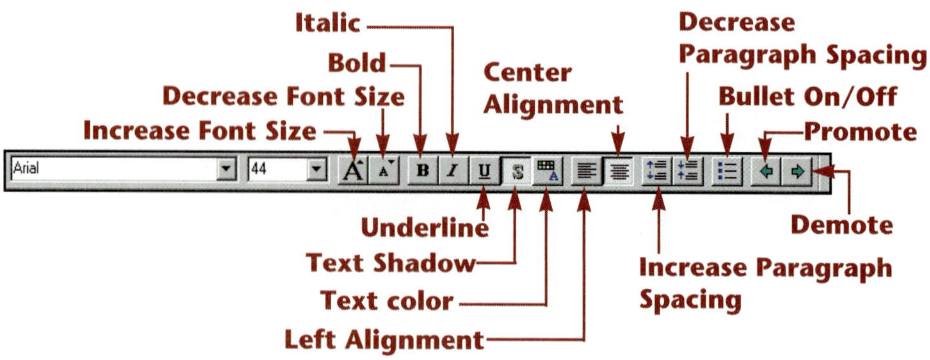

Figure 2.12
The Formatting toolbar.

Now try changing text characteristics in the Business Plan presentation.

To Change Text Characteristics

1. **Display the first slide of the Business Plan presentation in the Slide View.**

2. **Double-click the word *cutting*.**

   This selects the word so that you can change the formatting.

3. **Click the Italic, Bold, and Underline buttons on the Formatting toolbar.**

   Italic, bold, and underline effects are added to the selected word.

4. **Click and drag the mouse pointer to select the entire line, Tech Head Trends.**

5. **Move the mouse pointer to the Text Color button on the Formatting toolbar and click and hold down the mouse button.**

   The available text colors are displayed, as shown in Figure 2.13.

Figure 2.13
The text color palette of the Text Color button on the Formatting toolbar.

6. **Move the mouse pointer to the red color and release the mouse button.**

   Because the line is still selected, the change isn't seen immediately. Click anywhere else on the slide. As the text is deselected, you see the color change.

continues

To Change Text Characteristics (continued)

7 Select the text in the upper placeholder, Business Plan.

Notice that the Font Face and Font Size boxes on the Formatting toolbar indicate that this text is currently Arial 44 *points*, shown in Figure 2.14.

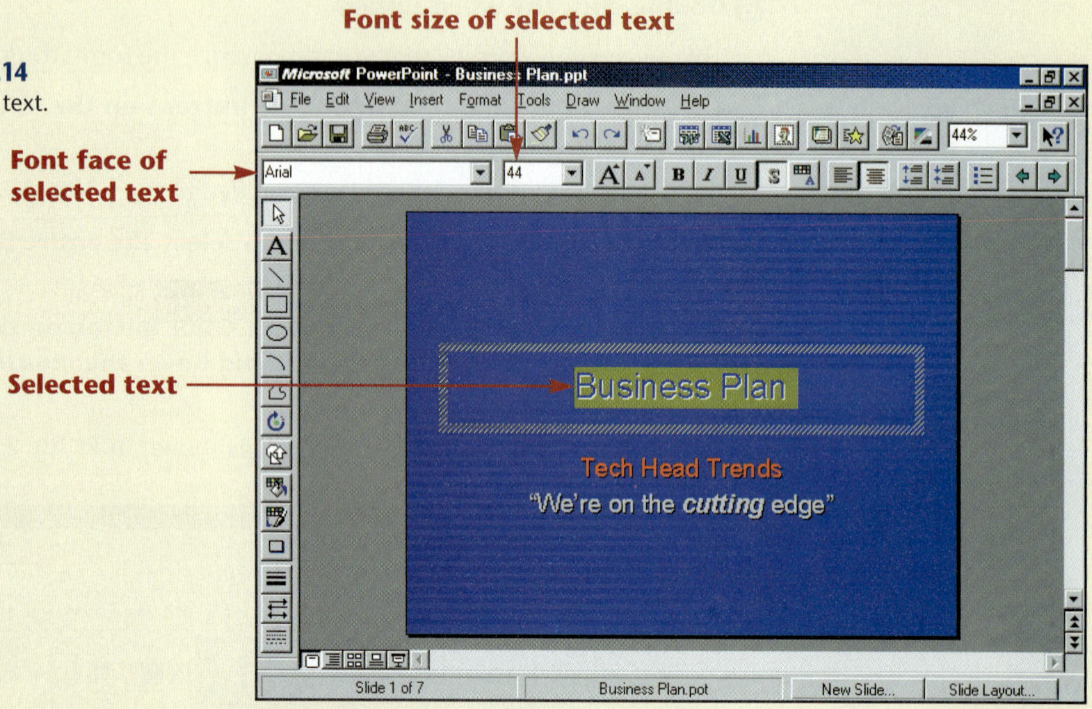

Figure 2.14
Selected text.

Font
The style (including size and appearance) of text

Point Size
The size of text as it will be printed is usually referred to in points. Text that is 72 points is 1 inch in height. The larger the point size, the larger the text.

8 Click the drop-down arrow to the right of the Font Size box on the Formatting toolbar, and select 66 as the point size.

The selected text changes to the larger point size.

9 Click the Font Face box drop-down arrow, and select Brush Script as the new font. If Brush Script is not available, select another script type font.

Business Plan is displayed using Brush Script text. This font (including size, appearance, and color) can be "painted" on to other text using the Format Painter. Think of the text that has the style you want to apply as a paint can. By clicking the Format Painter button, you are dipping your paint brush into the can. You then "paint" to apply the style to other text.

10 Make sure that the Business Plan text in Slide 1 is still selected, and click the Format Painter button on the Standard toolbar.

The mouse pointer changes to the Format Painter I-beam cursor.

11 Click and drag the cursor over Tech Head Trends.

The formatting styles associated with Business Plan are applied to Tech Head Trends. Leave the Business Plan presentation open for the next lesson.

If you have problems...

Make sure that the text containing the desired format is selected before you click the Format Painter button. Then click the text for which you want to apply the format.

INSIDE Stuff

The Format Painter is activated for only one occurrence. To keep it turned on so that you can format several sections of text, double-click the Format Painter button. To turn it off, click the Format Painter button again.

In addition to changing the text appearance on slides, you can change text alignment to left or center justification. You can also change paragraph spacing.

Now try changing the alignment of text in the Business Plan presentation.

To Change Alignment and Paragraph Spacing

1. **Display the first slide of the Business Plan presentation in the Slide View.**
2. **Click the first line on the slide, Business Plan.**
3. **Click the Left Alignment button on the Formatting toolbar.**

   The first line of the slide becomes left justified.
4. **Press PgDn.**

   This moves you to Slide 2, Company Differentiators.
5. **Select all bullet points in the lower placeholder on Slide 2.**
6. **Click the Increase Paragraph Spacing button on the Formatting toolbar four times.**

   The spacing between the bullet points increases each time you click the mouse.
7. **With the text still selected, click the Decrease Paragraph Spacing button.**

   The spacing between the bullet points decreases. Your slide should now look similar to Figure 2.15.
8. **Save changes to the Business Plan presentation and keep it open for the next lesson.**

continues

To Change Alignment and Paragraph Spacing (continued)

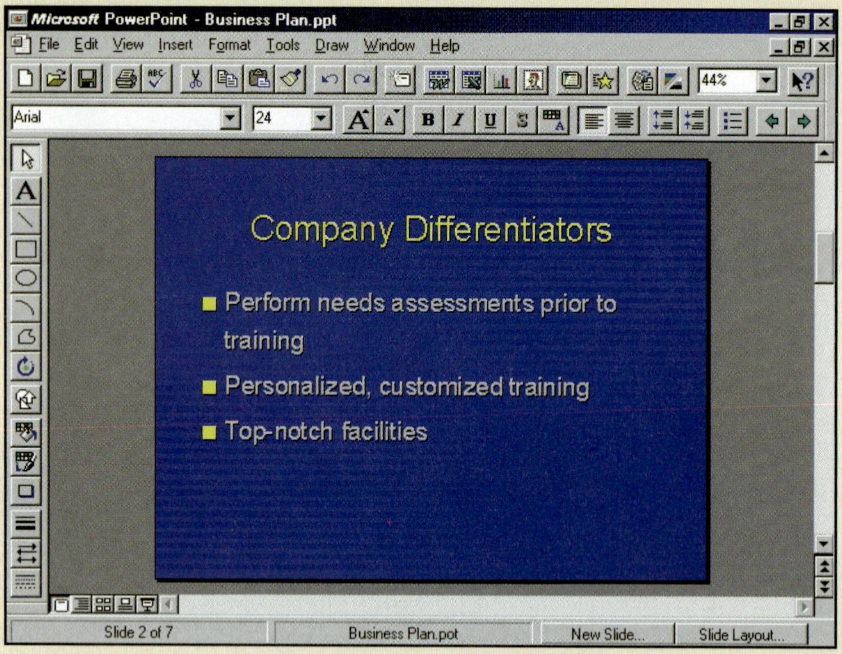

Figure 2.15
The slide with alignment and paragraph spacing features.

Jargon Watch

A number of terms are used in relation to computer text. Most of the terms originated in the printing industry. A **font** (sometimes referred to as a typeface, or face) is how text characters appear. A large number of alphabet fonts have been developed for use on the computer. **Point size** refers to how large or small text will print. Because 1 point is equivalent to 1/72", the larger the point size, the larger the text.

Demoting text means to indent the line of text, making it appear as a sub topic to the line above. When text is demoted in PowerPoint it is usually displayed smaller as well. **Promoting** text is the opposite—when text is promoted it is indented less, and usually increases in point size and relative importance.

Lesson 6: Printing an Outline

On occasion, especially when you are developing lengthy presentations, you will want to print the outline you have been working on. It's handy to have a printed copy of the outline to see the presentation's flow and sequence. Because the main purpose of the outline is to view the content, the printout will show only the text that has been typed. Graphics are not shown in this view. In addition, any text that is imported from other programs, or that has been added using the Text tool on the Drawing toolbar, will not appear.

To Print an Outline

1 With the Business Plan presentation open, choose File, Print.

The Print dialog box appears (see Figure 2.16).

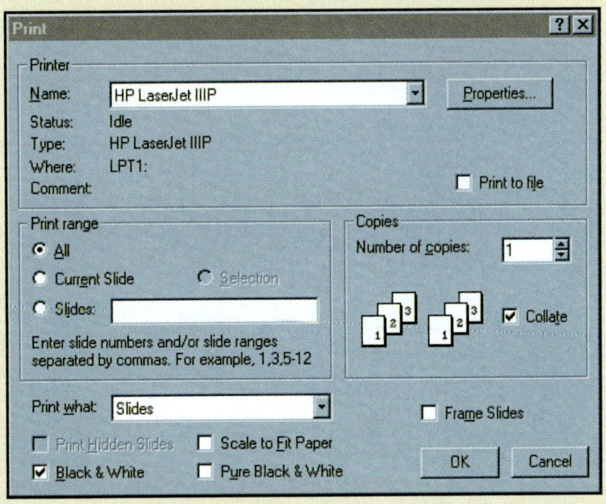

Figure 2.16
The Print dialog box.

2 Click the drop-down arrow to the right of the Print what text box.

A small window appears, showing three of the print choices. A small scroll bar associated with the drop-down list indicates that you have other choices as well.

3 Scroll down the open list, then select Outline View.

The Outline View is shown as the selection in the Print **w**hat text box.

4 In the Number of copies text box, make sure that the number of copies is set to 1.

5 In the Print Range area, make sure that the All option button is selected.

6 Check that the printer in the Name box of the Printer area is the correct one.

If the printer listed is not the one you want, click the drop-down arrow to the right of the **N**ame box to select the correct printer. If you are working on a network and have a variety of printers available, you can select one here based on your needs.

The completed Print dialog box appears (see Figure 2.17). The printer in the **N**ame text box will differ depending on the printer you are using.

continues

To Print an Outline (continued)

Figure 2.17
The completed Print dialog box.

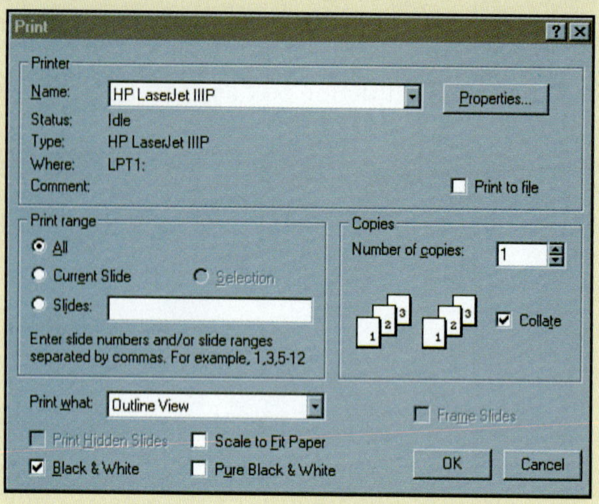

7 Choose OK.

This accepts the print settings and prints the outline. Keep the Business Plan presentation open for the next lesson, in which you print a slide.

Lesson 7: Printing a Slide

Printing a slide or series of slides is done in much the same manner as printing an outline. However, three additional factors need to be considered when printing in the Slide View—color, printing of backgrounds, and which slides should be printed.

More and more businesses and colleges are purchasing color printers, so chances are good that you will have access to one. However, printing in color is quite expensive on a per page basis. Therefore, most people save money by printing the bulk of their work in black and white, eliminating black backgrounds and printing more than one slide per page.

To Print a Slide

1 If necessary, move to Slide 1, Business Plan, of the Business Plan presentation and display it in the Slide View.

2 Click the B&W View button on the Standard toolbar.

The slide is displayed in black and white. The background color is white, the graphics are a default gray color, and the text appears in black. A miniature slide insert shows the slide with its original colors (see Figure 2.18).

Figure 2.18
The slide in B&W View.

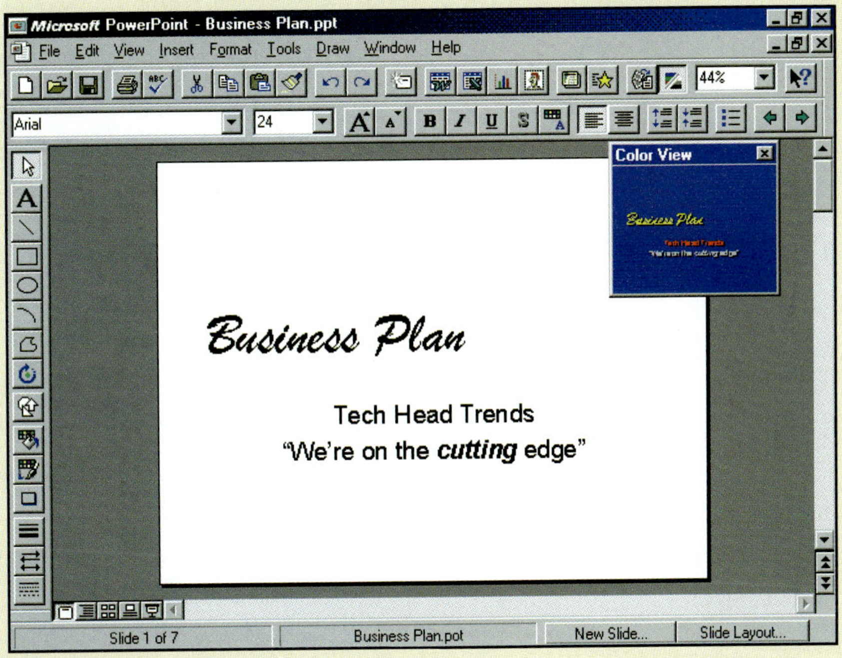

3. **Choose File, Print.**

   The Print dialog box appears (refer to Figure 2.16).

4. **Click the Current Slide option button in the Print range area.**

   This selects the current slide (Slide 1) to be printed.

5. **In the Print what text box, click the drop-down list arrow and select Slides.**

6. **Make sure that the printer is turned on, then choose OK.**

   A full-page printout of Slide 1 is printed. Now print a page that includes the first six slides.

7. **In the Print dialog box, click the Print what drop-down list arrow and select Handouts (6 slides per page).**

8. **In the Print range section, click the Slides option button.**

9. **Type 1-6 in the Slides text box.**

10. **Click the Black & White and Frame Slides check boxes at the bottom of the Print dialog box; then choose OK.**

    The first six slides are printed on one page. The slides should be approximately 2 by 3 inches, and have a box around the outer edge.

11. **Save and close the file.**

You can also select a specific slide to print by typing the slide number in the Sl**i**des text box of the Print range area. This text box also enables you to "pick and choose" slides by entering the slide numbers separated by commas. For example, entering 1-3,5,8 in the Sl**i**des text box would print slides 1, 2, 3, 5, 8.

Clicking the Print button on the Standard toolbar will print the presentation in the format of the present view.

Project Summary

To	Use
Open an Existing Presentation	Choose **F**ile, **O**pen from the menu.
Add a Slide to a Presentation	Click the New Slide button on the Standard toolbar.
Delete a Slide in a Presentation	Select the slide and choose **E**dit, **D**elete Slide from the menu.
Demote a Point (Indent More)	Click the Demote button on the Formatting toolbar.
Promote a Point (Indent Less)	Click the Promote button on the Formatting toolbar.
Move Text	In the Outline View and the Slide View, click the bullet icon to select the text, and drag to a new location.
Change Slide Order	In the Outline View, click the slide icon to select the entire slide, and drag to a new location.
	In the Slide Sorter View, click to select the slide, and drag to a new location.
Apply Text Characteristics	Select text, then click the Font Face, Font Size, Bold, Italic, Color, Shadow, or Alignment buttons on the Formatting toolbar.
Use the Format Painter	Click the word with the text characteristics you want to copy; click the Format Painter button, and click the text on which to apply the format.
Print	Choose **F**ile, **P**rint.

Applying Your Skills

Take a few minutes to practice the skills you have learned in this project by completing the following exercises.

Moving Slides and Text

You are in charge of new employee orientation at your company. You have previously created a presentation, but some benefits have recently changed.

You decide to revise the presentation. In doing so, you open an existing file and save it under a different name. You also move slides and text, and change the appearance of the text by applying fomatting features.

To Move Slides and Text

1. Open the presentation Proj0202 and choose the **F**ile, Save **A**s command to rename it **New Employees**.
2. Show the presentation in the Slide Sorter View. Delete Slide 3, History of Company, and Slide 4, Who's Who.
3. Move Slide 4, Benefits Review, between Slides 2 and 3 so that it becomes Slide 3.
4. Display the presentation in the Outline View and make the following changes to benefits:

    The fitness center has closed down so it is no longer a benefit. Eliminate the point associated with it.

    Change the text to show that you now get 3/4 sick day per month, rather than 1/2.

    Move the point for the 401(k) plan to just below the point for the vacation benefit.

5. Display Slide 1 in the Slide View and select the text, New Employee Orientation. Change the text as follows:

    Use 48 point, Univers font in bold and italic.

    Change the text color to red and add shadow.

6. Use the Format Painter to apply these text attributes to the presenter's name.
7. Print an outline of the presentation
8. Save and close the file.

Demoting and Promoting Bullet Points

For your class, you are required to give a presentation on the different personality types and how to effectively deal with them. You decide to use PowerPoint to help organize your thoughts. After creating your presentation, you promote and demote your bullet points. By using PowerPoint's capabilities to emphasize the importance of your topics, you can quickly revise a presentation to make the progression more logical.

To Demote and Promote Bullet Points

1. Open Proj0203. and save it as **People Skills.**
2. Display the presentation in the Slide Sorter View; then move Slide 3 to between Slides 1 and 2.
3. Delete Slide 2, Summary, from the presentation.
4. Show Slide 2, Skills, in the Slide View. Promote the last point listed, Communication Skills so that it is the same level as the other major points.

5. Move the bullet point for Communication Skills to the first point on Slide 2.
6. Demote the four points listed under Understanding Personality Types (the "Lion," the "Beaver," the "Golden Retriever," and the "Otter.")
7. Save, then close the file.

Using Formatting Features

You are working for a company that deals in computer ergonomic products—products that are designed to help people work more effectively on the computer. You decide to revise an existing presentaion that you developed to promote your products for a sales meeting. The existing presentation contains good information, but you want to add some spice by formatting it differently.

To Use Formatting Features

1. Open Proj0204 and save it as **Ergonomics in the Workplace**.
2. Display Slide 1 in the Slide View, then format Ergonomics with italic, bold and shadow features. Increase point size for Ergonomics to 60 point and change text color to purple.
3. Use the Format Painter to apply the formatting from Ergonomics to healthy on Slide 1.
4. Display Slide 2 and select all the bullet points. Center the text, then increase paragraph spacing so that the text fills up the slide area.
5. Print the first slide in black and white.
6. Save, then close the file.

Checking Your Skills

True/False

For each of the following, check *T* or *F* to indicate whether the statement is true or false.

__T __F **1.** Point size refers to the type of bullet used in a presentation.

__T __F **2.** Demote means to indent the line of text.

__T __F **3.** The Format Painter helps you to apply formatting features to text.

__T __F **4.** Slide Sorter View is the best view to use when moving text.

__T __F **5.** You add a new slide to a presentation by clicking the Promote button.

Multiple Choice

In the blank provided, write the letter of the correct answer for each of the following.

1. Which of the following is *not* an option on the Formatting toolbar? _______

a. italics

b. shadowing

c. undo

d. text color

2. To promote a point means _______.

a. to make the text larger

b. to change the font face

c. to indent it less

d. to indent it more

3. To save printing costs you can _______.

a. print color transparencies

b. print in black and white

c. print full-page slides with dark backgrounds

d. print several copies of each slide

4. To delete a slide you can _______.

a. click the Format Painter

b. show the presentation in the Slide Show View, then press Esc

c. select a slide in the Slide Sorter View, then press Del

d. choose **I**nsert, **D**elete Slide from the menu bar

5. To add a slide you can _______.

a. click the Slide Sorter View button, then press ↵Enter

b. press PgDn when in the Slide View

c. click the Get the New Slide button on the Slide Sorter toolbar

d. click the Insert New Slide button on the Standard toolbar

Completion

In the blank provided, write the correct answer for each of the following statements.

1. To move a point up one level in importance is to _______________ it.

2. Printing the ______________ View results in a printout with text only.

3. You can move a slide in the Slide Sorter View by ______________ it to the new location.

4. The ______________ and ______________ buttons are used to create various indent levels.

5. You can modify the appearance of selected text by changing the ______________, size, or style.

Project 3

Working With Charts and Tables

Objectives

In this project, you learn how to

- Select the Appropriate Chart Type
- Create Data Charts
- Change Chart Type, Size, and Location
- Import Data Charts from Excel
- Format Charts
- Create Tables
- Edit Tables
- Create Organization Charts
- Revise Organization Charts

Why Would I Do This?

As the old saying goes, "a picture is worth a thousand words." As you create your presentations, keep in mind that most people are more convinced by charts, presented in a clear, concise manner, than words. Business users want to know the bottom line—so use PowerPoint's capability to create pictorial charts to your advantage.

In this project, you use PowerPoint to create and use a variety of charts in new and existing presentations. You also use PowerPoint's formatting options to enhance charts, and you create and revise organization charts. Finally, you create Excel charts and Word tables and import them to a PowerPoint presentation. First, however, it's important to select the appropriate chart type for your presentations.

Lesson 1: Selecting the Appropriate Chart Type

You can select from 15 chart types to present your data clearly and effectively. As you develop your presentation, make sure that you format your data with the best chart type for what you're trying to convey. Because the most commonly-used chart types include the line, bar, column, and pie, the lessons in this project emphasize these chart types. Table 1.1 summarizes the main chart types available in PowerPoint.

Table 3.1 Available PowerPoint Chart Types

Button	Chart Type	Main Use	Example
	Area chart	Shows the relative importance of values over time.	Cumulative sales figures from several divisions.
	Bar chart	Shows comparisons between items in bar form. Bar charts can be stacked and also shown in 3-D.	Sales versus expenses for a 5-year period.
	Column chart	Similar to a bar chart, but its categories are organized horizontally, and its values organized vertically.	A company's profits versus revenue.
	Doughnut	Similar to a pie chart because its data shows the relationship of parts to a whole. However, it can show more than one data series.	Expenses broken down by category for several departments.
	Line chart	Shows trends or changes in data over time, usually in even intervals.	Yearly industrial production over several years.

Button	Chart Type	Main Use	Example
	Pie chart	Illustrates the relationship of parts to the whole. Pie charts can only show one data series.	Market share held by your company versus competitors.
	Radar chart	Shows frequencies or changes in data relative to each other and to a center point.	Comparison of how several products did in comparison with each other.
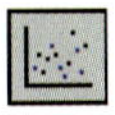	XY (Scatter) chart	Shows the relationship between values in several chart series.	The relationship between quantity and price.
	Organization chart	Shows the structure of an organization or process.	A chart showing job positions in an organization.

Lesson 2: Creating Data Charts

Peripheral program
A program with a specific function that is started every time a feature is accessed. Microsoft Graph is shared between all the Microsoft Office programs, which streamlines the process of creating charts.

PowerPoint has the capability to create different types of charts so that you can illustrate your points effectively. PowerPoint uses Microsoft Graph, a *peripheral program,* to create charts. Peripheral programs are started every time you access a feature within the main program, and place an object within the primary program. You can think of the object as being a doorway leading to the peripheral program, giving you access to its features and capabilities. PowerPoint shares Microsoft Graph with other Office programs. This makes chart development more uniform and efficient when working with the various Office products.

In PowerPoint, you can add charts in a variety of ways. You can use the chart placeholder on an existing or new slide, or use the Insert Chart button on the Standard toolbar. Because you actually start Microsoft Graph from within PowerPoint, you can choose the **I**nsert, Microsoft **C**hart command to start the program. Once you start Microsoft Graph, a *datasheet* results, enabling you to input information. When you are finished entering your data, you close the peripheral program, and your chart is embedded within the slide as an object.

Datasheet
A grid of columns and rows that enables you to enter numerical data into a PowerPoint chart. The intersection of a column and row is called a cell. Cells are always named by the column heading, followed by the row number, (for example, A1).

In this lesson, you use PowerPoint's peripheral program charting capability to add bar, line, and pie charts to a presentation. You also format the charts to improve their appearance. Try creating charts now.

To Create a Data Chart

1 Open the file Proj0301 and save it as Meeting.

2 Display Slide 3, Revenue, in the Slide View and click the Insert New slide button on the Standard toolbar.

continues

To Create a Data Chart (continued)

The New Slide dialog box appears. Notice that four of the AutoLayouts include a chart placeholder.

3. **Click the Graph AutoLayout (the fourth AutoLayout in the second row), as shown in Figure 3.1.**

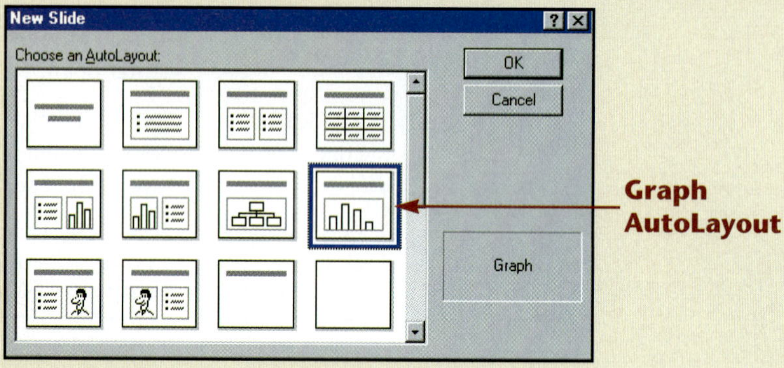

Figure 3.1
The New Slide dialog box.

4. **Choose OK.**

   A slide is inserted with placeholders for a title and a chart.

5. **In the top placeholder, type Revenues - 1994 vs. 1995.**

   This is the title for the chart.

6. **Double-click the lower placeholder to create a chart.**

   A datasheet is displayed with sample data. Note that the Microsoft Graph Standard toolbar is shown, and that the Drawing toolbar is activated (see Figure 3.2). The sample data is simply a guide and is easily replaced with your statistics.

7. **Click the cell containing the word *East*.**

   The darkened border around the cell indicates that this is the active cell—ready for an entry.

8. **Type 1994 and press ↓.**

   This enters 1994 in the cell and moves the mouse pointer down one cell.

9. **Click the row 3 heading.**

   The entire row is selected.

10. **Press Del.**

    The sample data from the entire row 3 is deleted. You can also click a column heading to select an entire column for deletion. Clicking the Select All button selects the entire datasheet. Try selecting different sections of the datasheet now.

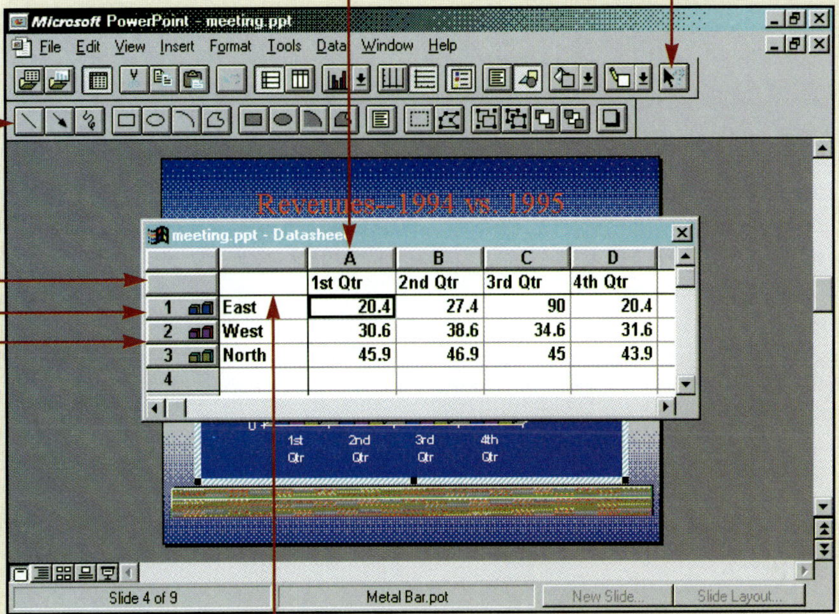

Figure 3.2 The datasheet and activated toolbars.

⑪ Enter the data shown in Figure 3.3 into your datasheet.

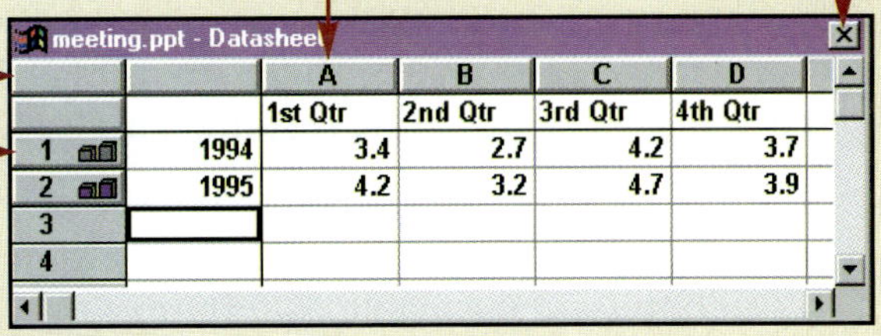

Figure 3.3 The completed datasheet.

⑫ Click anywhere outside the datasheet.

The datasheet view closes and a bar chart is created (the default chart type). The datasheet can also be closed by clicking the Close button in its upper right corner. The chart is embedded into the slide as an object. PowerPoint creates a bar or columnar chart by default. You should see white *selection handles* around the chart, indicating that the chart is selected, but that the Microsoft Graph program is closed. The white selection handles are used to resize and move the chart. (Black selection handles and a thick border surrounding the chart indicate that Microsoft Graph is still open so that you can work with specific chart elements.)

Keep the presentation open for the next lesson, where you learn how to resize, move, and change chart types.

Jargon Watch

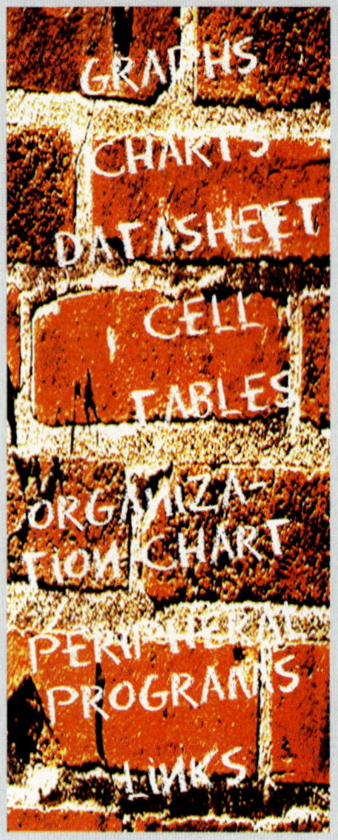

You encounter **graphs** or **charts** throughout everyday life because they are heavily used in magazines and advertising to emphasize certain points. Charts are typically used to graphically show numerical data. To create a chart, PowerPoint requires that you input numerical values into a **datasheet**, which appears similar to a spreadsheet with a series of columns and rows forming a grid. The intersection of a column and row, called a **cell**, is where you actually type in your data.

Like datasheets, **tables** consist of a series of columns and rows. However, tables excel at handling text rather than numbers. Another commonly used chart type is the **organization chart**, which shows the structure of an organization or process.

PowerPoint uses **peripheral programs** to facilitate creating charts. A peripheral program has a specific function that is started every time a feature is accessed. For example, Microsoft Graph is started every time you double-click a chart placeholder.

In addition to creating charts using the peripheral programs, PowerPoint can provide **links** to files created in other programs. You can think of a link as a pathway that joins two programs together so that information is passed back and forth freely. By using existing data from another program (for example, an Excel spreadsheet) you don't have to create it again.

Lesson 3: Changing Chart Type, Size, and Location

Because Microsoft Graph places a chart as an object on your slide, you can resize, move, and delete it like any other object. Most of the time you use the mouse with the white resizing handles to perform these commands.

You can also change the chart type to see the data displayed in different ways. There are two main methods of changing the chart type—the Chart Type command (available as a button or a menu choice), and the F**o**rmat **A**utoFormat command.

To Change Chart Type, Size, and Location

1. **Select Slide 5, Profit, in the Meeting presentation, and click the Insert Graph button on the Standard toolbar.**
2. **Click the Select All button in the upper left corner of the datasheet and press Del.**
3. **Enter information into the datasheet so that it appears like the one shown in Figure 3.4.**

Figure 3.4
The completed datasheet.

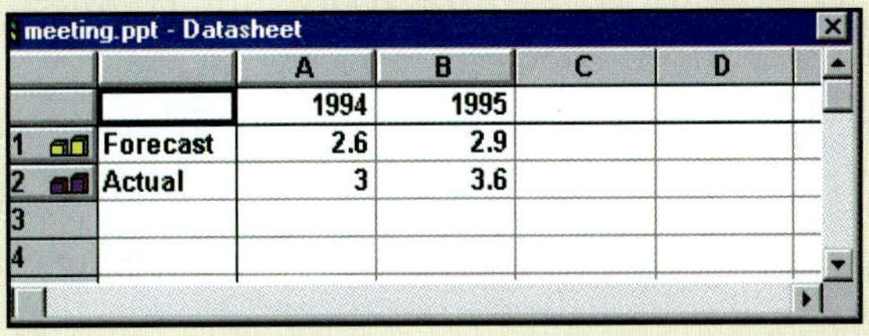

4 Click anywhere outside the datasheet.

This embeds the chart within the slide. The chart is placed over existing text. The square resizing handles on the chart placeholder indicate that it is a selected object. At this point, the chart can be moved or resized. Next, you resize the chart because it's covering existing text.

5 Move the mouse pointer over the upper right corner resizing handle until it turns into a two-sided arrow.

6 Drag to resize the chart towards the center of the chart and redisplay the text.

The chart is resized. You can use any of the white resizing handles to change the chart's size. If you also need to move the chart, move the mouse pointer into the middle of the selected chart, click and drag to the new location.

7 Double-click to activate the chart, then click the Chart Type drop-down list button to show the different chart types, as shown in Figure 3.5.

Figure 3.5
The Chart Type drop-down list showing the available chart types.

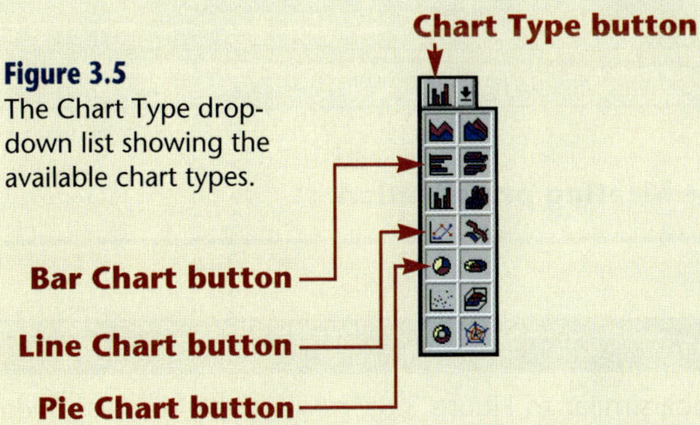

8 Click the Line Chart button.

The chart appears as a line chart. You decide that the chart is difficult to read, and that a horizontal bar chart would display better.

9 Click the Bar Chart button; then click outside the chart.

The Microsoft Graph Program is closed and the chart is displayed as a horizontal bar chart on Slide 5.

continues

To Change Chart Type, Size, and Location (continued)

10 Double-click the chart on Slide 7, Market Share; then click the Pie Chart button from the Chart Type drop-down list.

The chart is shown as a pie chart. The chart selects the first range of data as "slices" of the pie. Notice also that you can select a 3-D pie chart. The 3-D version of the pie chart is usually used to emphasize data associated with the facing wedge. Your completed slide should look similar to Figure 3.6.

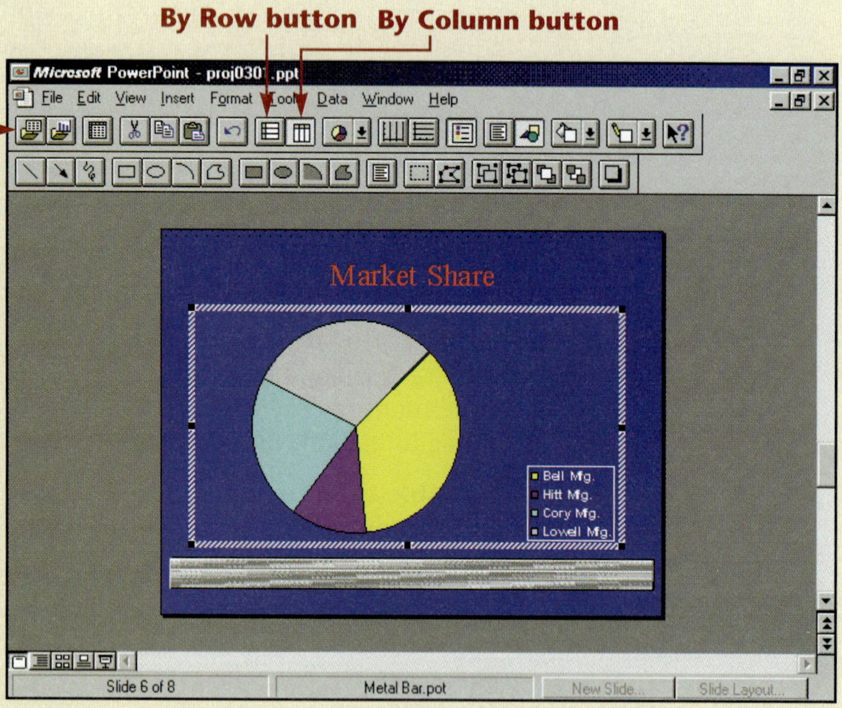

Figure 3.6
The pie chart slide.

11 Save and close the Meeting presentation.

If you have problems...

If your chart doesn't look similar to Figure 3.6, the data may be displayed by row rather than by column. Click the By Column button on the Microsoft Graph Standard toolbar to redraw the chart.

Choose F**o**rmat, **A**utoFormat to view and select the *subtypes* associated with each chart type. A subtype is simply a variation of a chart type. For example, a bar chart's subtypes would include 3-D charts or stacked bar charts. In the AutoFormat dialog box, you can choose the subtype you want by double-clicking it. The subtype is applied to the selected chart.

To give you a ready reference for using the Microsoft Graph Standard toolbar, a list of their functions follows in Table 3.2.

Table 3.2 Microsoft Graph Standard Toolbar Buttons

Toolbar button	Name	Function
	Import Data	Imports data from other programs.
	Import Chart	Imports Excel charts.
	View Datasheet	Activates the datasheet window so that you can enter, edit, or format the data.
	By Row	Associates chart data series with horizontal rows on the datasheet.
	By Column	Associates chart data series with vertical columns on the datasheet.
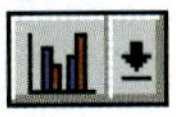	Chart Type	Gives you quick access to 14 different chart types. Click the drop-down list arrow to the right of the button; then click the chart type desired.
	Vertical Gridlines	Controls whether vertical gridlines are visible on the chart.
	Horizontal Gridlines	Controls whether horizontal gridlines are visible on the chart.
	Legend	Toggles on and off to display or remove a legend for the selected chart.
	Text Box	Enables you to draw a text box on the chart in order to enter text.
	Drawing	Toggles to display or remove the Drawing toolbar while you are working in Microsoft Graph.
	Color	Changes the foreground color of an object through use of a drop-down pallet.
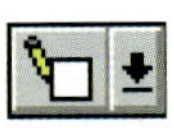	Pattern	Changes the pattern and pattern color of a graphic object or chart item.

Lesson 4: Importing Data Charts from Excel

You have just learned how to create charts by entering data directly into a PowerPoint datasheet. In this lesson, you learn how to import Microsoft Excel (a powerful spreadsheet program) data into a PowerPoint presentation. Because Excel has the capability to perform complicated calculations, you can create extensive Excel worksheets and import them into PowerPoint without having to retype them. Microsoft programs are integrated so that you can easily import data between programs. Importing an existing Excel chart is more efficient than creating one from scratch and enables you to show the result of complicated formulas.

When an Excel chart is imported into PowerPoint, an object is placed on the slide and a link can be created between the two programs. The link enables changes in the Excel worksheet to be reflected in the PowerPoint chart as well. Think of a PowerPoint chart object as a door between two rooms—a "PowerPoint room" and an "Excel Room." Creating the link opens the door between programs, so that information is freely shared between them. Make sure that Excel is available on your system, then try creating a linked chart now.

To Import a Data Chart From Excel

1 Make sure that PowerPoint is open, then start the Excel program by clicking the Start button on the Taskbar and choosing Excel from the Programs menu.

The Excel worksheet appears with its menu and toolbars. Note the similarity of the toolbar buttons to PowerPoint, especially New, Open, Save, Cut, Copy, and Paste.

2 Open the file Proj0302.xls and save it as Salespro.xls.

3 Click the chart, then click the Copy button.

Excel copies the chart to the *Clipboard*.

Clipboard
A temporary storage area in memory where information that is cut or copied from a document is stored until you paste the material elsewhere.

4 Click the PowerPoint button on the Taskbar (see Figure 3.7).

PowerPoint becomes the active program.

5 Click the New button on the Standard toolbar.

The New Slide dialog box appears with the available AutoLayouts.

6 Double-click the Blank AutoLayout (on the third row and last column).

A blank slide is created.

7 Choose Edit, Paste Special from the menu bar.

The Paste Special dialog box is displayed (see Figure 3.8).

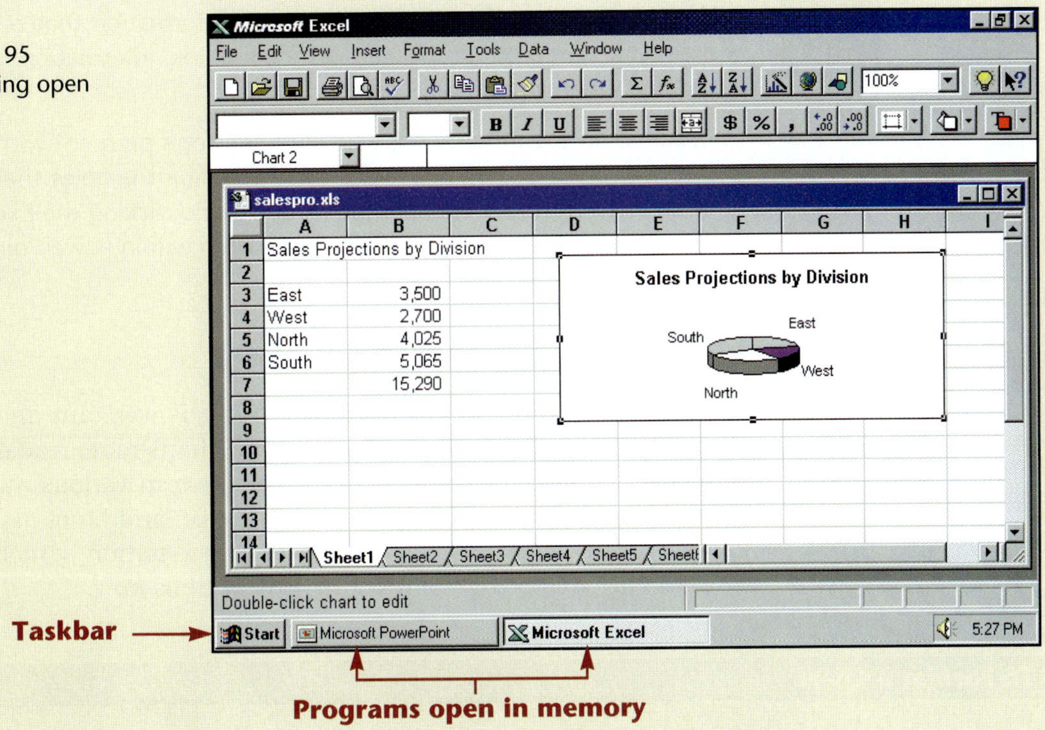

Figure 3.7
The Windows 95 Taskbar showing open programs.

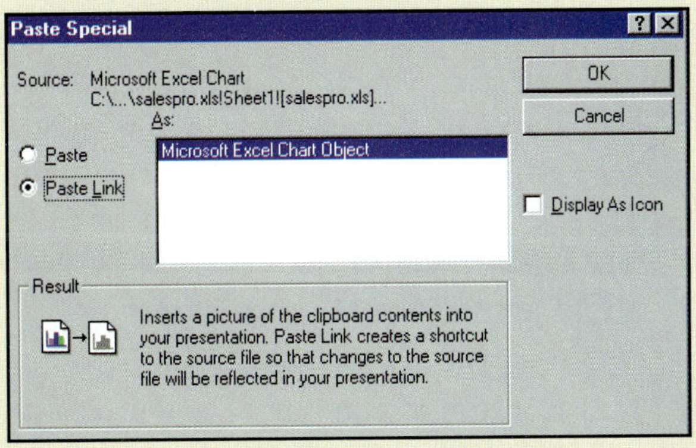

Figure 3.8
The Paste Special dialog box.

8 Click the Paste Link option button so that any future changes made to the original Excel file will be reflected in your PowerPoint chart, then click OK.

The Excel chart is placed in your PowerPoint slide as a linked object. Any changes made to the Excel chart will be reflected in your presentation chart.

9 Save the PowerPoint file as Link.ppt, then close it.

10 Switch to Excel, save the Salespro.xls file and close the program.

All Microsoft programs have the capability to perform *Object Linking and Embedding* (OLE). *Linking* refers to inserting information that retains a connection to data stored in another file. When you link, information in the target file is updated when you modify the source file.

Embedding, on the other hand, actually opens one program within another. For example, embedding an Excel chart in PowerPoint enables the Excel program to be opened from the PowerPoint slide. Double-clicking the Excel chart after it was embedded in PowerPoint opens Excel from within PowerPoint.

Lesson 5: Formatting Charts

You now know how to create charts within PowerPoint and to link Excel charts to a PowerPoint slide. To make your charts more readable and understandable, you need to be able to format them in various ways. In this lesson, you learn how to change the Text, Color, and Lines associated with a chart. You work with a Safety Campaign Presentation, which includes bar, line, and pie charts. Try some formatting options now.

To Format a Chart

1 Open the file Proj0303 and save it as Safety.

2 Double-click the chart on Slide 4, Total sick days per facility.

Microsoft Graph is activated, as shown by the black handles around the chart. The chart is currently a 3-D Column chart, however, you are most interested in showing not only the number of sick days per facility, but also the total for your entire company. You decide to change the chart type to a stacked column.

3 Choose Format, AutoFormat.

The AutoFormat dialog box is activated, as shown in Figure 3.9. Notice that you have a graphical list of choices on how to display the chart.

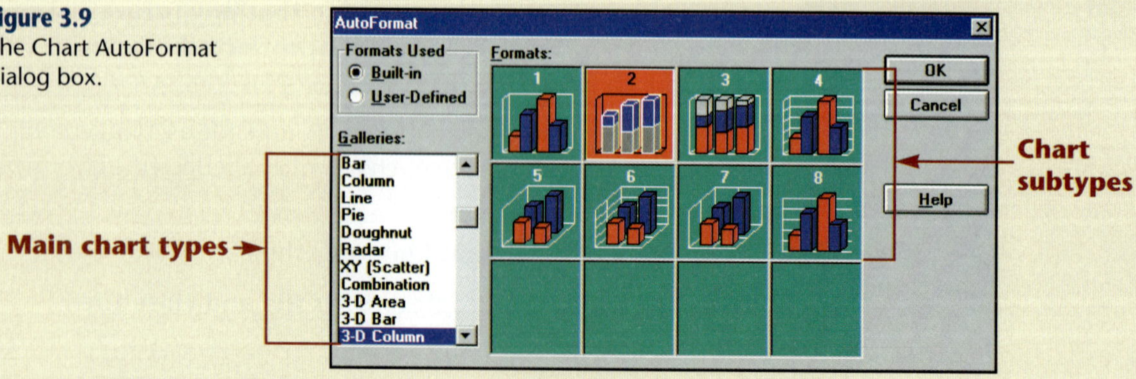

Figure 3.9
The Chart AutoFormat dialog box.

4 Double-click number 2, which shows a stacked, 3-D chart.

The chart changes to the selected format. Now change the color associated with the data series.

5 Double-click the red portion of the bar (the lowest section).

The Format Data Series dialog box appears, as shown in Figure 3.10. Another way of performing the same command is to right-click the data series and choose Format Data Series from the shortcut menu. Note the tabs, which indicate two pages of related information contained in this dialog box—Patterns and Data Labels.

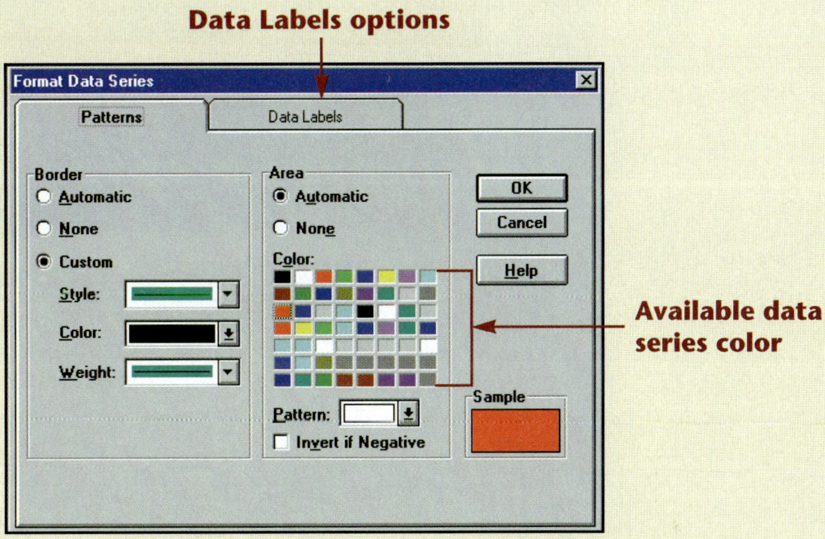

Figure 3.10
The Format Data Series dialog box.

6 Click the Patterns tab if it isn't already in front.

7 In the Color palette of the Area section, click the second color down in the fifth column (purple), and then click OK.

The Danville data series should now be purple. You can also change color by selecting a data series, clicking the Color button drop-down arrow on the Standard toolbar, and selecting a color.

8 Double-click the chart on Slide 5, Sick Days - 1994 vs. 1995.

You want to add a legend and horizontal gridlines to this chart so that it's more understandable.

9 From the Graph toolbar, click the Horizontal Gridlines button and then the Legend button.

Horizontal gridlines and a legend are placed on the chart.

10 Double-click the pie chart on Slide 7, then click the red pie slice until you see handles around it, as shown in Figure 3.11.

continues

To Format a Chart (continued)

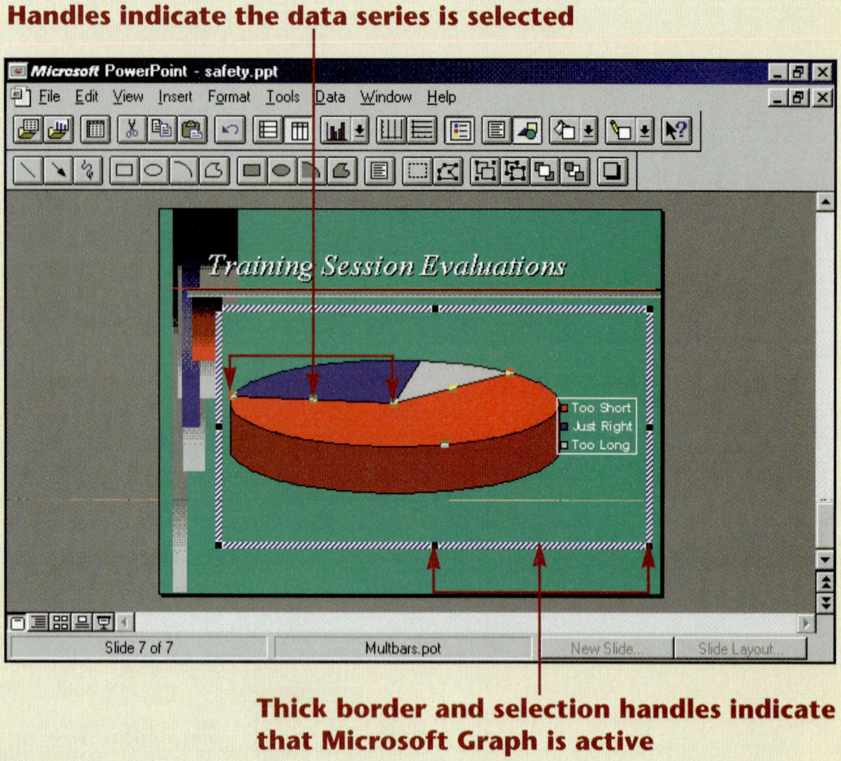

Figure 3.11
The pie chart with a data series selected.

11. **Move the mouse pointer to the middle of the selected wedge and drag to move the slice away from the rest of the chart.**

    The data series represented is emphasized.

12. **Save and close the file.**

INSIDE Stuff

When you double-click different sections of your chart, dialog boxes appear that are related to formatting each section. For example, double-clicking a legend activates a dialog box related to formatting legends.

Table 3.3 is a handy reference guide showing common ways to use the Microsoft Graph peripheral program.

Table 3.3 Summary of Graph Charting Features

To	Use
Start Microsoft Graph	Choose **I**nsert, Microsoft **G**raph from the menu.
	Click the New Slide button and select an AutoLayout format containing a chart placeholder.
	Click the Insert Graph button on the Standard toolbar.
Change the chart type	Click the Chart Type button and select the desired chart from the drop-down list.

To	Use
	Choose **F**o**r**mat, **C**hart Type, or F**o**rmat, **A**utoFormat from the menu bar.
Resize a chart	Move the mouse pointer over a selected chart handle until it changes to a double-sided arrow, then drag to resize.
Move a chart	Move the mouse pointer to the middle of a chart that has white selection handles and drag to a new location.
Delete a chart	Click a chart so that the white selection handles are displayed, then press Del.
Change data in a datasheet	Click the View Datasheet button.
	Choose **V**iew, **D**atasheet from the menu bar.
Delete data from a chart	View the datasheet, select the cells, column(s) or row(s) that you want to erase and press Del.
Change the series color or pattern	Select object(s) within a chart to recolor, then click the Color or Pattern button on the Microsoft Graph Standard toolbar.
	Double-click the object you want to change to activate the Format Data Series dialog box.
Insert titles	Choose **I**nsert, **T**itles and select the title you want to add (chart, X or Y axis).
Change chart orientation	Activate Microsoft Graph, then click the By Row or By Column button on the Standard toolbar.
Show gridlines	Choose **I**nsert, **G**ridlines from the menu bar.
	Click the Horizontal Gridlines or Vertical Gridlines button on the Microsoft Graph Standard toolbar.
Add a legend	Choose **I**nsert, **L**egend.
	Click the Legend button.
Activate features for any part of a chart	Double-click the area of the chart to reformat.
Delete objects on a chart (for example, the legend)	Click the object until selection handles surround it, then press Del.

Lesson 6: Creating Tables

Tables provide another method of working with text in PowerPoint. A table is simply a grid with columns and rows for entering data. A table gives you more flexibility in handling text. You can also group related information together easily when using a table. Another advantage of using a table is that you can resize the columns to display the data better.

To create a table in PowerPoint, you actually use Word toolbars and commands. Therefore, you need to have Word on your system to complete the tutorials in this lesson and Lesson 7. Assuming that you have access to Word, try creating and editing a table now.

To Create a Table

1 Open Proj0304 in the Slide View and save it as Table.

2 Move to the last slide in the presentation, then click the New Slide button on the status bar.

The new slide dialog box is shown, with the available AutoLayouts. Because you need space for a table, select the Title Only AutoLayout, located on the third row down, the third AutoLayout from the left.

3 Double-click the AutoLayout for Title Only.

A blank slide with only the title is inserted after the last slide.

4 In the title placeholder, type Teams.

5 Move the mouse pointer to the Insert Microsoft Word Table button and press and hold down the left mouse button until the pallete is shown.

The palette results so that you can indicate the number of columns and rows for your presentation. Notice that as you drag the mouse pointer down or to the right that the grid is highlighted, indicating the number of columns and rows that you will have in your finished table. Don't be fooled by the initial size of the palette when you first click the button—if you continue to drag down and to the right, Word will create a table as large as six rows by twelve columns. For practical purposes, however, you will probably want a smaller, more readable table for presentations.

6 Drag to indicate a table two columns by four rows in size (see Figure 3.12).

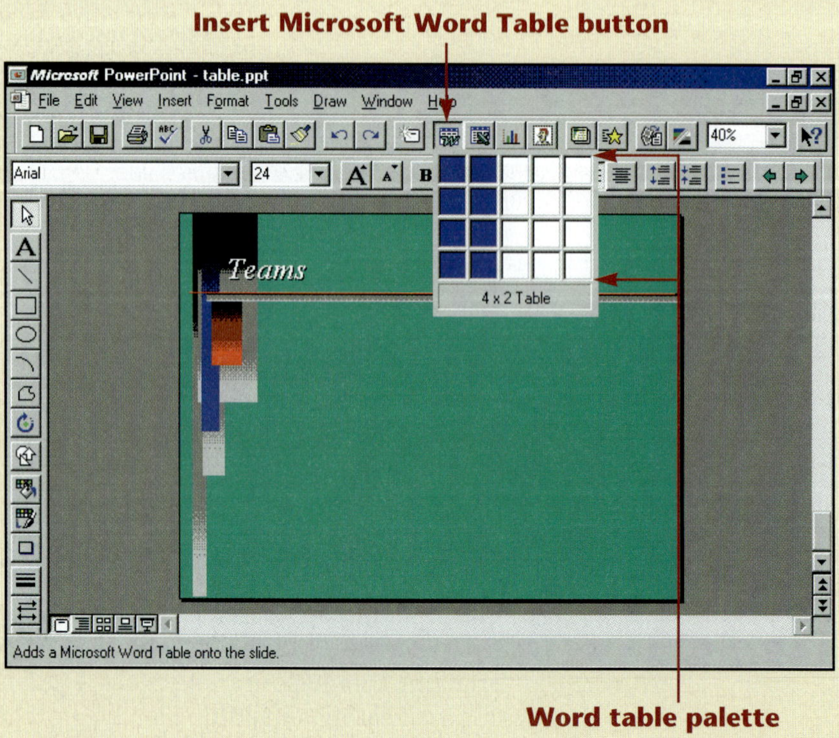

Figure 3.12
The Insert Microsoft Word Table button.

7 Release the mouse button.

A Word table of the indicated size is embedded into your slide. You should see a total of eight cells in your table. Also note that the toolbars reflect Word's functions whenever the table is active.

If you have problems...

If you have trouble indicating the correct number of columns and rows using the palette, choose the **I**nsert, Microsoft **W**ord Table from the menu instead. The resulting dialog box will give you more control over the number of columns and rows.

8 Enter the following information into your table. Press Tab or Shift+Tab to move forward or backward between cells.

Teams	Members
Production	
Sales	
Engineering	

Your table should now appear similar to the one shown in Figure 3.13.

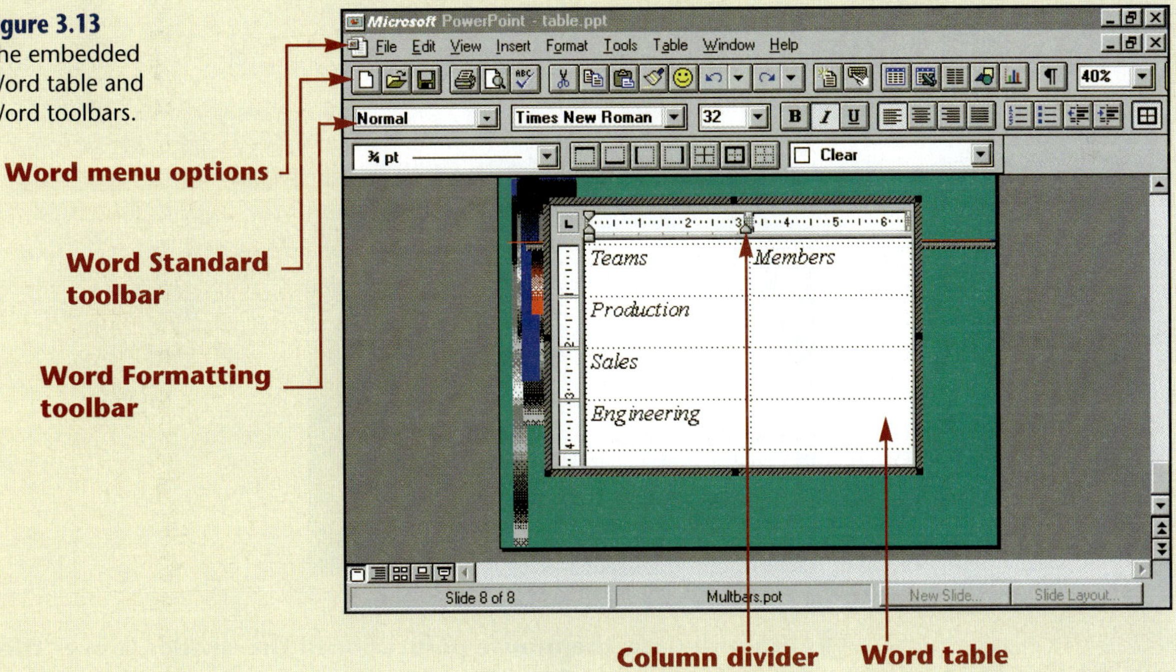

Figure 3.13
The embedded Word table and Word toolbars.

continues

To Create a Table (continued)

9 When you are finished entering information, click anywhere outside the table.

The table is embedded in the slide. Keep the file open for the next lesson, where you learn how to edit a table.

Lesson 7: Editing Tables

You have just created a table as an embedded Word object within your slide. To make the table look truly outstanding, you can resize, move, and reformat the table. In addition, you can add or delete text. Whenever you edit the table, you are using the embedded Word object. Try editing your table now.

To Edit a Table

1 Double-click in the middle of the table area on your slide.

The Microsoft Word Table is activated, as indicated by the black handles around the border of the table.

2 Move the mouse pointer to the column divider on the Word ruler, as shown in Figure 3.14.

When the mouse pointer crosses over the divider, it changes to a two-sided resizing arrow.

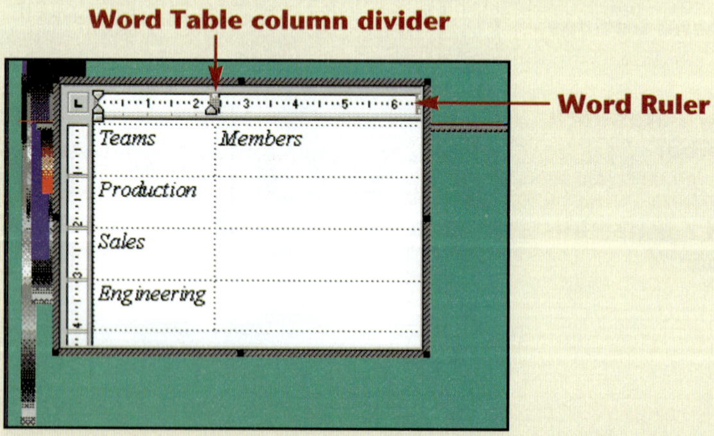

Figure 3.14
The Word Table with column dividers.

3 Click and drag the mouse pointer until the divider is over the 2.5-inch mark on the ruler; then release the mouse button.

The columns are resized with the left column ending at the 2.5-inch mark on the ruler. In some cases, the text may be reformatted and wrapped to the next line in each cell.

4 Click the cell to the right of Production, type Lucinda Hitt, then press [Enter].

The text is entered on the first line of the cell. Pressing [Enter] expands the cell by creating a new line. Word's capability to expand cells insures that related information (in this case, the Production Team Members) stays together.

5 Finish entering the rest of the personnel, as shown in Figure 3.15.

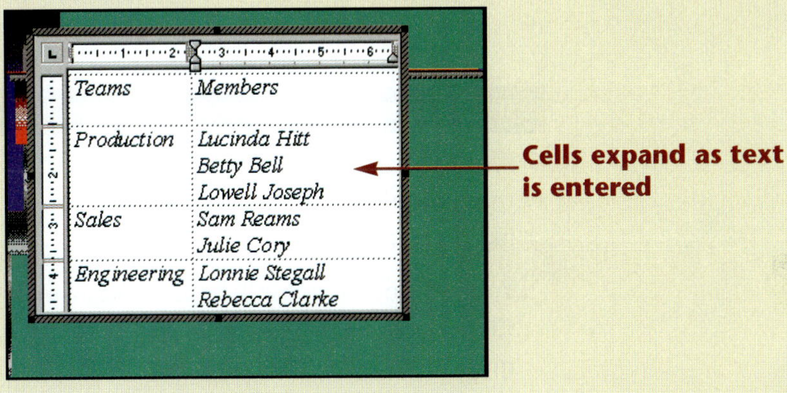

Figure 3.15
The activated table with expanding cells to accommodate new text.

6 Choose Table, Select Table.

All the text in the table is shown in reverse video, indicating that it is selected. Once selected, the text may be formatted just as in a Word document. You can change the size, font, text color, and other text characteristics. Try making some changes now.

7 Click the Font Face and Font Size buttons on the Formatting toolbar, change the font to 28-point Univers.

The text changes to conform to the selected formatting.

8 Select the names in the right column, then click the Bullet button on the Formatting toolbar.

The names are formatted with bullets, making the table more readable.

9 Click outside the table.

The Word Ruler and toolbars are replaced by PowerPoint's commands as Word is closed. The table is embedded as an object on the slide, but remains selected, as indicated by the white selection handles. Use these to move or resize the table as any other object.

Save and close the file. Keep PowerPoint open for the next lesson.

Lesson 8: Creating Organization Charts

Organization charts show the structure and relationships between people or functions in an organization. PowerPoint creates organization charts by starting a peripheral program, called Microsoft Organization Chart, in its own window on a slide. When Microsoft Organization Chart is activated, it also displays its own toolbar and menu options.

The organization chart is created by selecting an AutoFormat with the Organization Chart placeholder. Alternately, choose **I**nsert, **O**bject and choose Microsoft Organization Chart from the displayed list. Once created, the organization chart can be modified in content or format. Create an organization chart now.

If you have problems...

If you get a message when trying to start up Microsoft Organization Chart that PowerPoint can't start the program, you may have one of the following problems:

Your computer doesn't have enough memory to run another program. Close down all the programs (and other presentations) in order to free up more memory on the computer.

The program that PowerPoint is trying to find has been deleted or relocated on a network device that is not hooked up. See your network administrator to troubleshoot the problem.

To Create an Organization Chart

1. **Create a new presentation by clicking the New button on the Standard toolbar.**

   The New Slide dialog box results, with available AutoLayouts. The Organization Chart AutoLayout is on the second row, third from the left.

2. **Double-click the Organization Chart AutoLayout.**

   A new slide is created with a placeholder for the organization chart in the lower portion of the slide.

3. **In the title placeholder, type Team Structure, then double-click the Organization Chart placeholder to activate Microsoft Organization Chart.**

   The chart program is started and the Microsoft Organization Chart window is displayed (see Figure 3.16). Notice that the top level box is selected, as indicated by a highlight.

Figure 3.16
The Organization Chart window.

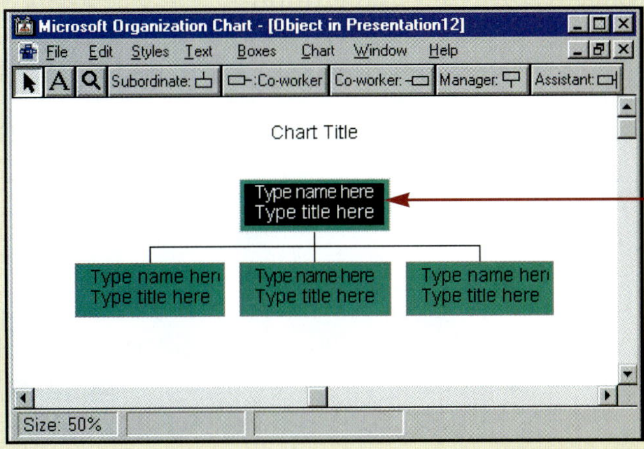

4 **Type Joyce Michaels, press Enter, then type President.**

This enters the name and title into the top level box.

5 **Click the lower level boxes and enter the information shown in Figure 3.17.**

Figure 3.17
The Microsoft Organization Chart dialog box.

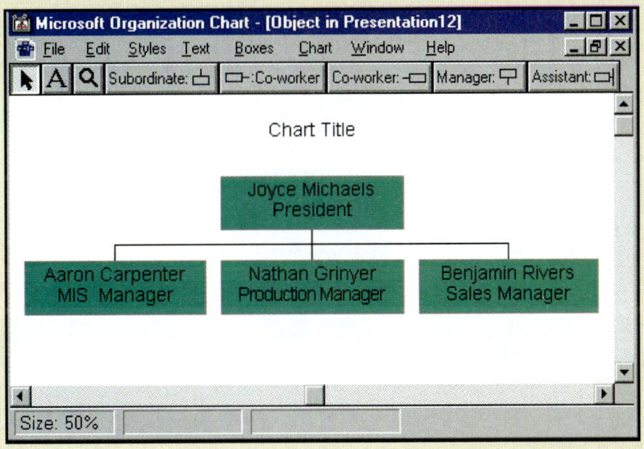

Notice that clicking outside a selected box (either the background or another box) deselects it. Using the Organization Chart toolbar, you can add assistants, coworkers or subordinates. Use the Organization Chart toolbar to add a subordinate now.

6 **Click the Assistant button on the Organization Chart toolbar.**

The mouse pointer displays the assistant symbol.

7 **Click the box containing the name Benjamin Rivers.**

The Assistant Box becomes attached to the selected box, as shown in Figure 3.18. Coworkers, subordinates, and managers are attached in the same way.

continues

To Create an Organization Chart (continued)

Figure 3.18
Attaching an Assistant box.

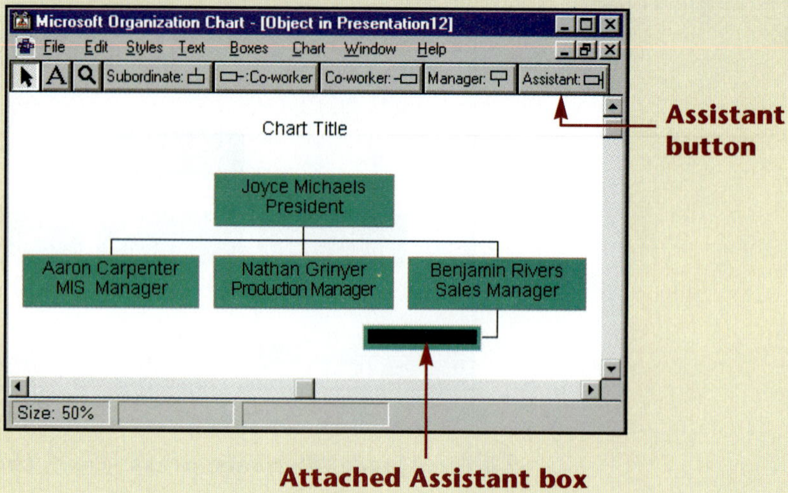

8 With the Assistant Box still selected, press Del.

The selected box is deleted. Leave the presentation open for the next lesson, in which you add formatting features.

Lesson 9: Revising Organization Charts

Once created, an organization chart can be modified for better display. In this lesson, you align text, change color, and modify lines and boxes to improve the appearance of your organization chart.

To Revise an Organization Chart

1 In the presentation open from the previous lesson, select the President's box and choose Text, Left.

All the text in the box is left-aligned.

2 Place the mouse pointer in the upper left corner of the chart, then drag down and to the right until a selection box encompasses the entire chart.

All boxes in the chart are selected. Another way to pick multiple objects is to press and hold Shift, then click each box you want to select.

3 From the menu bar choose Boxes, Shadow.

A pop-up menu showing available shadow appearances appears, as shown in Figure 3.19.

Figure 3.19
The choices associated with Box Shadows.

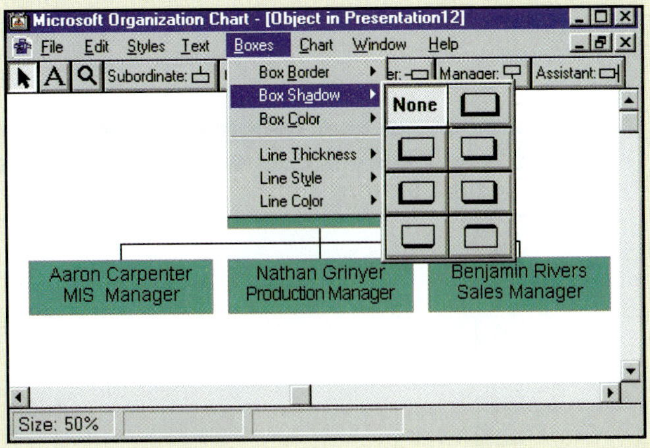

4. **Select the box shadow located below the None button.**

   The shadow appearance is applied to the selected boxes. It may be hard to see the change until the boxes are deselected. If you do deselect the boxes to view the modification, make sure to re-select them for the next step.

5. **Choose Boxes, Color.**

   A listing of available box colors is displayed.

6. **Select white.**

   The selected boxes are changed to white. If you want, you can select one of your corporate or school colors instead.

7. **Choose Chart, Background Color.**

   Another listing of colors is shown—this time for the background portion of the chart.

8. **Choose either red (or one of your organization's colors).**

9. **Choose File, Exit and Return to Presentation.**

   A confirmation box prompts you to update the organization chart in the presentation with those changes you made in the Microsoft Organization Chart program.

10. **Choose Yes to save the changes, then click outside the object.**

    Congratulations! You have just added an organization chart to the presentation. If you later want to revise the chart, simply double-click the organization chart object to re-enter the MS Organization Chart program.

11. **Save the presentation as Orgchart, then close it.**

Table 3.4 summarizes the buttons available on MS Organization Chart's toolbar. Use this as a quick reference guide when working with organization charts.

Table 3.4 Organization Chart Toolbar Buttons

Toolbar Button	Command
	Selects objects.
	Adds a text object to the organization chart.
	Zoom button.
Subordinate:	Adds a box directly below the selected box.
:Co-worker	Adds a box to the left and at the same level of the selected box.
Co-worker:	Adds a box to the right and at the same level of the selected box.
Manager:	Adds a box directly above the chosen box.
Assistant:	Adds a box below and to the left of the selected box.

Project Summary

To	Use
Create a data chart	Click the New Slide button on the status bar and select an AutoLayout format containing a chart placeholder.
Edit a data chart	Double-click a chart object to activate Microsoft Graph.
View a datasheet	Click the View Datasheet button.
Change chart type	Click the Chart Type button and select the desired chart from the drop-down list.
Change chart color or pattern	Select object(s) within a chart to change, then click the Color or Pattern button on the Microsoft Graph Standard toolbar.
Import an Excel chart	Copy the Excel Chart to the clipboard; in PowerPoint choose **E**dit, Paste **S**pecial.
Resize a chart	Move the mouse pointer over a selected chart handle until it changes to a double-sided arrow, drag to resize.

To	Use
Move a chart	Move the mouse pointer to the middle of a chart that has white selection handles and drag to a new location.
Delete data from a chart	View the datasheet, select the cells, column(s) or row(s) you want to erase and press Del.
Insert title on a chart	Choose **I**nsert, **T**itles from the Microsoft Graph standard toolbar.
Show gridlines	Click the Vertical or Horizontal Gridline button on the Microsoft Graph Standard toolbar to add or remove gridlines.
Delete a chart	Click the chart placeholder to display the white selection handles, then press Del.
Create a table	Click and hold the left mouse button while pointing to the Insert Word Table button; drag to select the number of columns and rows desired.
Edit a table	Double-click while pointing to the table.
Move within a table	Press Tab or Shift+Tab to move forward or back by cell.
Select table cell(s)	Drag over multiple cells.
Select a table row	Position the mouse pointer in the row to select; choose T**a**ble, Select **R**ow from the menu.
Select a table column	Position the mouse pointer in the row to select; choose T**a**ble, Select **C**olumn from the menu.
Apply formatting to Table Cells	Select cell(s), then apply formatting, such as bullets, bold, italic, fonts.
Resize table columns	Drag the column marker on the horizontal ruler.
Create an organization chart	Use the Organization Chart, AutoLayout Chart when creating a new slide.
Edit an organization chart	Double-click the organization chart object.
Add a job position to an organization chart	Click the appropriate job position button; then click the box to which it will be attached.
Add box color	Select box(es), then choose **B**oxes, C**o**lor.
Add background color	Choose **C**hart, **B**ackground Color.
Add box shadowing	Choose **B**oxes, Shado**w**.

Applying Your Skills

Take a few minutes to practice the skills you have learned in this project by completing the following exercises.

Creating Data and Organization Charts

You need to create a presentation that includes sales data and the structure for your company, Lowell Manufacturing. Because PowerPoint excels at creating great-looking charts, you decide to use it for your presentation. You create a placeholder for the graph using the Graph AutoLayout; then enter and edit data. You also change chart type and format the graph in various ways.

To Create a Data and Organization Chart

1. Create a new blank presentation and select the Graph AutoLayout.
2. Create a columnar chart with the title, **Five Year Summary**, using the following data:

	1991	1992	1993	1994	1995
Sales	104	135	125	140	150
Expenses	65	89	67	60	88

3. Change the chart type to line, then to a 2-D horizontal bar chart.
4. Change the color for the expense data series to red.
5. Add a new Organization Chart slide and enter the following data:

   Title Placeholder: Lowell Manufacturing

   Joseph Lowell, President

   Jessica Lyles, Admin. Assistant to Pres.

   Brittany Cory, Sales Manager

   Michael Luther, Production Manager

6. Change the box color to white, and the background color to blue.
7. Save the presentation as **Lowell Manufacturing**; then close it.

Creating a Line Chart

You need to show your boss that the cost of living is constantly rising, while your wages (adjusted for inflation, of course!) are falling. You decide to create a line chart to emphasize your point.

To Create a Line Chart

1. Click the New button on the Standard toolbar to show the New Slide dialog box.
2. Choose the AutoLayout to create a slide with title and chart placeholders.
3. Enter the title **Why I Need a Raise** in the place holder.

4. Double-click to activate Microsoft Graph. Enter the following information in the datasheet:

	Jan	Feb	March	April	May	June
Income	**2000**	**1980**	**1967**	**1945**	**1930**	**1900**
Cost of Living	**2000**	**2100**	**2150**	**2180**	**2240**	**2280**

5. Click outside the datasheet to show the chart as a columnar bar chart.
6. Change the chart type to a line chart.
7. Save the file as **Living Expenses**, then close it.

Changing Data Series

As part of your job, you track expenses as a percentage of income. You have previously created a bar chart that shows this information in chart form. But now you have a new boss whom you want to impress by changing the colors and patterns of your chart. You also want to add gridlines to further enhance the chart's appearance.

To Change Data Series

1. Open Proj0305 and save it as **Income**.
2. Activate the Microsoft Chart program by double-clicking the chart placeholder.
3. Double-click the data series for income (currently shown in green) to display the Format Data Series dialog box.
4. Change the data series to a color and pattern of your choice.
5. Add horizontal gridlines by clicking the Horizontal Gridlines button on the Standard toolbar.
6. Save, then close the file.

Working with a Pie Chart

As part of your job at the Bell Manufacturing Company, you track how your company does in relation to the competition. Every quarter, you revise a pie graph that shows your company's percentage of the market share. Last quarter, you beat the competition in several key markets. Now you want to change the graph to emphasize how well your company is doing.

To Work with a Pie Chart

1. Open proj0306 and save it as **Market Share**.
2. Double-click the chart placeholder area to activate the Microsoft Graph program.
3. Use the Chart Type button on Microsoft Graph's Standard toolbar to change the pie chart to 3-D.
4. Change the color and pattern for the Bell Mfg. data series.
5. Select the wedge for Bell Mfg., then drag to separate it from the rest of the pie.
6. Save, then close the file.

Checking Your Skills

True/False

For each of the following, check *T* or *F* to indicate whether the statement is true or false.

__T __F **1.** PowerPoint uses a peripheral program to create charts.

__T __F **2.** Word tables have chart toolbars available.

__T __F **3.** You can create an organization chart by using Word, a peripheral program.

__T __F **4.** Data is entered in a chart by using a datasheet.

__T __F **5.** Once you create a chart you cannot change the chart colors.

Multiple Choice

In the blank provided, write the letter of the correct answer for each of the following.

1. The peripheral program that PowerPoint uses to create or revise data charts is called _______.

- **a.** Microsoft Datasheet
- **b.** Microsoft Organization Chart
- **c.** Microsoft Graph
- **d.** Microsoft PowerGraph

2. The peripheral program that PowerPoint uses to create or revise tables is called _______.

- **a.** Microsoft Graph
- **b.** Microsoft Word
- **c.** Microsoft TableAdd
- **d.** Microsoft Organization Chart

3. Which of the following changes can you *not* make to a chart once it is created? _______

- **a.** changing the color of the data series
- **b.** changing the chart type
- **c.** changing the gridlines
- **d.** none of the above

4. How do you activate Microsoft Graph to edit an existing data chart?

a. Double-click the placeholder that contains the chart.

b. Click the Graphing Programs button on the status bar.

c. Choose **F**ile, **G**raph from the menu bar.

d. none of the above

5. To add a subordinate to an organization chart, ______.

a. click the Subordinate button on the Organization Chart toolbar, then click the box to which it will be attached

b. choose **A**ttach, **B**ox, **S**ubordinate from the menu

c. click the Attach a Job Position button on the status bar

d. click the box to attach the subordinate to, then click the Add a Job Position button

Completion

In the blank provided, write the correct answer for each of the following statements.

1. The temporary storage area in memory where you can cut or copy information is called ______________.

2. The intersection of a column and row in a datasheet is called a ______________.

3. A group of related information in a chart is called a data ______________.

4. A type of chart that shows the relationship of one part to the whole is called a ______________ chart.

5. A program with a specific function that is started every time a feature is accessed is called a ______________ program.

Project 4

Changing the Appearance of a Presentation

Objectives

In this project, you learn how to

- Use Templates
- Work with Color Schemes
- Work with Slide Masters
- Create Drawn Objects
- Select and Modify Drawn Objects
- Work with Multiple Drawn Objects
- Use Clip Art

Why Would I Do This?

Slide Master
A framework slide that controls how a slide will look and enables you to place items, such as a date, name, and/or logo, to each slide automatically.

You can strengthen the impact of your presentations by enhancing the color and design. PowerPoint contains a number of color schemes and design layouts created by graphic artists to make your presentation truly outstanding. You can use these preset color schemes, or create your own. You can use PowerPoint's *Slide Master* to add design elements, such as date or time, to every slide in your presentation. If you make a change, such as switching fonts or increasing a font size, that modification will be reflected in all the other slides in your presentation.

Another way to add interest to a presentation is to include drawings and illustrations. PowerPoint comes with a set of art, called *clip art*, that you can add to emphasize parts of your presentation. You can also use PowerPoint's drawing tools to create simple or complex illustrations. These features combine to quickly and easily produce an impressive presentation. Try using these options for creating an exciting presentation now.

Lesson 1: Using Templates

Template
In PowerPoint, a pattern that includes the text, color, and graphics needed to create standardized presentations. The template can be used to automate the creation of these presentations in the future.

PowerPoint provides an extensive group of predesigned *templates* for your presentations. Because these templates have been created by professional graphic artists, they can help you create a presentation with a consistent, well-designed look. This allows you to concentrate on content, rather than on layout and design.

You can choose to use a template at any time while creating a presentation. For example, if you have created a presentation, but want to see how other color schemes look, you can apply various templates until you find one you like. You can also create and save your own template. Try working with templates now.

To Use Templates

1. **Start PowerPoint and click the Template option button in the PowerPoint start-up dialog box.**

   The New Presentation dialog box appears, with three tabs. This dialog box also appears when you choose the **F**ile, **N**ew command.

   The General tab is used to create a blank presentation, and has no particular template associated with it. The Presentations tab is a listing of files that the AutoContent Wizard uses to make its presentations. The Presentation Designs tab includes a listing of available templates.

2 Click the Presentation Designs tab.

This brings the Presentation Designs page with the available templates to the front (see Figure 4.1).

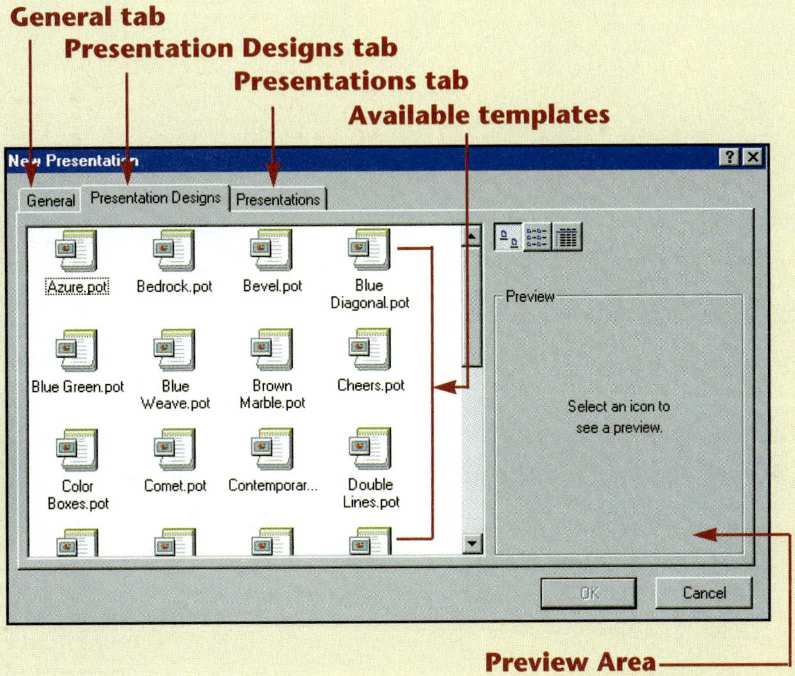

Figure 4.1
The New Presentation dialog box.

3 Click the Azure.pot template file.

The preview window shows an example of the selected template. Click several template files to preview them.

4 Choose the Comet.pot template and click OK.

The New Slide dialog box appears so that you can select a slide AutoLayout.

5 Select the Title Slide.

A title slide with the selected template is produced. Other slides that you add to this presentation will also use the Comet template.

6 In the title placeholder, type your company name; then enter your own name in the subtitle area.

The slide is complete, but now you want to see how the existing presentation would look if you applied other templates to it. Try changing template patterns now.

continues

To Use Templates (continued)

7 Right-click the slide. From the shortcut menu, choose Apply Design Template.

The Apply Design Template dialog box results with a listing of all available templates (see Figure 4.2). Notice that this is the same list of files that you saw previously. You can preview the files by clicking them, just as you did earlier.

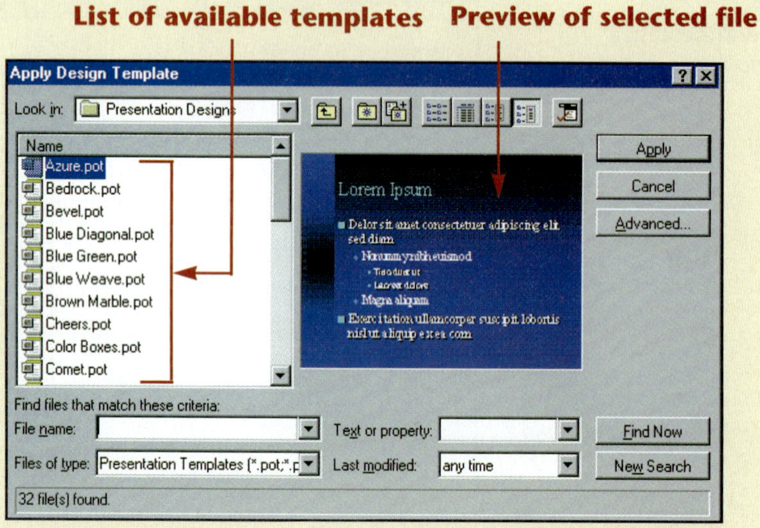

Figure 4.2
The Apply Design Template dialog box.

8 Double-click Bevel.pot.

The new template design is applied to the slide. If you want, try applying other templates. Close the presentation without saving it.

INSIDE Stuff

You can apply design templates by choosing F**o**rmat, Apply Design Te**m**plate, or by clicking the Apply Design Template button on the Standard toolbar.

If you are artistically inclined (or just want to create a custom look for your presentations), you can create your own template. To create your own template, change whatever features of a slide you'd like—color, text, graphics—of a presentation. Choose **F**ile, Save **A**s and enter a name for your new template. Then choose Presentation Templates from the Save as **t**ype drop-down list so that it will be saved as a template and not a file.

Lesson 2: Working with Color Schemes

Knowing how to change *color schemes* is handy for a couple of reasons. You may be about to give a presentation on the road and the LCD or computer screen doesn't have the contrast of your office computer. Being able to change the color scheme could literally save your presentation!

Color Scheme
A set of eight colors you can assign to slides, note pages, and handouts in a presentation.

You can also have similar presentations, but add customized slides for different audiences; one set for sales, one for marketing, and one for advertising. By changing the color scheme for each audience, you can instantly tell that you are running the correct version of your presentation.

Try customizing the color scheme of an existing presentation now.

To Customize Color Schemes

1 Open Proj0401 and save it as Hickory.

2 Display the presentation in the Slide Sorter View so that the new color schemes are easier to see.

Color schemes are most commonly applied in the Slide View or the Slide Sorter View. However, you can also apply color schemes to the Notes Pages View to change the color for the Notes Pages area.

3 Choose Format, Slide Color Scheme.

The Color Scheme dialog box is displayed, as shown in Figure 4.3. You can also open this dialog box by choosing Slide Color Scheme from the shortcut menu.

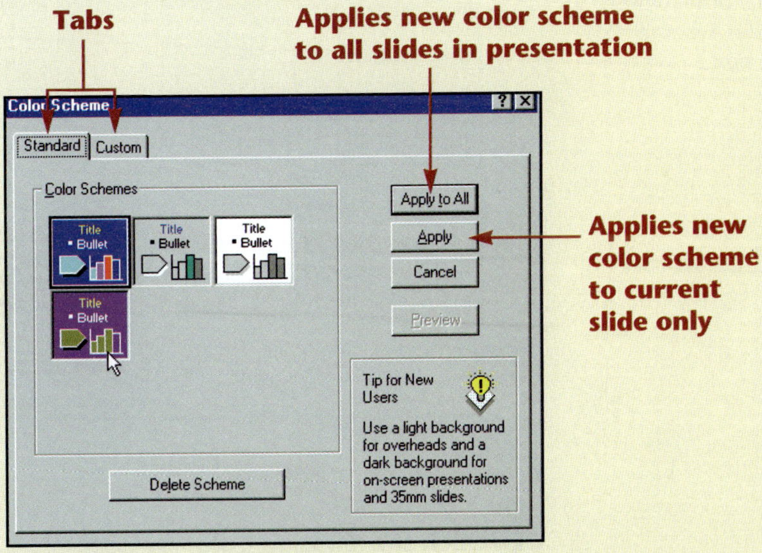

Figure 4.3
The Color Scheme dialog box.

Like many dialog boxes, Color Scheme has more than one page, indicated by the tabs. You choose the Standard tab to select a predesigned color scheme. However, if you want to change only one element of the color scheme (for example, Title Text) click the Custom tab.

In general, you should select a scheme with a light background and dark text for overheads. Select a dark background with contrasting text for on-screen display and 35mm slides. Try selecting a color scheme for on-screen display now.

continues

To Customize Color Schemes (continued)

4 With the Standard tab displayed, select the dark maroon color scheme on the second row; then choose Apply to All.

The presentation is shown with the dark maroon color scheme applied to all slides. If you chose Apply, the color scheme for only the displayed slide would change.

If you like a color scheme, but want to change one element, click the Custom tab in the Color Scheme dialog box to display the custom options. Try customizing your scheme now.

5 Double-click Slide 2, Our Objectives.

Slide 2 of the presentation is shown in the Slide View.

6 Activate the Color Scheme dialog box and click the Custom tab.

The Custom page comes to the front.

7 Click the Title Text color box (see Figure 4.4).

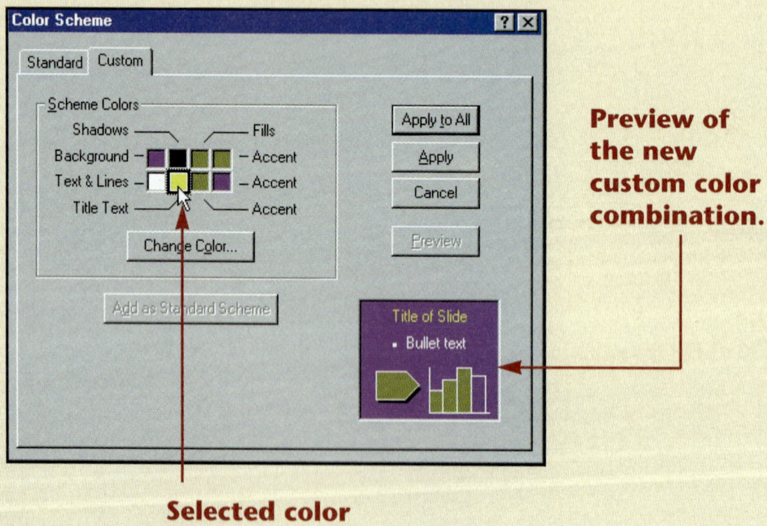

Figure 4.4 The Custom tab of the Color Scheme dialog box.

8 Click the Change Color button.

The Title Text Color dialog box results, with the current color indicated.

9 Select the light blue color (see Figure 4.5).

10 Choose OK.

The Color Scheme dialog box is redisplayed. Notice that a preview of the new color scheme is shown in the lower right corner of the dialog box. If you don't like the new look, just click Cancel, or select another color. You can choose Apply to place the modified color scheme on the currently displayed slide, or Apply to All to change it on all slides.

Figure 4.5
The Title Text Color dialog box.

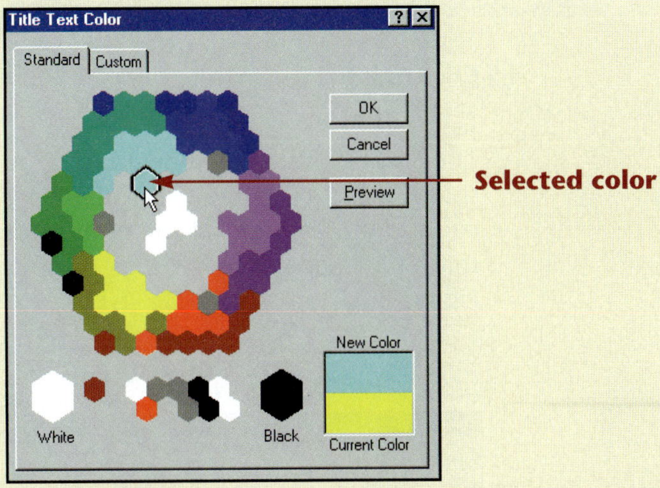

⓫ **Choose Apply to All.**

The color scheme is applied to all slides in the presentation. Save and close your presentation.

PowerPoint for Windows 95 has some great options for changing the background color and pattern of your slides. You can add shadow effects, textures, and patterns to the background. Try changing some of these features now.

To Change the Background Color

❶ **Open Proj0402 and save it as Logging.**

❷ **While viewing Slide 1, choose Format, Custom Background.**

The Custom Background dialog box results, as shown in Figure 4.6. Note the drop-down list arrow under the background fill area of the box.

Figure 4.6
The Custom Background dialog box.

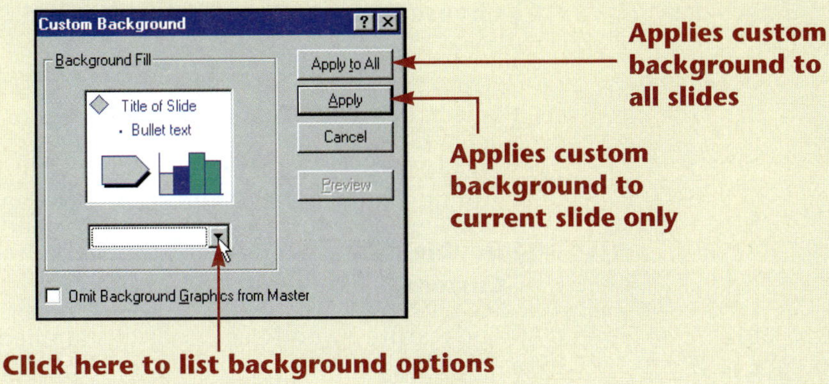

continues

To Change the Background Color (continued)

3 Click the drop-down list arrow for background options, and select Shaded from the list.

The Shaded Fill dialog box appears, showing options related to the shaded fill pattern results. Experiment with different looks for your background by clicking the option buttons for shade styles. Notice that each shade style has a group of variants associated with it (see Figure 4.7).

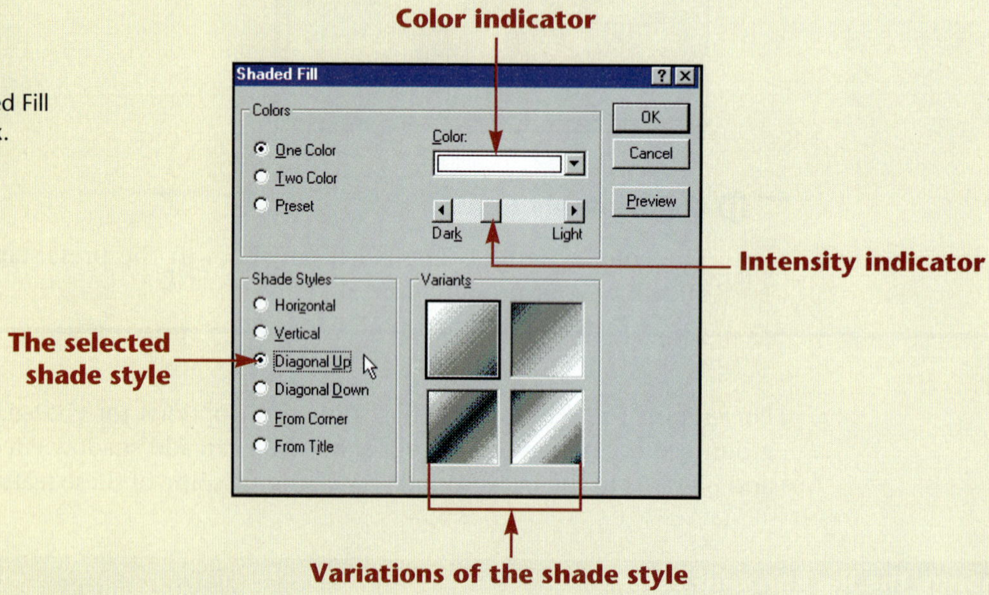

Figure 4.7 The Shaded Fill dialog box.

4 Click the Diagonal Up option button. In the Variants section, click the upper left variant (refer to Figure 4.7) and choose OK; then choose Apply from the Custom Background dialog box.

The chosen background style is applied to Slide 1. You can also add one of a number of textures to the background.

5 Choose Format, Custom Background.

The Custom Background dialog box appears again.

6 Select Textured from the background options drop-down list.

The Textured Fill dialog box results, showing natural-looking backgrounds, such as wood and stone (see Figure 4.8).

7 Double-click the Oak option; then choose Apply to All in the Custom Background dialog box.

The textured wood background is applied to all slides in the presentation. Save and close the file.

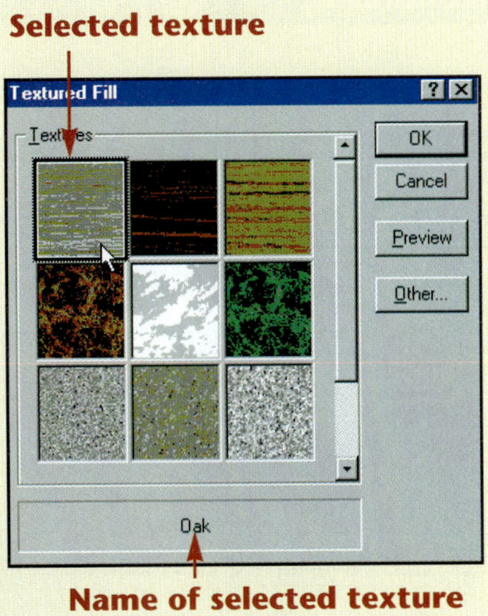

Figure 4.8
The Textured Fill dialog box.

Lesson 3: Working with Slide Masters

As discussed briefly in the introduction to this project, PowerPoint provides a simple tool called the Slide Master that makes creating presentations a simple process. Every presentation has a Slide Master that is determined when a presentation is created. The Slide Master contains instructions (such as background color, background design, text, color, font, and font size) that gives each slide in the presentation identical properties.

In every presentation you have four masters available—the Slide, Title, Handout, and Notes Pages Masters. The Slide Master and Title Master are used the most. True to their names, the Slide Master dictates the format on all slides except the Title Master, which controls how the title slide will appear.

In this lesson, you use and modify Slide Masters. Try using this powerful feature now.

To Work with a Slide Master

1. **Open Proj0403 and save it as Star.**

2. **Choose View, Master, Slide Master.**

   The master slide for the presentation is shown (see Figure 4.9). It contains a title object and a body object that you can use to specify the default format for the title and body text. You can also add other objects to the Slide Master that would then be placed in all presentation slides.

continues

To Work with a Slide Master (continued)

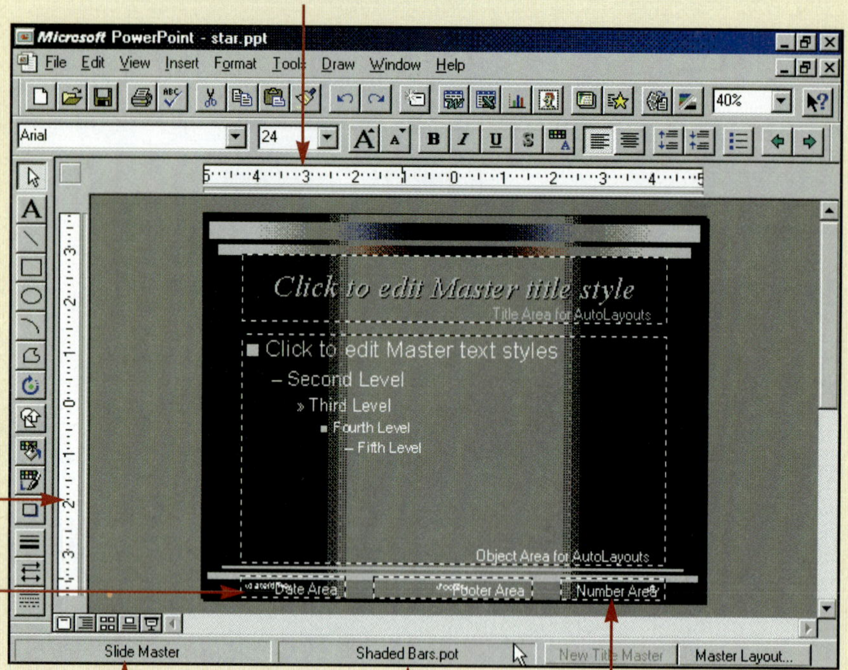

Figure 4.9
The Slide Master.

3. **Slowly drag the vertical scroll bar downward, (see Figure 4.10).**

   The view changes from the Slide Master to the Title Master.

4. **Make sure the Slide Master is on-screen, then click the object entitled, Click to edit Master title style.**

   The title area is selected, as indicated by the thickened border. This area is currently formatted in italics.

5. **Click the Italic button.**

   This removes the italic formatting.

6. **Click the Date area at the bottom of the Master slide.**

   The Date Area is selected. Like most objects, the selection is shown as a thickened, striped border.

7. **Drag to select the contents of the Date area and press Del.**

   The contents of the Date Area are deleted.

8. **Choose Insert, Date and Time.**

   The Date and Time dialog box appears.

Figure 4.10
Moving between the Title Master and Slide Master views using the scroll bar.

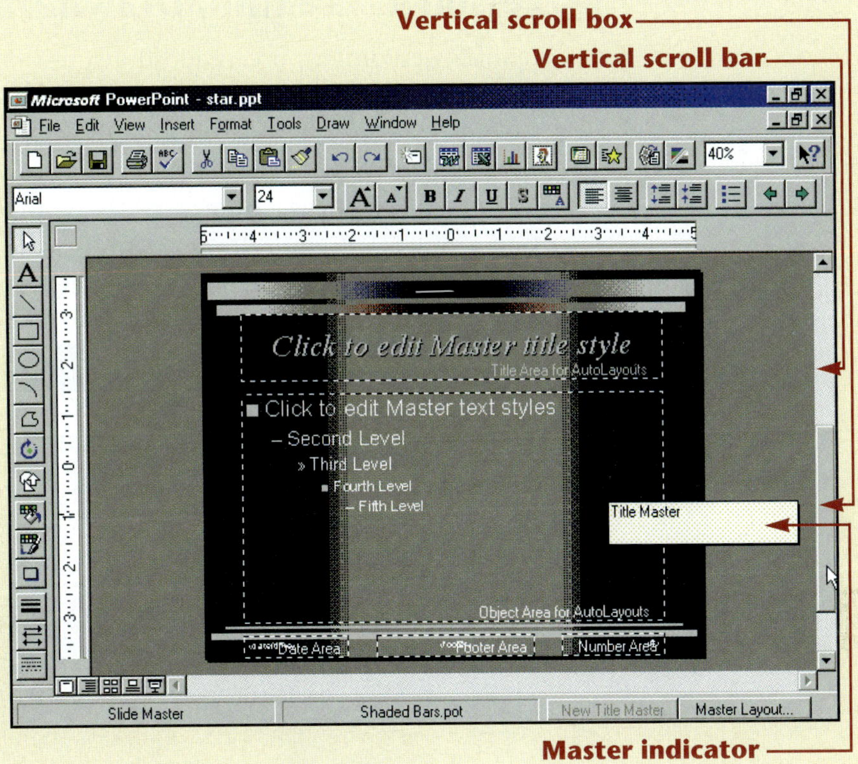

9 Select a date format and click OK.

The current date is inserted into the Slide Master so that it can be viewed on all slides.

10 Choose View, Slides.

The date is inserted into each slide in the presentation. Scroll through the slides to see the date on each slide. Save and close the presentation.

INSIDE Stuff

To quickly toggle between the Slide Master and the Slide View, move the mouse pointer to the Slide View button, press and hold down Shift and click the Slide View button. The Slide Master is displayed. Clicking the Slide View button again returns the presentation to the Slide View.

Jargon Watch

A **template** is a design or blueprint for developing your presentation slides. Templates contain colors, patterns, and text features that help you create a uniform presentation.

Slide Masters enable you to control the elements contained on a slide and dictate how they appear. For example, you can insert the date or slide numbers onto the Slide Master, and they will display on each slide in a presentation.

Drawn objects are items that you create using the Drawing toolbar to enhance your slide by emphasizing certain information. The **AutoShapes** toolbar enables you to quickly reproduce professionally-created shapes.

Lesson 4: Creating Drawn Objects

With PowerPoint, you can add drawings to your presentation. PowerPoint has a variety of drawing tools that enable you to create simple to complex illustrations to enhance the presentation. Once created, you can move, resize, copy, or delete the objects.

You use the Drawing toolbar to draw and modify objects. Examples of drawn objects include lines, arrows, rectangles, and ellipses. Table 4.1 describes the tools found on the Drawing toolbar.

Table 4.1 The Drawing Tools

Button	Name	To
	Selection tool	Select drawn objects.
	Text tool	Add a text object.
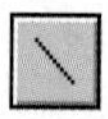	Line tool	Draw a line.
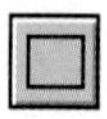	Rectangle tool	Draw a rectangle.
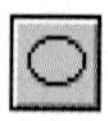	Ellipse tool	Draw an ellipse.
	Arc tool	Draw an arc.
	Freeform tool	Draw freeform shapes.
	Free Rotate tool	Rotate a selected object.
	AutoShapes tool	Add AutoShapes.
	Fill Color tool	Fill a selected object with a texture, color, or pattern.
	Line Color tool	Change the color of a selected line.
	Shadow On/Off tool	Add or remove shading for a selected object.
	Line Style tool	Change the thickness of a line.
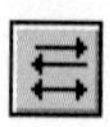	Arrowheads tool	Add arrowheads to a selected line.
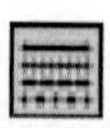	Dashed lines tool	Create dashed or dotted line effects

To Create Drawn Objects

1 Start a new presentation and display a blank slide.

2 Choose View, Ruler.

The ruler guides are shown on-screen. The 0" marks on the horizontal and vertical rulers represent the center of the slide.

3 Click the Rectangle tool on the Drawing toolbar, then move the mouse pointer to the slide area.

The mouse pointer changes to a cross-hair, so that you can accurately place the drawn object.

4 Starting with both ruler markers at 0", click and drag until the horizontal ruler marker is 3", and the vertical ruler marker is 2"; then release the mouse button.

A rectangle is added to your presentation. The color and line colors are whatever is currently specified in the Fill Color and Line Color buttons.

5 Using the Line and Ellipse tools, draw a line and ellipse (see Figure 4.11).

Figure 4.11
The drawn objects.

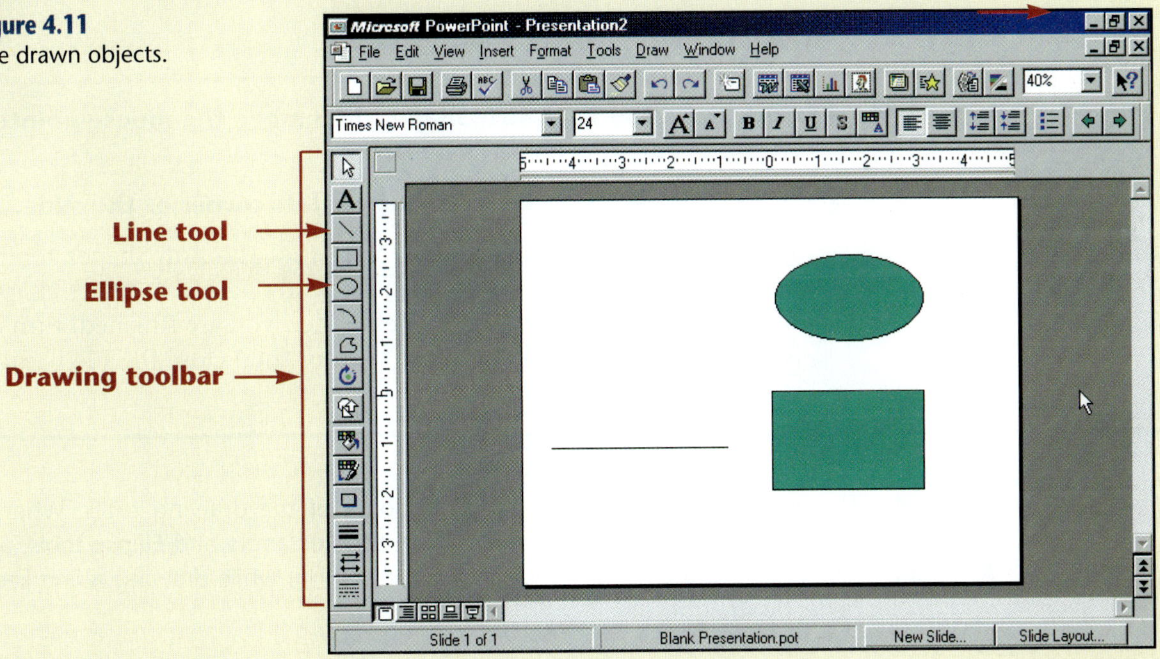

In addition to creating objects from scratch, you can use PowerPoint's AutoShape tool to place pre-drawn shapes on your slide.

continues

To Create Drawn Objects (continued)

6. **Click the AutoShape tool.**

All available AutoShapes are displayed, as shown in Figure 4.12. Move the mouse pointer over any of the AutoShapes for a moment and a Tooltip will display the AutoShape's name.

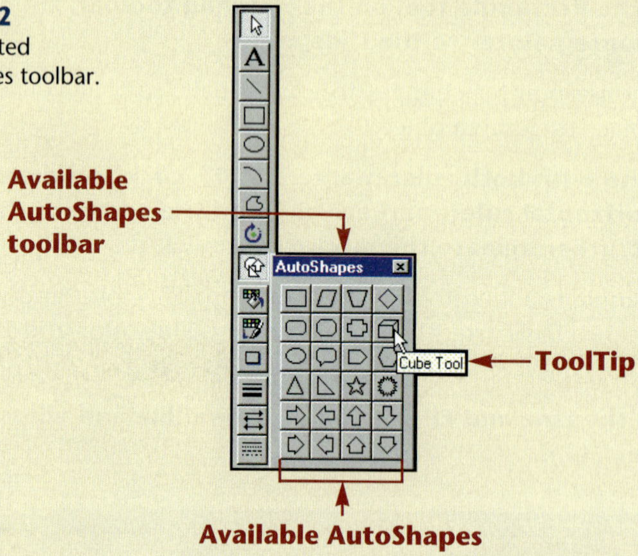

Figure 4.12 The activated AutoShapes toolbar.

7. **Click the Cube Tool AutoShape, then move the mouse pointer to the drawing area.**

8. **Drag to draw the cube in the upper left corner of the slide.**

The cube is placed on the slide. Note that the AutoShapes toolbar remains active so that you can have ready access to other shapes. Experiment with other AutoShapes. When you are finished, turn off AutoShapes by clicking the Close button, then close the file without saving it.

INSIDE Stuff

The Shift key changes the action of some of the drawing tools. When you press and hold down Shift while using the Rectangle and Ellipse tools, a perfect square and circle are formed. Pressing Shift while drawing a line keeps it perfectly straight.

Lesson 5: Selecting and Modifying Drawn Objects

Once created, you can modify drawn objects in a number of ways. You can move, resize, or delete objects. Before modifying an object, it must be selected. Table 4.2 contains useful methods for selecting and deselecting objects.

Table 4.2 Methods of Selecting Objects

Use	To
Select an Object	Click an object.
Select Multiple Objects	Press and hold down Shift while clicking objects.
	Use the selection arrow to draw a box around all objects.
Deselect One Object	Hold down Shift, click the object, release Shift.
Deselect All Objects	Click outside the selected objects.

In this lesson, you learn how to select drawn objects using some of the techniques listed in Table 4.2. Once the objects are selected, you can modify them in a number of ways. Try selecting and changing objects now.

To Select and Modify Drawn Objects

1. **Open Proj0404 and save it as Drawing.**
2. **Click the diamond object.**

   The diamond is selected, as indicated by the white selection handles around the border.
3. **Press and hold down Shift and click the rectangle object; then release Shift.**

   The rectangle is selected in addition to the diamond.
4. **Make sure that the Selection tool on the Drawing toolbar is in effect, then drag from the upper left to lower right corner of the slide and release the mouse button.**

   A dashed border indicates the area being selected. When the mouse button is released, all encompassed objects are selected.
5. **Click outside the objects.**

   All objects are deselected.
6. **Click the rectangle to select it, then move the mouse pointer across the top center handle until it becomes a two-sided resizing arrow (see Figure 4.13).**

continues

To Select and Modify Drawn Objects (continued)

Figure 4.13
The selected object with resizing arrow.

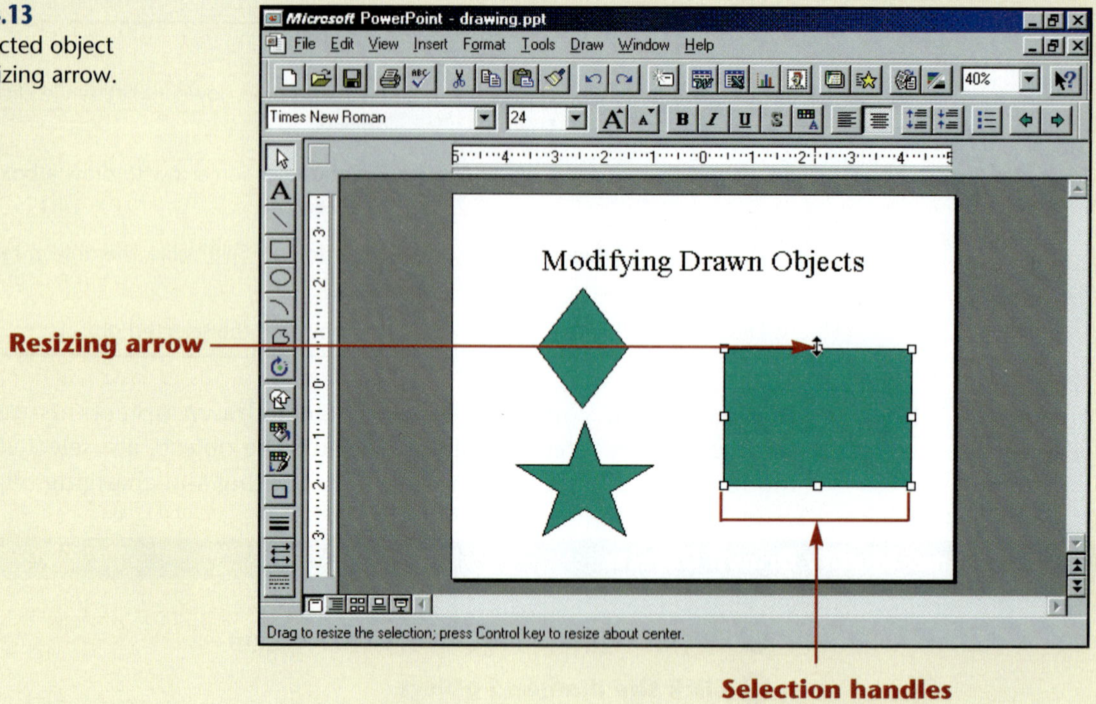

7. **Drag the upper border of the rectangle downward to resize it; then release the mouse button.**

   The rectangle is resized. You can also resize around the center of any drawn object by pressing Ctrl while resizing.

8. **With the rectangle still selected, move the mouse pointer inside the rectangle until it changes to a white selection arrow.**

9. **Hold down and drag the rectangle object until it touches the bottom border of the slide.**

   The drawn object is moved. If you make a mistake as you move or resize an object, choose **E**dit, **U**ndo to reverse the action.

10. **Select the rectangle if it isn't already, then press Del.**

   The selected object is deleted. Selecting several objects before pressing Del erases all the objects at once. If you accidentally delete an object, click the Undo button. Keep this file open for the next exercise.

Once the objects are selected, you can also change the color and lines associated with them. Changing lines and colors helps to emphasize certain information in your presentation. Try changing lines and colors for drawn objects now.

To Change Drawn Object's Lines and Colors

1. **In the Drawing presentation that you revised in the previous exercise, select the star object.**

2. **Click the Fill Color tool on the Drawing toolbar.**

   A pop-up list of choices results, as shown in Figure 4.14. The options you select will be applied only to the selected object(s).

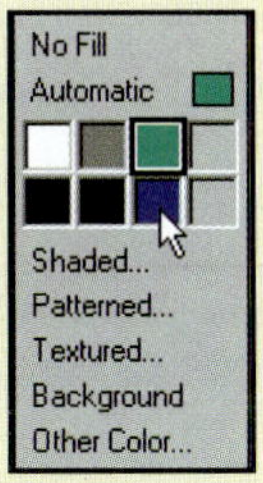

Figure 4.14
The Fill Color button options.

3. **Click the blue color.**

   The Fill Color menu closes and the selected color is applied to the object.

4. **With the star object still selected, choose Format, Colors and Lines.**

   The Colors and Lines dialog box results, as shown in Figure 4.15. (The same dialog box results if you choose the Colors and Lines option from a selected object's shortcut menu.)

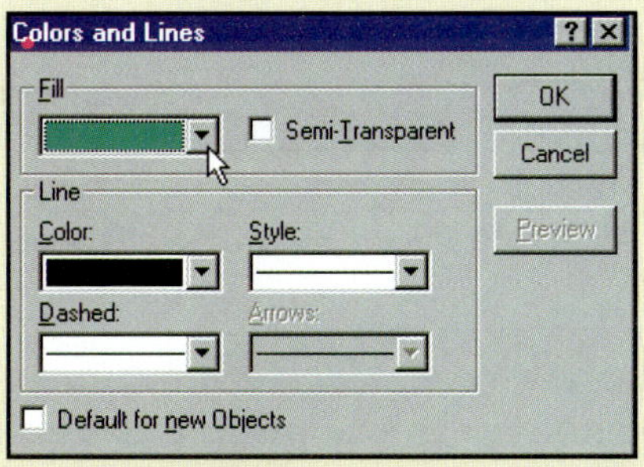

Figure 4.15
The Colors and Lines dialog box.

5. **Click the Fill drop-down list and select Patterned.**

   The Patterned Fill dialog box results, with various options for applying a pattern to the selected object.

   Note that the **F**ill drop-down list also has options for applying shading, textures, and other colors. Selecting No Fill results in the object being shown with only the outline border.

6. **Click a pattern of your choice, and click OK.**

   The Patterned Fill dialog box closes, but the Colors and Lines dialog box is still open. Note that you can change Line Style or Color, and can also make it dashed. Try changing the line style now.

continues

To Change Drawn Object's Lines and Color (continued)

7. **Click the Line Style drop-down arrow, and select one of the thicker lines.**

   Assuming that you can still see at least part of your drawn object behind the Colors and Lines dialog box, you can preview the results of your changes before returning to your presentation. If needed, move the dialog box so that you can see the star. Then click the **P**review button.

8. **Click the Preview button in the Colors and Lines dialog box.**

   The line style for the star changes on-screen. If you want, you can change the line style and click the **P**review button again.

9. **Click OK to accept the changes; then save and close the presentation.**

You can apply color and line options to several objects at once by selecting them, then applying the attributes to the entire group.

Lesson 6: Working with Multiple Drawn Objects

Not only can you work with single drawn objects, but you work with groups of them. You can group, ungroup, and layer objects for different effects. PowerPoint also has commands for lining up drawn objects so that you can display them better. Try working with multiple drawn objects now.

To Work with Multiple Drawn Objects

1. **Open Proj0405 and save it as Objects; then move to the first slide.**

2. **Select the circle, drag to move it on top of the rectangle; then move the star to the middle of the circle.**

   A stack of drawn objects is created. Notice that the star is the selected object.

3. **Choose Draw, Send to Back.**

   The star object is sent to the bottom of the stack of objects. Note the location of the selection handles, indicating that the star is still selected, even though you can't see it.

4. **Select Draw, Bring to Front.**

   The star object becomes the top layer. You can send objects to the top or bottom of the stack, or bring them forward or back one layer at a time.

In addition to layering objects, you can group, or connect objects so that they act as one. If you need to work with them individually at a later time, you can ungroup them. Try grouping and ungrouping objects now.

5. **Move to Slide 2 and select the arrow.**

6. **Move the arrow so that it is connected to the right side of the rectangle; then select both objects by holding down the Shift key as you click them (see Figure 4.16).**

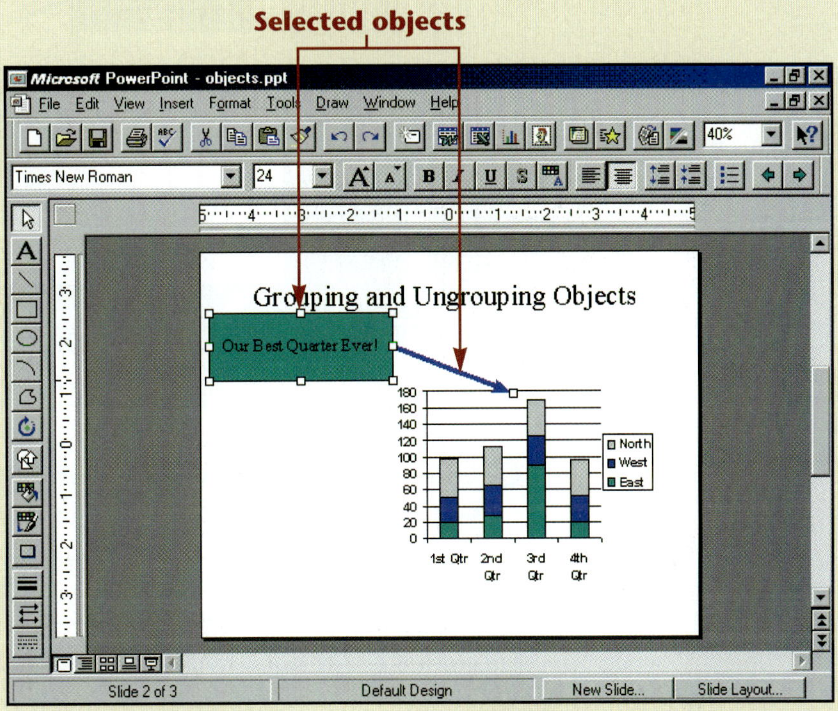

Figure 4.16 Multiple selected objects, ready for grouping.

Notice that the arrow was able to move independently of the rectangle, because it was the only selected item. Once it is grouped with the rectangle, however, they will act as one unit.

7. **Choose Draw, Group.**

The selected objects are combined into one object, as indicated by the selection handles that encompass the entire group (see Figure 4.17). When objects are grouped, any command will apply to the entire group. For example, you can move, resize, or delete all objects in a group at once. In this exercise, grouping the arrow with the rectangle prevents you from accidentally moving them individually. Try moving the grouped object as a unit, and notice how all components move together.

continues

To Work with Multiple Drawn Objects (continued)

Figure 4.17
The grouped object.

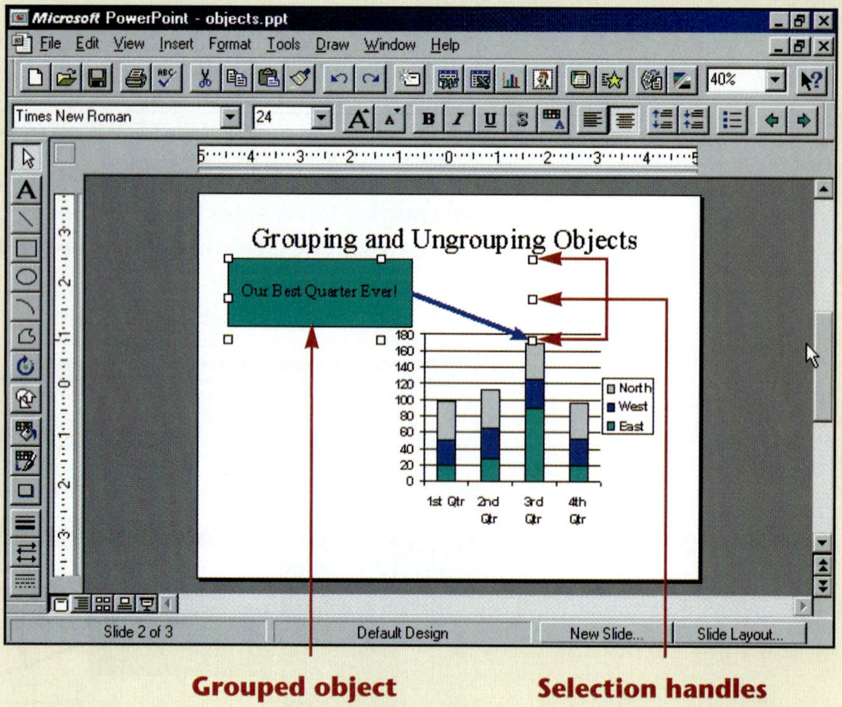

8. **Choose Draw, Ungroup to separate the objects so that you can work with them individually.**

   The objects each have selection handles around them. To work with only one object, click outside the objects to deselect them, then select the one you want. When you have multiple drawn objects, you can also line them up in various ways. Try aligning objects now.

9. **Move to Slide 3, and select all objects.**

10. **Choose Draw, Align, Middles.**

    All objects are lined up at a center point on the slide. Save, then close the presentation.

INSIDE Stuff

To add text to an AutoShape, click the shape to select it, then type the text. To change an AutoShape, select the AutoShape to replace, then choose **D**raw, **C**hange AutoShape from the menu and click the AutoShape that you want.

Lesson 7: Using Clip Art

PowerPoint includes a good selection of electronic clip art in its ClipArt Gallery that you can use to spice up your presentations. In addition, inclusion of clip art can help hold audience attention and reinforce your main points. The ClipArt Gallery includes a variety of pictures for personal and business use. If you need more choices, you can purchase additional clip art programs.

Once clip art is placed on a slide, you can change its location, size, and appearance. Clip art can also be ungrouped into its component parts so that you can work with each part as an individual object. For example, you can recolor parts of a map to highlight data associated with it. Try your hand at clip art now.

To Use Clip Art

1. **Open Proj0406 and save it as Clipart.**
2. **Choose Insert, New Slide.**
3. **In the New Slide dialog box, select the AutoLayout for Text and ClipArt—the first slide on the third row down (see Figure 4.18).**

   A new slide is inserted with a clip art placeholder.

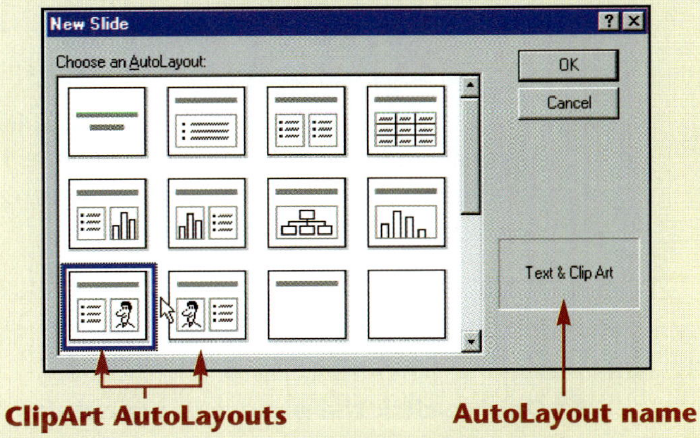

Figure 4.18
AutoLayouts with clip art placeholders.

4. **Double-click the clip art placeholder.**

   The Microsoft ClipArt Gallery dialog box results, with a graphical listing of available pictures. The ClipArt Gallery on your computer may appear differently than the one illustrated here, depending on what art has been installed. If you have a slide without a clip art placeholder, choose **I**nsert, **C**lipArt from the menu. Once in the ClipArt Gallery, you can view all the available pictures, or select a category. To view a specific category, click its name. To display all the images again, click (All Categories).

5. **Click the Currency category, then select the image indicated in Figure 4.19 (the stacked coins) by double-clicking it.**

continues

To Use Clip Art (continued)

Figure 4.19
The ClipArt Gallery with the Currency category selected.

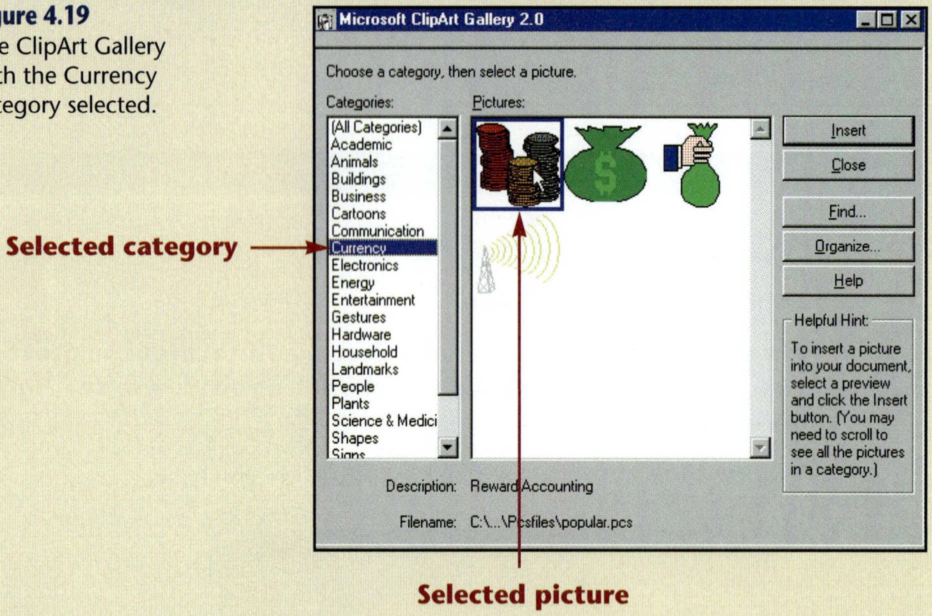

The selected image is inserted into the slide. The white selection handles indicate that the image can currently be resized, moved, or deleted.

If you want to replace the image in your slide with another, double-click it to re-enter the ClipArt Gallery. Try replacing the displayed picture now.

6 Double-click the picture in your slide.

The ClipArt Gallery is displayed.

7 From the Currency category, select the picture of the money bag.

The clip art is replaced by the new picture. Once the image is on the slide, you can change its colors. For example, you may like a picture but don't like how the color combination looks on the slide background. Use PowerPoint's Recolor command to change the image colors. Try recoloring the current clip art image now.

8 Right-click the picture and choose Recolor from the shortcut menu.

The Recolor Picture dialog box appears, as shown in Figure 4.20. Every color used for the picture is listed.

Figure 4.20
The Recolor Picture dialog box.

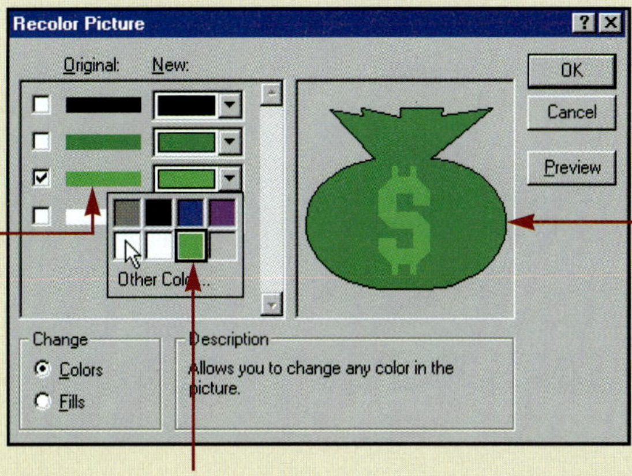

9 Click the drop-down arrow for the lime green dollar sign (in the third row), and select white as the replacement color.

The sample image in the Recolor Picture dialog box shows the result of the change.

10 Click OK.

The clip art is redrawn according to the colors you specified. Save your changes before closing the presentation.

INSIDE Stuff

You must be in either the Slide View or the Notes Pages View to add clip art. Not only can you double-click a clip art placeholder, you can also click the Insert ClipArt button on the Standard toolbar or choose **I**nsert, **C**lipArt.

Project Summary

To	Use
Apply a template	Click the Apply Design Template button on the Standard toolbar.
Apply a color scheme	Choose F**o**rmat, Slide **C**olor Scheme.
Change the background color or pattern of a slide	Choose F**o**rmat, Custom Back**g**round.
View the Slide Master	Choose **V**iew, **M**aster, **S**lide Master.
Show slide	Choose **V**iew, **S**lides.
Insert date into a Slide Master	Select the Date area placeholder on the Slide Master, then choose **I**nsert, D**a**te and Time.

continues

To	Use
Insert footer into a Slide Master	Select the footer area placeholder on the Slide Master, then type in text.
Insert slide numbers into a Slide Master	Select the Number area placeholder on the Slide Master, then choose **I**nsert, Slide **N**umber.
Modify a Slide Master	Select the placeholder and format or change text.
Make a drawn object	Click a tool from the Drawing toolbar, click and drag to draw.
Select a drawn object	Click object.
Select multiple objects	Hold down Shift while clicking objects.
	Using the selection arrow, draw a box around all objects.
Deselect one object	Hold down Shift, click the object, release Shift.
Deselect all objects	Click outside selected objects.
Resize an object	Move the mouse pointer across a selection handle until it turns into a two-sided arrow; drag to resize.
Move an object	Move the mouse pointer to the middle of the selected object; drag to move.
Delete an object	Select the object; then press Del.
Change an object's colors	Click the Fill Color button on the Drawing toolbar.
Change an object's line style	Click the Fill Line button on the Drawing toolbar.
Make an object the bottom layer	Choose **D**raw, Send to Bac**k**.
Make an object the top layer	Choose **D**raw, Bring to Fron**t**.
Group objects	Select objects; then choose **D**raw, **G**roup.
Ungroup objects	Select objects; then choose **D**raw, **U**ngroup.
Insert clip art	Double-click a clip art placeholder.
Recolor clip art	Right-click the clip art object and choose Recolor.

Applying Your Skills

Take a few minutes to practice the skills you have learned in this project by completing the following exercises.

Working with Templates, Slide Masters, and Color Schemes

As an employee of Cory Financial Services, you have been chosen to present information on the company at the next chamber of commerce meeting. You have already developed a presentation about the company, but need to change the template and color scheme so that the presentation will display better on the equipment at the chamber meeting. You also decide to change the Slide Master to show the current date.

To Work with Templates, Slide Masters, and Color Schemes

1. Open Proj0407 and save it as **Cory Financial Services**.
2. Change the design template to Azure.pot.
3. Apply a new custom background for slide 1. Use Shaded Fill, with the Shade Style set to Diagonal Down.
4. Add a date to the Slide Master.
5. Add a clip art image to Slide 3, Financial Stability. Select the stacked coins picture from the Currency category.
6. Recolor the clip art picture to your choice of colors.
7. Use the AutoShapes to add the Thin Right Arrow Tool to the right of the title on Slide 6.
8. Save and close the presentation.

Working with Drawn Objects

You are using your computer skills to earn some extra money by designing logos for small businesses. You have accepted a job to create a logo for Star Storage Company. To make the logo, you use PowerPoint's AutoShapes. You then recolor, move, and resize the objects to create the perfect logo.

To Work with Drawn Objects

1. Create a new presentation with a blank slide.
2. Use the AutoShapes toolbar to add a cube and star to the slide.
3. Change the cube color to blue shaded.
4. Change the fill for the star to textured marble.
5. Resize the cube so that it is bigger than the star; then drag the star on top of the cube.
6. Save the presentation as **Logo**; then close it.

Grouping and Ungrouping Objects

One of your many job responsibilities includes creating manuals outlining training procedures for your company. You create flow charts using PowerPoint's drawn objects to clarify the training progress and provide documentation for quality assurance. By grouping the drawn objects, you can move, resize, or recolor the objects more easily than leaving them as individual objects.

To Group and Ungroup Objects

1. Open Proj0408 and save it as **Training Procedures**.
2. Select all the green flow chart boxes on Slide 1.

3. Connect the objects as one unit.
4. Change the color for the grouped object to shaded blue.
5. Change the font of the grouped object to 28 points.
6. Move the grouped object down so that the bottom border is touching the bottom of the slide.
7. Disconnect the objects.
8. Save, then close the file.

Using Clip Art

You want to create a flyer to send out to everyone announcing your upcoming college graduation. You decide to create it using PowerPoint's clip art Gallery. You then modify it to suit your needs.

To Use ClipArt

1. Create a new presentation with a blank slide.
2. Choose **I**nsert, **C**lipArt to enter the ClipArt Gallery.
3. Choose the Academic category, then double-click the clip art that looks like a diploma.
4. Right-click the inserted clip art and choose Recolor from the shortcut menu.
5. Change the red ribbon to blue.
6. Save the file as **Diploma**, then close the file.

Checking Your Skills

True/False

For each of the following, check *T* or *F* to indicate whether the statement is true or false.

__T __F 1. You can create predrawn objects in your presentation using the AutoShapes toolbar.

__T __F 2. In most cases, a predesigned template frees you to concentrate on the content of the presentation without having to worry about the structure and design.

__T __F 3. The Design Template enables you to select and print handouts for a presentation.

__T __F **4.** Customizing the template design before building your presentation is usually best because you can't change the template at a later time.

__T __F **5.** You can dictate common elements for all slides by using the Design Master.

Multiple Choice

In the blank provided, write the letter of the correct answer for each of the following.

1. You insert pictures into your presentation by using _______.

a. AutoLayout

b. ClipArt

c. Templates

d. Master Color Schemes

2. One category of predesigned templates not provided by PowerPoint is _______.

a. color overheads

b. 35mm slides

c. color on-screen presentations

d. color story boards

3. To make two drawn objects act as one unit you can _______.

a. deselect them

b. group them

c. send them to back

d. apply AutoShapes

4. By changing the design elements on the Master Slide, you change the template to a custom design and automatically apply that design to all _______.

a. the text slides in the presentation

b. the slides in the presentation

c. future presentations built in the current session

d. title slides in currently active multiple presentations

5. Objects placed on the Master Slide are _______.

a. displayed on all the slides

b. displayed if the Master On switch is used

c. hidden unless clicked

d. always blue

Completion

In the blank provided, write the correct answer for each of the following statements.

1. You can select several objects by holding down the ______________.
2. You can tell that a drawn object is selected because it has ______________ around its borders.
3. The set of eight colors associated with a slide design is called its ______________ ______________.
4. PowerPoint contains electronic pictures referred to as ______________.
5. A blueprint or pattern for slide design is called a ______________.

Project 5

Adding Multimedia Features

Objectives

In this project, you learn how to

- Use Transitions in the Slide Sorter View
- Use Transitions in the Slide View and the Slide Show View
- Use the Build Feature
- Use the Animation Effects Toolbar
- Use Sound
- Insert Movie Clips
- Play Movie Clips in the Slide Show

Why Would I Do This?

When you are actually presenting your slide show to an audience, you want to make the greatest impression possible. One way to do this is to use PowerPoint's transition effects between slides. The transition effects vary the way slides advance during a presentation. Another way to create anticipation is to use the build feature, which displays your bullet points one at a time. Animation, sound, and movie clips are also attention-grabbers. By using these multimedia features, you change your presentation from merely good to outstanding.

Lesson 1: Using Transitions in the Slide Sorter View

In Lessons 3 and 6 of Project 1, you learned how to move through a presentation in the Slide Show View. By now you have probably run some other slide shows. As you click the mouse button or press ↵Enter to move to a new slide, you probably noticed that each slide replaced the previous one.

The transition effects help you make more of an impact by varying the way one slide replaces another. For example, you can specify a slide to fade, wipe, or dissolve into another. You can also add sound (as long as your computer has a sound card) as the slide changes, which is guaranteed to keep the attention of the audience. Table 5.1 describes some transition effects.

Table 5.1 Popular Transitional Effects

Transition Effect	Description
Blinds	Opens the screen in wide, even strips horizontally or vertically.
Box In or Out	Redraws the screen from the center outward or from the outside to the center, using a box shape.
Checkerboard	Changes the screen with a checkerboard pattern, either across or down.
Cover	Redraws the screen as the new slide covers up the previous one.
Fade Through Black	Fades away the old slide, shows black momentarily, then fades in the new slide.
Random Bars	Similar to blinds, except that the strips are thin and uneven.
Split	Redraws the screen by splitting it in different directions.
Strips	The new slide rolls over the old one, usually diagonally.
Uncover	Opens the screen like a curtain, in a variety of directions.
Wipe	Sweeps the screen in a choice of directions.

You can access the transition commands in several ways. You can choose the **T**ools, Slide **T**ransition command or use features available in Slide Sorter View. Try adding some transition effects now.

To Use Transitions in the Slide Sorter View

1 Open Proj0501 and save it as Retail.

2 Display the presentation in the Slide Sorter View.

The slides are shown in miniature. Notice the Slide Sorter toolbar that automatically displays when the Slide Sorter View is used (see Figure 5.1). The Slide Sorter toolbar makes it easy for you to add or change transition effects.

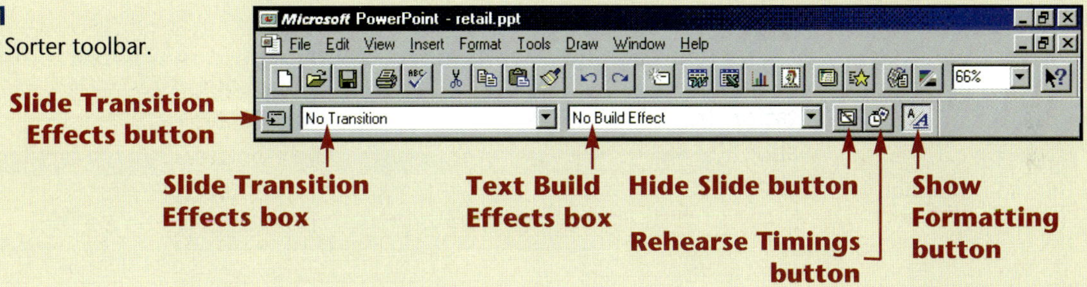

Figure 5.1
The Slide Sorter toolbar.

3 With the first slide selected, click the Slide Transition Effects button.

The Slide Transition dialog box is displayed, as shown in Figure 5.2. Notice that this dialog box contains categories for selecting the effect, speed, advance, and sound for the selected slide.

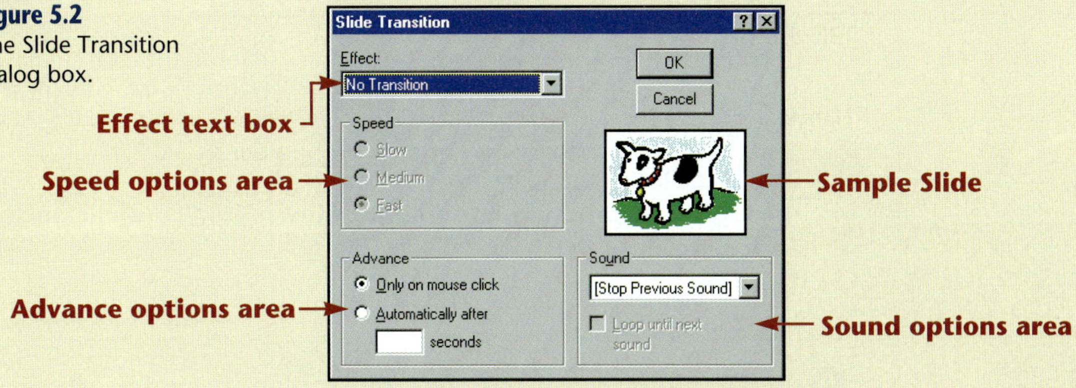

Figure 5.2
The Slide Transition dialog box.

4 Click the Effect text box drop-down arrow.

A list of available effects appears.

5 Select Blinds Horizontal; then click the miniature sample slide in the dialog box.

A preview of the effect is shown. This is a handy way of viewing the various effects before committing to them. If you want, you can

continues

To Use Transitions in the Slide Sorter View (continued)

change the speed to slow and click the sample slide again to see the change.

6 Make sure that the Only on Mouse Click option button is selected in the Advance area, then choose OK.

The transition effect is applied to Slide 1. Notice that a miniaturized version of the Slide Transition icon is shown at the bottom of Slide 1. This indicates that this slide has an effect associated with it. Furthermore, clicking the Slide Transition icon will display the transition.

Another method of applying transition effects in the Slide Sorter View is to use the Slide Transition Effects button on the Slide Sorter toolbar.

7 Click the Slide Transition Effects drop-down list arrow and select Checkerboard Across (see Figure 5.3).

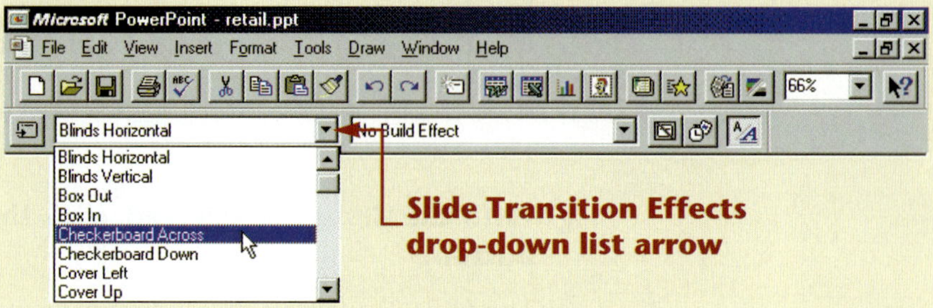

Figure 5.3 The Slide Transition Effects drop-down list.

The effect is seen immediately on Slide 1. Try out some different transition effects on Slide 1. When you are finished, make sure that Checkerboard Across is selected.

If you want to apply the same effect to several slides, select the slides before selecting the transition. Now try changing the transition effect for several slides at once.

8 Deselect Slide 1 by clicking outside it, then select Slides 2 through 6 by pressing and holding down Shift and clicking each slide.

A thick black line appears around each of the slides, indicating that they are selected.

9 Use the Slide Transition Effects button on the Slide Sorter toolbar and select Dissolve.

As the transition effect is applied, the first slide in the selected series shows the change. You can see the effect again by clicking the Slide Transition icon at the bottom of any transitional slide (see Figure 5.4).

Figure 5.4
Click the Slide Transition icon to see the transition effect.

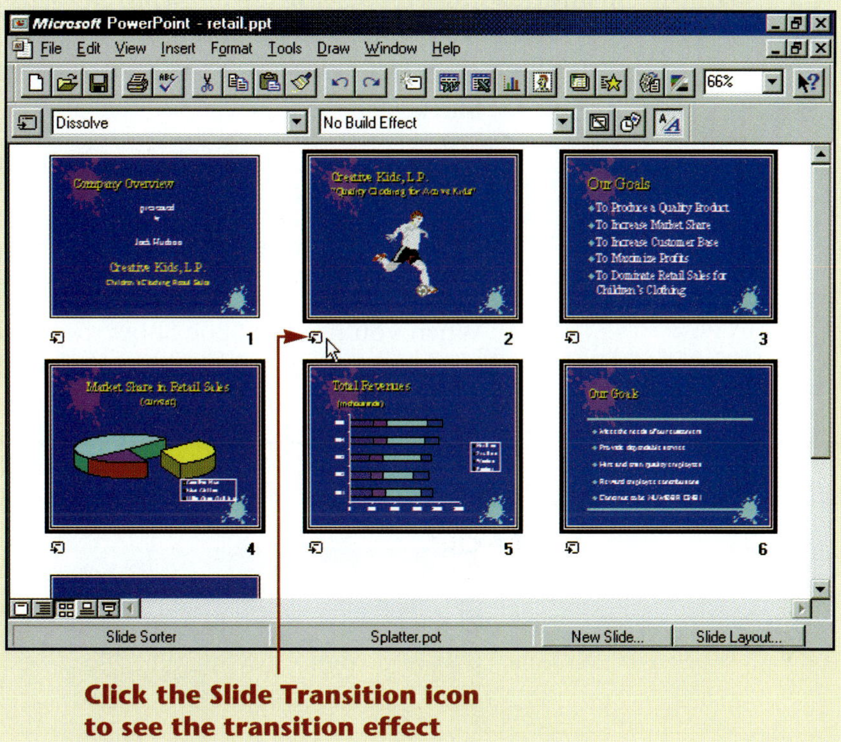

Save the file and keep it open for the next exercise.

Lesson 2: Using Transitions in the Slide View and the Slide Show View

The easiest way to set your transition effects is in the Slide Sorter View. However, using the Slide View is helpful if you want to change only one slide at a time. To add or change transition effects in the Slide View, choose the **T**ools, Slide **T**ransition command from the menu bar.

The Slide Show displays the results of your hard work. You can preview your slide transition changes full-screen when you run the slide show. Try these features now.

To Use Transitions in the Slide View and the Slide Show View

1 In the Retail presentation, double-click Slide 7.

This displays Slide 7 in the Slide View.

2 Choose Tools, Slide Transition from the menu bar.

The Slide Transition dialog box is displayed.

continues

To Use Transitions in the Slide View and the Slide Show View (continued)

3 Click the Effect drop-down list arrow and select Fade Through Black.

A preview of the selected effect is shown. Another way that you can vary transitions is to add sound.

4 Click the Sound drop-down list arrow, and select Applause (see Figure 5.5).

When you run the Slide Show the Applause sound will be activated at the slide transition (assuming that you have the appropriate equipment to take advantage of this feature).

Now that you have added special effects, you want to preview them as a complete electronic slide show.

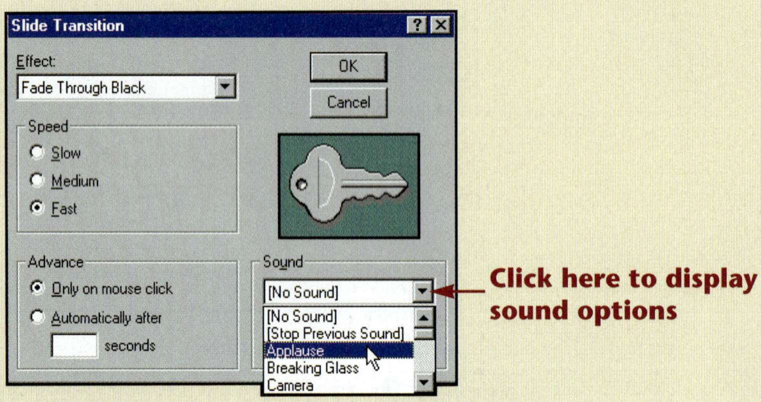

Figure 5.5
The Slide Transition dialog box.

5 Click OK to close the Slide Transition dialog box, then choose View, Slide Show, Show.

The slide show begins.

6 Click the left mouse button to advance through the slides.

The slide show is displayed, using the transitional effects you applied.

You can change the transition effects at any time during presentation development. After the slide show ends, select the slide, choose **T**ools, Slide **T**ransition, and then change the effects in the dialog box. Try changing some effects now.

7 Change the transition effect in Slide 5 to Box Out.

8 Remove the transition from Slide 2 by selecting No Transition in the Effects drop-down list of the Slide Transition dialog box.

9 Run the slide show.

By running the slide show, you can view the changes. Save the file and keep it open for the next lesson.

Table 5.2 is a handy reference guide that you can use when you add slide transitions to your presentations.

Table 5.2 Summary of Slide Transition Commands

To	Use
Add Slide Transitions in the Slide View	Choose **T**ools, Slide **T**ransition.
Add Slide Transitions in the Slide Sorter View	Choose Slide Transition from the shortcut menu for any slide.
	Click the Transition Effects box on the Slide Sorter toolbar.
	Click the Slide Transition button on the Slide Sorter toolbar.
View Slide Transitions (Slide Sorter View).	Click the Slide Transition icon below the slide.
	Choose **V**iew, Slide Sho**w**, **S**how.
	Click the sample slide in the Slide Transition dialog box.
Change Slide Transitions	Select slide(s), choose **T**ools, Slide **T**ransition.
	Select slide(s), use the special features on the Slide Sorter toolbar.
Remove Slide Transitions	Choose No Transition in the **E**ffect area of the Slide Transition dialog box.
	Choose No Transition in the Slide Transitions Effect Box on the Slide Sorter toolbar.

Lesson 3: Using the Build Feature

Another way to keep an audience's attention is to use PowerPoint's popular Text Build Effects. The Text Build Effects creates the slide one item at a time. Use this feature to have your bullet points appear one by one. This has great advantages over displaying the entire slide. It prevents your audience from reading ahead on a slide (and losing attention). An additional option is to dim or even hide previous points as you move to a new one. The build feature operates independently from transition effects you learned in Lessons 1 and 2. Try some of these effects now.

To Use the Build Feature

1 Make sure that the Retail presentation is open in the Slide Sorter View, then select Slide 3.

Because Slide 3 has bullet points, you can specify that PowerPoint build them separately. You can also indicate what build effect you would like.

2 From the Slide Sorter toolbar, click the Text Build Effects drop-down arrow.

A list of available methods for building your text points is shown. Selecting one of the effects from this list will automatically specify that the slide will have the text displayed one point at a time.

3 Select Fly From Left (see Figure 5.6).

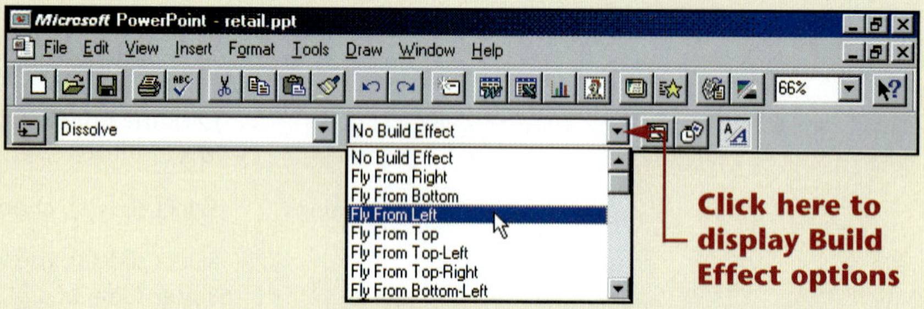

Figure 5.6
The Build Effect drop-down list

The Text Build Effects drop-down list closes, and a special build icon appears at the lower left corner of Slide 3. This indicates that it is a build slide (see Figure 5.7).

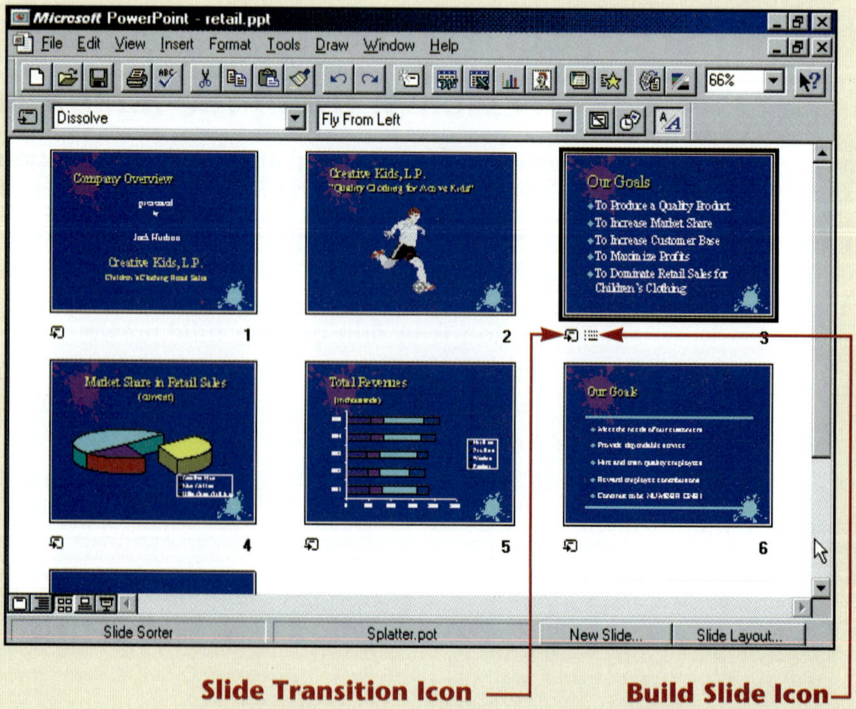

Figure 5.7
The Build Slide indicator.

4 Click the Slide Show button.

The slide show begins.

5 Click the left mouse button several times.

The bullet points are displayed, one at a time.

In addition to using the basic build feature, you now want to dim the previous bullet points so that the bullet you are talking about is emphasized.

6 Press Esc to return to Slide Sorter View; then select Slide 3 if necessary.

7 Choose, Tools, Build Slide Text, Other.

The Animations Settings dialog box appears. The lower right corner of the dialog box contains options for dimming the previous point when you move to a new one. You can select a color to show the points or choose to hide them when the new one is shown.

8 Click the After Build Step drop-down arrow, select the aqua blue color shown in Figure 5.8.

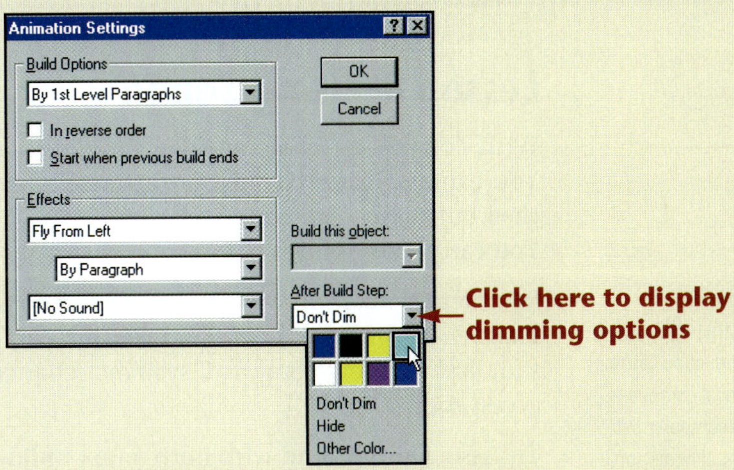

Figure 5.8
The Animations Settings dialog box with the Dim options activated.

9 Choose OK.

This returns you to the Slide Sorter View

10 Click the Slide Show button to run the slide show, starting at Slide 3; then click the left mouse button several times to advance through the slide show.

The bullet points are shown in a build sequence. As each new line is displayed, the previous one is dimmed (see Figure 5.9). Save the file before closing it.

continues

To Use the Build Feature (continued)

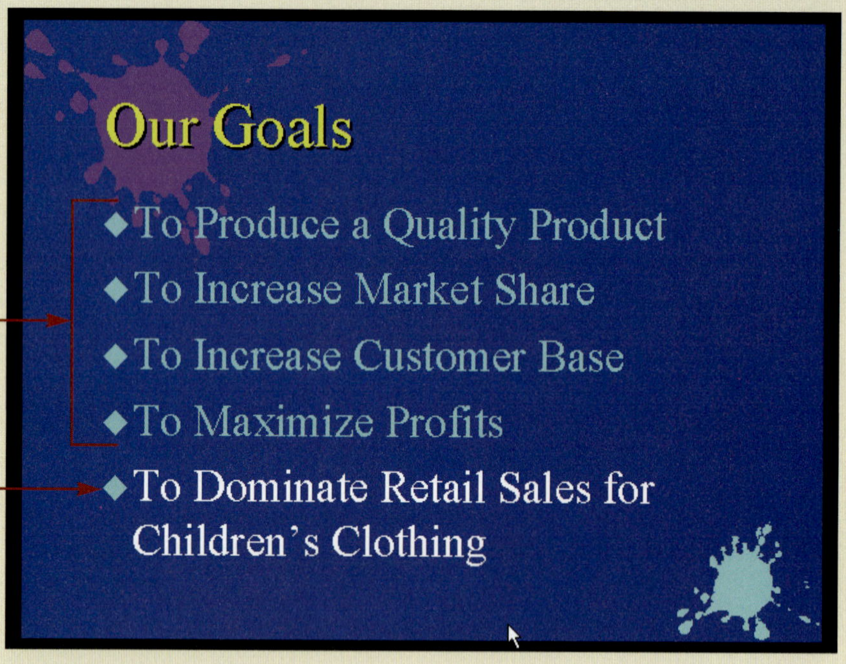

Figure 5.9
The Slide with dimmed options in effect.

The previous points (dimmed)

The current point (emphasized)

Lesson 4: Using Sound

With PowerPoint, you can play sounds or music during your presentation. You can associate the sound with a number of things—your text points as they build, the transition to a new slide, or even with an object on-screen. You can set up sounds to play automatically, or only when you specify.

Sound Board
An adapter that adds digital sound reproduction capabilities to personal computers, making the computer better suited for multimedia applications.

In order to take full advantage of the sound features, you need to have a *sound board* and speakers. Because this equipment is becoming part of the standard for new computer systems, chances are good that you will have access to it.

Try associating sound with both a text build and a slide transition now.

To Use Sound

1. **Open Proj0502 in the Slide Sorter View and rename it Sound.**
2. **Select Slide 3, and use the Slide Sorter toolbar to add Fly From Bottom Right as the build effect.**
3. **Choose Tools, Build Slide Text, Other.**

   The Animation Settings dialog box results. Note that the Build Options and Effects are already indicated because you already selected them (Figure 5.10).

Figure 5.10
The Animation Settings dialog box.

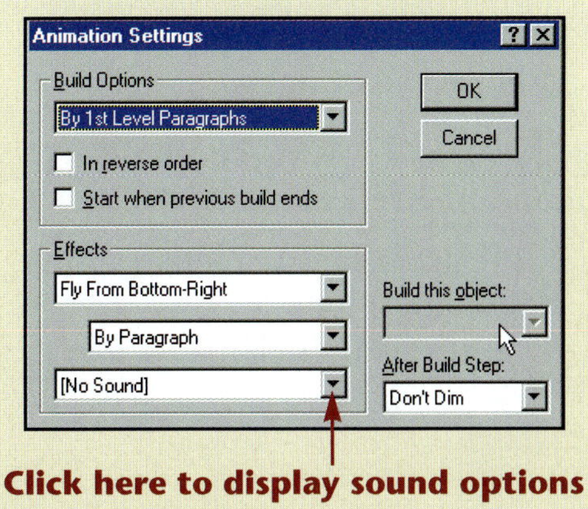

4. **In the Effects drop-down list associated with sound, select Whoosh; then click OK.**

5. **Select Slide 5, then choose Tools, Slide Transition.**

   The Slide Transition dialog box opens.

6. **Select Box In as the transition effect, and Cash Register as the sound; then click OK.**

   When the transition is made from Slide 4 to Slide 5, the Cash Register sound will result.

7. **Choose View, Slide Show, Show to run the slide show from the beginning.**

   When the text builds in Slide 3, the "Whooshing" sound is heard. When the transition is activated between Slide 4 and 5, the sound of a cash register is heard. Save and close the presentation.

To find out what multimedia equipment is installed on your system, activate the Control Panel in Windows 95. Then double-click the Multimedia and Sound icons.

Lesson 5: Using the Animation Effects Toolbar

The Animation Effects button on the Standard toolbar is a quick way to add animation effects to selected areas of slides. Clicking the button activates the Animations Effects toolbar. With the toolbar you can indicate sounds and effects, then preview them in the Slide Show. To have one of the sounds play when certain text or an object appears on-screen, you can select the text and then click the Animation Effects button that represents the sound you want.

Try using the Animation Effects toolbar now.

To Use the Animation Effects Toolbar

1. **Open Proj0503 in the Slide View and save it as Animate.**

2. **Select the bullet text placeholder in Slide 3; then click the Animation Effects button on the Standard toolbar.**

   The Animation Effects toolbar results (see Figure 5.11). You can hold the mouse pointer over each of the toolbar buttons for a moment to see the ToolTip for each.

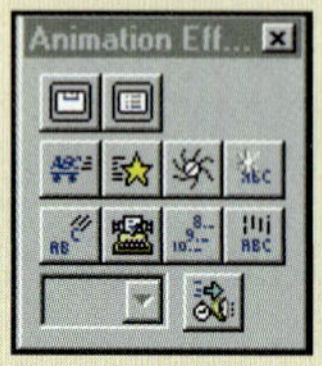

Figure 5.11
The Animation Effects buttons.

3. **Click the Typewriter Text Effect button.**

   The selected text will be "typed" onto the screen during a slide show, including the appropriate sound. Notice that the Build Slide Text button at the top of the Animation Effects toolbar is pushed in, indicating that the bulleted area of text has animation effects associated with it.

4. **Move to Slide 6, Our Goals, and select the title area placeholder.**

5. **Click the Flying Effect button on the Animation Effects toolbar.**

   The Animate Title button on the Animation Effects toolbar is depressed, indicating that the title area has a special effect applied to it.

6. **On the same slide, select the bulleted text placeholder area and select the Drop-In Text Effect.**

   The Build Slide Text button appears pushed in as soon as the effect is applied to the bullet portion of the slide. Also notice that the Animation Order button on the Animation Effects toolbar shows that this area of the slide will be built after the title.

7. **Choose View, Slide Show, Show to run the presentation from the beginning.**

8. **Save, then close the presentation.**

If you decide that you don't want the animation effect, you can remove it for a slide. Select the slide area for which you want to remove the effect, then click the Animate Title or Build Slide Text buttons to deactivate them.

Table 5.3 summarizes the buttons available on the Animation Effects toolbar. Use this as a reference guide when adding animation effects to your presentation.

Table 5.3 Animation Effects Toolbar

Use	To
Animate Title	Make the title drop in from the top during a slide show.
	Indicate when the title has an animation setting associated with it.
Build Slide Text	Make the text points build one at a time during a Slide Show.
	Indicate when the body text has an animation setting associated with it.
Drive-in Effect	Make the selected object fly in from the right accompanied by the sound of a car.
Flying Effect	Make the selected object fly in from the left accompanied by a "whooshing" sound.
Camera Effect	Give the effect that a camera shutter is opening on the slide.
Flash Once	Make the selected object flash once upon completion of the build during a Slide Show.
Laser Text Effect	Make the selected object fly in from the upper right corner accompanied by the sound of a laser.
Typewriter Text Effect	Make the selected text appear to be typed in accompanied by the sound of a typewriter.
Reverse Text Build	Make the selected text build from the bottom of the list upward.
Drop-in Text Effect	Make the selected text drop in one word at a time from the top of the slide.
Animation Order	Show the order that the selected text or object appears on a slide.
Animation Settings	Display the Animation Settings dialog box so that you can change more advanced options.

Lesson 6: Inserting Movie Clips

One of the multimedia capabilities of PowerPoint is that you can actually show movie or video clips during your presentation. You can insert movies by creating or using a slide with a Media Clip placeholder. You can also place a movie object on a slide by choosing the **I**nsert, **M**ovie menu command. In either case, the Media Player, a program that is part of Windows 95, controls the settings and display of the media clip.

Because the movie clip is an object, it can be resized, moved, or deleted in the same way as any other object. The video can be previewed in the Slide View, in the Media Player, or as part of the Slide Show itself. Try inserting movie clips now.

To Insert a Movie Clip

1 Open Proj0504 and save it as Movie.

2 Display Slide 2 in the Slide View, then choose Insert, Movie.

The Insert Movie dialog box results. The dialog box looks very much like the one that results from the **F**ile, **O**pen command. Movie clips have an extension of .avi. The file you want to insert, Kayaker.avi should be available on your data disk that came with this book.

If you want to find other movie clips, look in the Media folder that comes with Windows 95.

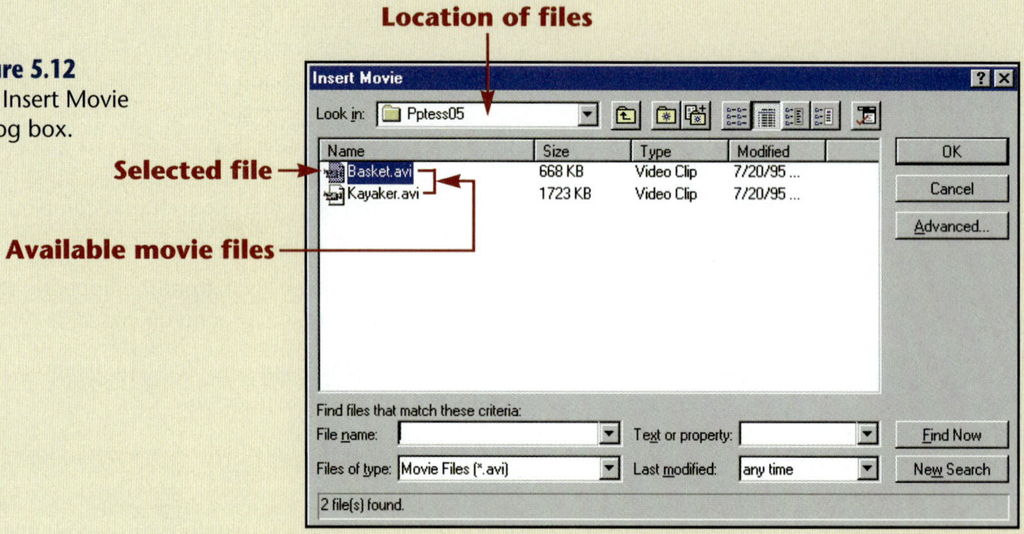

Figure 5.12
The Insert Movie dialog box.

3 Choose Kayaker.avi from the displayed list and click OK.

The file is inserted into your slide as an object, as shown in Figure 5.13. The movie clip is inserted as a poster, which means that the first frame of the movie is shown on-screen. Because the movie is an object, you can resize it by dragging any of the handles.

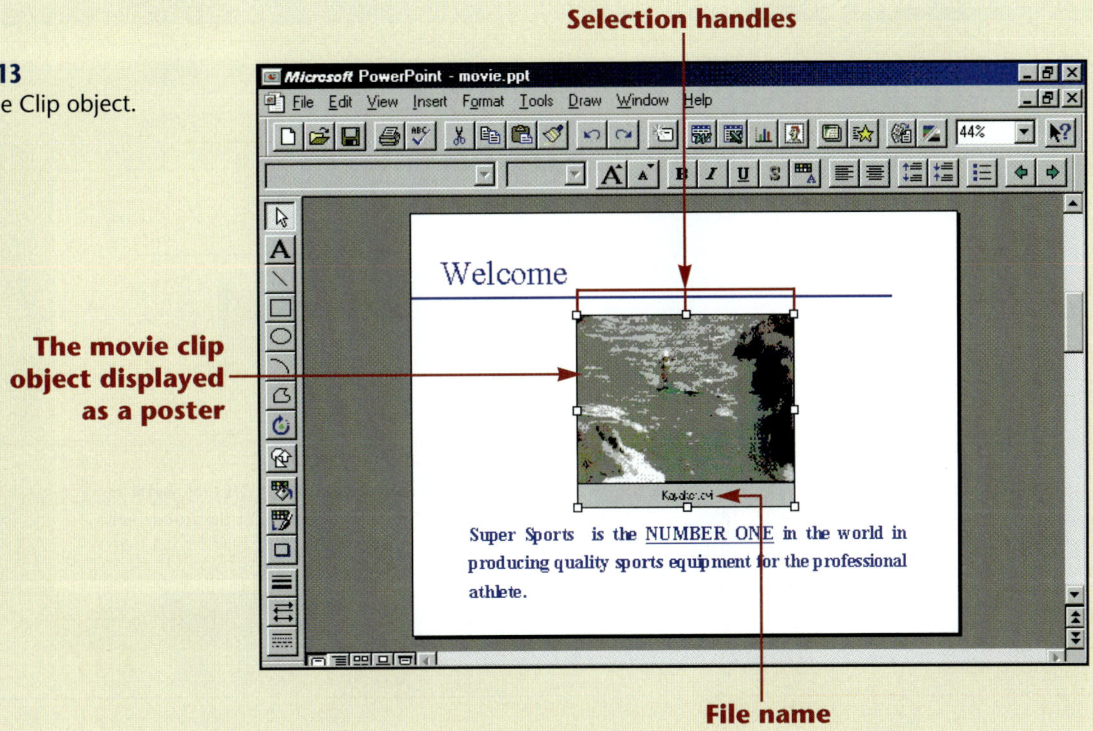

Figure 5.13
The Movie Clip object.

❹ **Drag any selection handle to resize the movie object; then move it if necessary so that it is in the middle of the screen.**

❺ **Double-click the object.**

The video clip plays, including accompanying sound. Note the Pause and Stop buttons that enable you to pause or end the video (see Figure 5.14). The moving bar to the right of the media control bar shows the progression in time of the movie.

continues

To Insert a Movie Clip (continued)

Figure 5.14
Media buttons.

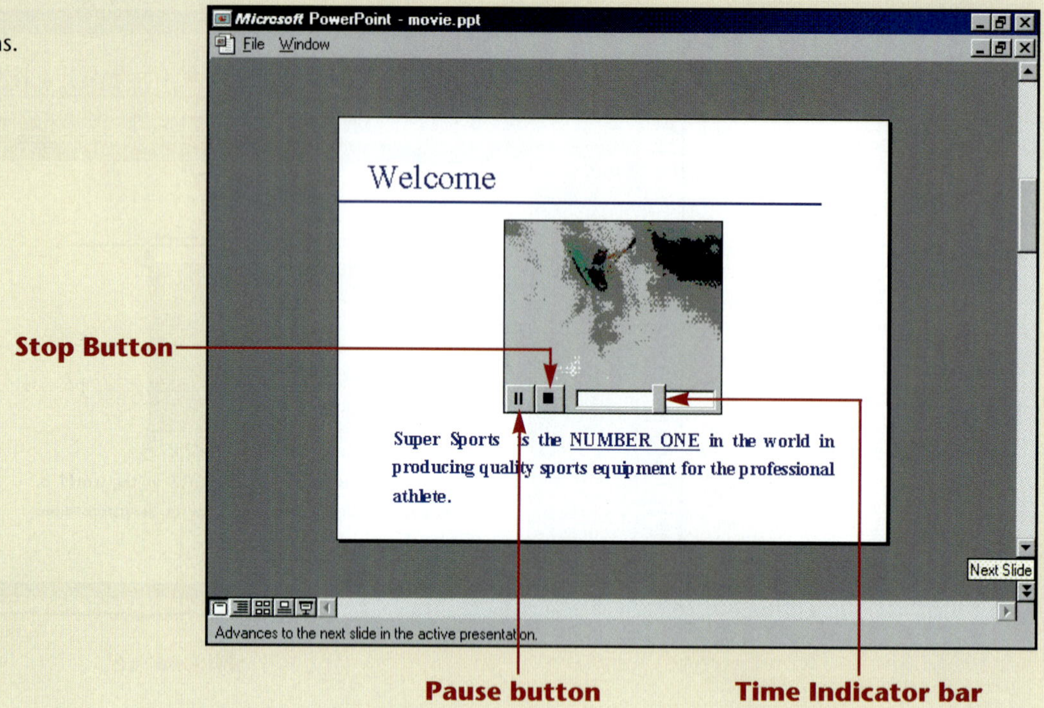

6 Display Slide 6; then double-click the Media Clip placeholder.

The Media Player is activated on-screen, with appropriate menus (see Figure 5.15).

Figure 5.15
The Media Player Screen.

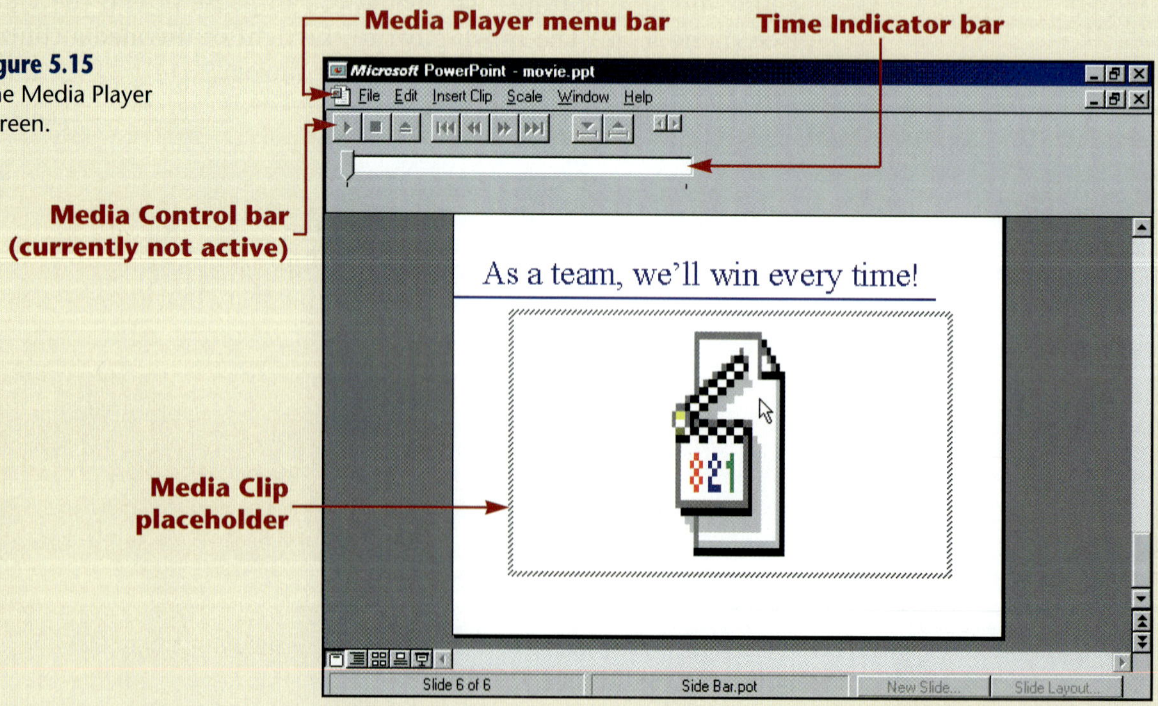

7 Choose Insert Clip, 4 Video for Windows from the Media Player menu bar.

The Open dialog box results, with a listing of available video files.

8 Select Basket.avi.

The first frame of the selected video clip is shown. A control bar with a number of buttons related to playing, rewinding, and fast-forwarding the video becomes active, similar to the buttons on a VCR (see Figure 5.16).

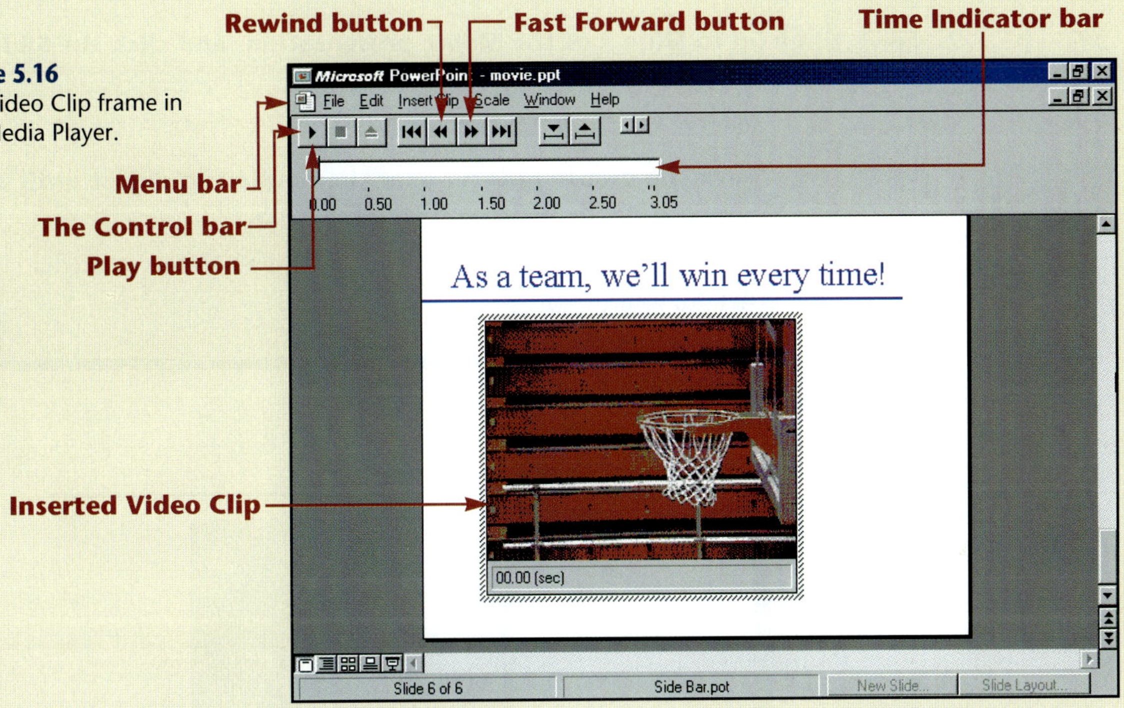

Figure 5.16
The Video Clip frame in the Media Player.

9 Click the Play button.

The video clip runs. As it is running, the Pause and Stop buttons both become active. When the clip is finished, the Play button is again shown.

10 Click outside the video clip placeholder.

The video clip is placed as an object on the slide, as indicated by the selection handles. If you want to edit or change settings related to any video clip, right-click the object; then choose Edit Media Clip Object. Save the presentation and keep it open for the next lesson.

INSIDE Stuff

If you want to add slides with a Media Clip placeholder, choose **I**nsert, **N**ew Slide. From the Insert New Slide dialog box, select an AutoLayout with a Media Clip placeholder.

Lesson 7: Playing Media Clips in the Slide Show

Once inserted, the media clips are most impressive when they are actually run as part of the slide show. You can set up the video clip to run automatically when a slide is displayed during a presentation, or run only when you click the mouse.

In addition, you can suppress the display of the media control bar so that it isn't seen during a Slide Show. Try working with these options now.

To Play Media Clips in the Slide Show

1. **Go to Slide 2 of the Movie presentation, and click the Slide Show button.**

   The second slide is shown on-screen.

2. **Move the mouse pointer over the media clip object until a hand pointer is displayed (see Figure 5.17).**

   The hand pointer indicates that you can activate the media clip by clicking it.

Figure 5.17
The Media Clip Object in Slide Show View.

Click here to start video

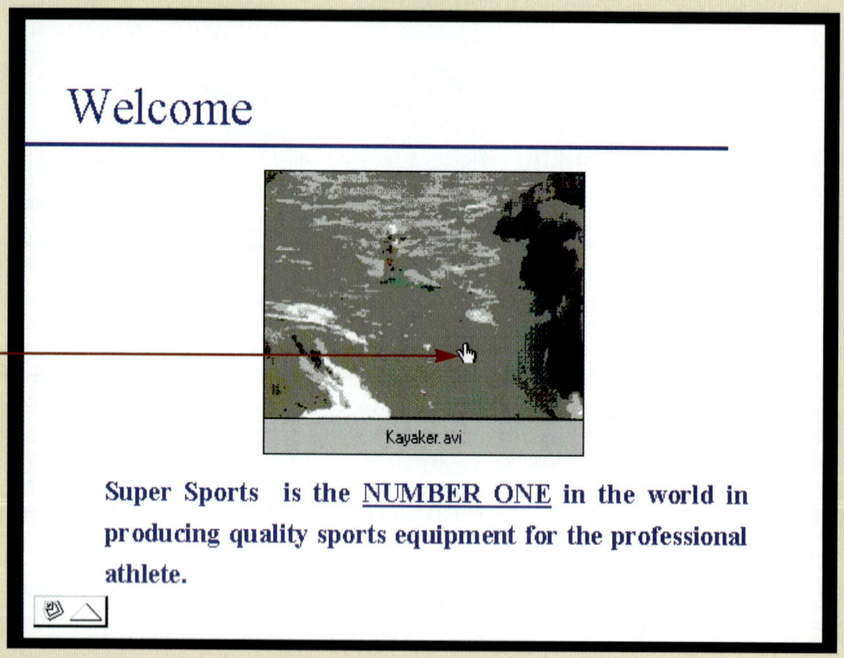

3. **Click the media clip object.**

   The video plays as part of the slide show. Notice the Play, Pause, and Stop buttons that are available as the video plays.

4. **Continue to click through the Slide Show until you return to the Slide View.**

   The remainder of the Slide Show displays. Notice that Slide 6 also contains a media clip, which must be activated manually by clicking it.

In addition to playing a video clip manually, you can change settings so that the video will run automatically during a slide show. This is especially useful if you have developed an on-screen display. Try automating your movie now.

5 Move to Slide 2, if necessary, and select the media object.

Selection handles indicate that the object is selected.

6 Choose Tools, Animation Settings.

The Animation Settings dialog box is shown. Notice that the bottom of the dialog box contains **P**lay Options related to how the object should display.

7 Select Play from the Play Options drop-down list, then click the More button.

The More Play Options dialog box results (see Figure 5.18). In the Start area, notice that you can indicate that you want PowerPoint to start the video a certain number of seconds after the slide is shown.

Figure 5.18
The More Play Options dialog box.

Use this option button to start a video clip automatically

8 In the Start area, click the Automatically option button, then enter 1 as the number of seconds to wait after the slide is displayed (refer to Figure 5.18).

9 Click OK in both dialog boxes.

Both dialog boxes close.

10 Run the slide show again from Slide 2.

The video clip in Slide 2 runs automatically instead of requiring a mouse click. Save, then close the presentation.

INSIDE Stuff

If you don't want the movie title and the control bar to be displayed on-screen, you can remove it. You can right-click the movie object and choose Crop Picture from the shortcut menu. Then position the cropping tool over the bottom left corner handle, and drag upward until the movie's name is cut off. This also suppresses the display of the control bar when the video plays.

Another method is to activate the Media Player by right-clicking the media object and choosing Edit Video Clip Object. From the Media Player menu bar choose **E**dit, **O**ptions and remove the check mark next to **C**ontrol Bar on Playback. Because the control bar is distracting to most people, it is a good idea to remove it.

Jargon Watch

Communication media, such as the telephone, fax, and computer, are becoming more and more interwoven. Most personal computers, for example, are now equipped with sound and video capabilities. This means that you can use your computer to take phone messages, send faxes, or play your latest CD. The computer's capability to integrate various ways of communicating with people is called **multimedia**.

Certain equipment is needed in order for your computer to be a multimedia machine. An internal **sound board** is an adapter that adds digital sound reproduction capabilities to personal computers. Speakers are usually used with the sound board so that you can hear the sounds created. Because video and music files are often too large for a 31/2-inch disk a CD-ROM, which holds much more data, is typically used. A **CD-ROM Drive** is used to read CDs. This read-only disk drive reads the data encoded on CD-ROMs and transfers this data to a computer.

Project Summary

To	Use
Add slide transitions in the Slide View	**T**ools, Slide **T**ransition.
Add slide transitions in the Slide Sorter View	Select slide, then click the drop-down list from the Transition Effects Box on the Slide Sorter toolbar.
View slide transitions	Choose **V**iew, Slide Sho**w**, **S**how.
Change slide transitions	Select slide(s), choose **T**ools, Slide **T**ransition.
Remove slide transitions	Choose No Transition in the Effect area of the Slide Transition dialog box.
Build text	Select the slide, then choose **T**ools, **B**uild Slide Text.
Add sound to a transition	Choose **T**ools, Slide **T**ransition, Sound.
Add sound to a build sequence	Use the Animation Effects toolbar.
Use the Animation Effects	Click the Animations Effects button to activate the Animations Effect toolbar.
Insert a movie clip	Choose **I**nsert, **M**ovie.
Play a movie clip in the Slide View	Double-click the Media Clip object.
Edit a movie clip	Right-click the object to activate the shortcut menu and choose Edit Media Clip Object.

To	Use
Play a movie clip manually in the Slide Show View	Move the mouse pointer over the media object until a hand pointer is displayed, then click.
Play a movie clip automatically in the Slide Show View	Use **T**ools, A**n**imation Settings, set Play Option, **M**ore, **A**utomatically.

Applying Your Skills

Take a few minutes to practice the skills you have learned in this project by completing the following exercises.

Using Multimedia Effects

You are conducting a brief sales presentation for ABC Training Company and want to add multimedia effects to your presentation. Your goal is to convince as many people as possible to attend an upcoming seminar. To help you do this, you decide to use PowerPoint's transition and build effects. You also add a movie to the presentation.

To Use Multimedia Effects

1. Open Proj0505 and save it as **Media**.
2. Show the presentation in the Slide Sorter View. Add transition effects as follows for each slide from the Slide Sorter toolbar:

   Slide 1: Box Out

   Slide 2: Checkerboard Across

   Slide 3: Checkerboard Down
3. Add the Random Bars Vertical build effect to Slide 2.
4. Add the sound of chimes to the build effects in Slide 2.
5. Activate the Animation Effects toolbar, then click the Animate Title button for Slide 2.
6. Display the presentation in the Slide View. Add a media clip to Slide 3. Use Basket.avi as the media clip file.
7. Enlarge the media clip object so that it displays better on Slide 3.
8. Run the slide show from the beginning. Change transition effects and build options and play it again.
9. Save and close the file.

Using Slide Transitions

You are scheduled to conduct a brief presentation at your company's annual meeting. By adding animation and slide tranisition effects, you hope to catch people's attention.

To Use Slide Transitions

1. Open Proj0506 and save it as **Best Food in America**.
2. Using the Slide Sorter View, add Box Out as the transitional effect for Slide 1.
3. Select Slides 2 and 3; then add Box In as the transitional effect for both slides.
4. Add the Dissolve Build Effect for Slide 2.
5. Add the Fly from Left Build Effect for Slide 3.
6. Add the Checkerboard Across transitional effect for Slide 4.
7. Run the slide show to see the effects.
8. Save, then close the file.

Using the Animation Effects Toolbar

For one of your classes, you are to conduct a presentation on the advantages and disadvantages of Windows 95. You hope to impress the teacher and keep fellow students' attention by adding sound effects to the slides.

To Use the Animation Effects Toolbar

1. Open Proj0507 and save it as **Windows 95 Presentation**.
2. Make sure the presentation is shown in the Slide View; then click the Animation Effects toolbar to activate it.
3. Click the sub-title placeholder on slide 1, then add the Drive-In effect.
4. Select the bulleted text placeholder in Slide 2, then add the Typewriter effect.
5. Select the bulleted text placeholder in Slide 3, then add the Camera effect.
6. Display the slide show to see the effects.
7. Save, then close the presentation.

Adding a Video Clip and Animation Effects to a Presentation

You have developed a presentation for your company, Super Sports. To add some excitement and impress your CEO, you add both animation effects and a video clip.

To Add a Video Clip and Animation Effects to a Presentation

1. Open Proj0508 and rename it **Super Sports**.
2. Using the Animation Effects toolbar, add the following effects:

   Slide 2, bulleted text area: Laser Text Effect

   Slide 3, bulleted text area: Camera Effect
3. In Slide 4, double-click the media clip placeholder to activate the media player.

4. Insert basket.avi in the media clip placeholder and exit the Media Player.
5. Resize and move the video clip to better see it.
6. Run the slide show to see the animation effects and video clip.
7. Save, then close the presentation.

Checking Your Skills

True/False

For each of the following, check *T* or *F* to indicate whether the statement is true or false.

__T __F **1.** The Media Minder is used to insert videos into your presentation.

__T __F **2.** To resize a video object without distorting its proportions, use the handles on the side or top of the surrounding box.

__T __F **3.** The Animation Effects toolbar is used to add drawings to your presentation.

__T __F **4.** PowerPoint slides can include sounds, such as applause, that are saved as computer images.

__T __F **5.** Slide transition effects can only be added when running the slide show.

Multiple Choice

In the blank provided, write the letter of the correct answer for each of the following.

1. Which of the following is *not* an animation effect available in PowerPoint? _______
   - **a.** Camera Effect
   - **b.** Laser Effect
   - **c.** Shadow Effect
   - **d.** Drive-In Effect
2. The command to add slide transitions in the Slide View is _______.
   - **a. S**lide View, **T**ransitions
   - **b. T**ools, Slide **T**ransition
   - **c. E**dit, **T**ransition Effect
   - **d. I**nsert, **T**ransition Effect

3. The program used to insert video, or movie clips is called _______.
    a. Media Minder
    b. Media Player
    c. Video Player
    d. Video Minder
4. To play the video in a slide show, _______.
    a. move the mouse pointer over the object until it becomes a hand, then click
    b. move the mouse pointer over the object, then activate Media Minder
    c. move the mouse pointer over the object, then activate the Video Player
    d. rest the mouse pointer over the object until the video begins to play
5. Animation Effects can be added to a slide by _______.
    a. using the Slide Transitions toolbar
    b. playing a video clip in the Slide Show View
    c. using the Animation Effects toolbar
    d. using the Drawing Effects toolbar

Completion

In the blank provided, write the correct answer for each of the following statements.

1. The toolbar button that is used to activate the Animation Effects toolbar is called the _______________ button.
2. One way to add a video clip is to add a new slide with a _______________ _______________ placeholder.
3. You can preview the slide transition effects without running the slide show by using the _______________ _______________ View.
4. You can select several slides to apply transition effects to in the Slide Sorter View by holding down the _______________ key while clicking on the slides.
5. PowerPoint uses the _______________ program to insert video clips onto a slide.

Project 6

Putting It All Together

Objectives

In this project, you learn how to

- Lay Out and Design a Slide Show
- Choose the Output Type
- Prepare Notes Pages and Handouts
- Use Hidden Slides
- Time the Slide Show Presentation
- Use the Slide Show Shortcut Keys
- Use the Annotation Pen
- Use the Meeting Minder

Why Would I Do This?

The end result of learning PowerPoint is to create and deliver the best possible presentation. You have learned a number of skills related to using the program—now you pull these skills together.

Lesson 1 of this project provides you with practical tips to design charts and slides. Learning a few basic design principles will help immensely as you develop the presentation.

PowerPoint can also help you create handouts and notes pages. Handouts are passed out to your audience so that they can follow your presentation better. Notes pages are developed in conjunction with the slides so that you have speaker notes when you talk.

Hidden slides are another useful PowerPoint feature. Hidden slides are created as additional support material just in case you need it. You can also time the slide show and turn on automatic advancement so that the slide show runs by itself.

When you present the slide show, you can use techniques such as blackening out the display or using the annotation pen to write on the presentation. You can also keep track of meeting notes on-screen with the Meeting Minder.

Using these various techniques will help ensure your success with PowerPoint. Try some of these techniques now.

Lesson 1: Laying Out and Designing a Slide Show

By learning a few design principles, you can develop a better presentation. Because PowerPoint has so many features you can easily overuse them and overwhelm the audience. Remember that you are trying to communicate a specific, targeted message with a slide. Therefore, the overall and text designs need to be carefully crafted.

The slide's overall look should be designed with care. Avoid using too many colors and objects or the slide becomes cluttered and without focus. If you aren't artistically inclined you probably will want to rely on the designs included in PowerPoint to ensure design balance and uniformity.

Typeface
The distinctive design of a set of type, distinguished by its weight (such as bold), posture (such as italic), and type size.

Potentially, there are several design pitfalls related to text. Using too many *typefaces*, including a mix of color, style, and sizes make the slide lack a uniform design. A text point size of less than 18 points is hard to read for most people. Also avoid using all capital letters, which is significantly harder to read than a mix of upper- and lowercase. Don't include more than six bullet points on a slide. Finally, use phrases rather than full sentences in your text areas.

In this lesson, you fix a number of problems with a presentation so that the message is clear. Try using layout and design principles now.

To Lay Out and Design a Slide Show

1 Open Proj0601 and save it as Design.

Slide 1 contains a number of design problems (see Figure 6.1) that you can fix. The first thing you probably notice is that the slide lacks focus, partly because it is too cluttered. Eliminating extraneous material will help sell your message. The chart, for example, has no direct relation to the slide's main message and should be removed.

Figure 6.1
A slide with a number of design problems.

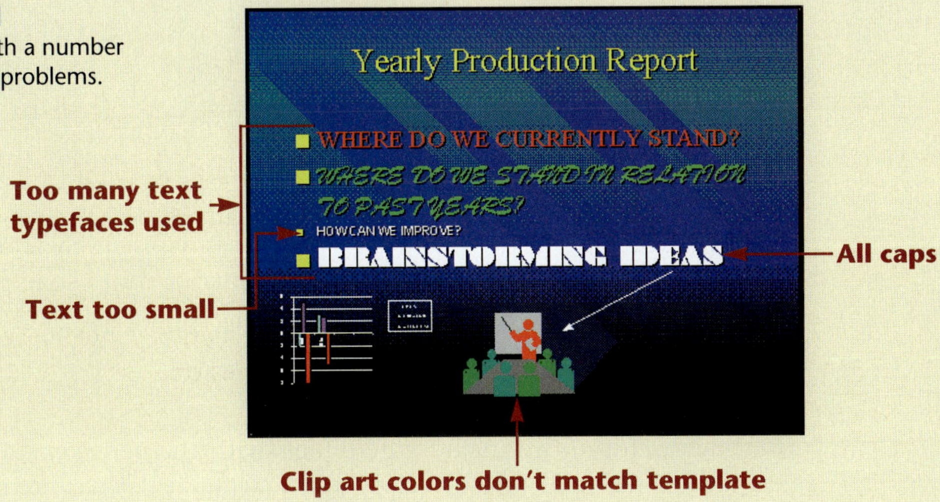

2 Click the chart placeholder to select it, then press Del.

The chart is removed from the slide. The arrow can also be removed without lessening the slide's impact.

3 Click to select the arrow, then press Del.

The arrow is erased. The clip art graphic is a good enhancement, but the colors should be changed to better match the template.

4 Select the clip art graphic; then right-click it and choose Recolor from the shortcut menu.

The Recolor Picture dialog box appears.

5 Change the pea green color to white and the aqua blue-green color to blue, as shown in Figure 6.2; then choose OK.

continues

To Lay Out and Design a Slide Show (continued)

Figure 6.2
The Recolor Picture dialog box.

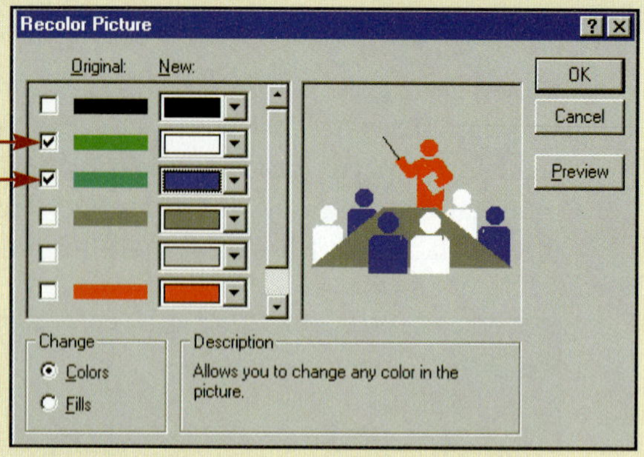

Change these colors to better match the template colors

The clip art graphic colors match the templates.

The slide also has several design problems involving text. Too many typefaces have been used, including a mix of color, style, and sizes that make the slide lack uniformity. Fix the text design problems now.

6. **Click and drag over the body text.**

   Be careful not to include the bullets with the body text. The body text is selected. Once selected, you can change its characteristics.

7. **Use the Formatting toolbar to change the following:**

   Click the Font Face drop-down list arrow and select Times New Roman.

   Click the Font Size drop-down list arrow and select 32.

   Click the Text Color button and change the color to white.

   Click the Bold button.

   The body text is now uniform in size, color, and typeface. The text is displayed in all caps, however, which makes it less readable. Rather than retyping the information, use a PowerPoint formatting feature to change the selected text to *sentence case*.

Sentence Case
The first letter of each selected sentence is uppercase.

8. **With the body text still selected, choose Format, Change Case.**

   The Change Case dialog box appears, with a variety of case options (see Figure 6.3). Sentence case is already selected.

Figure 6.3
The Change Case dialog box.

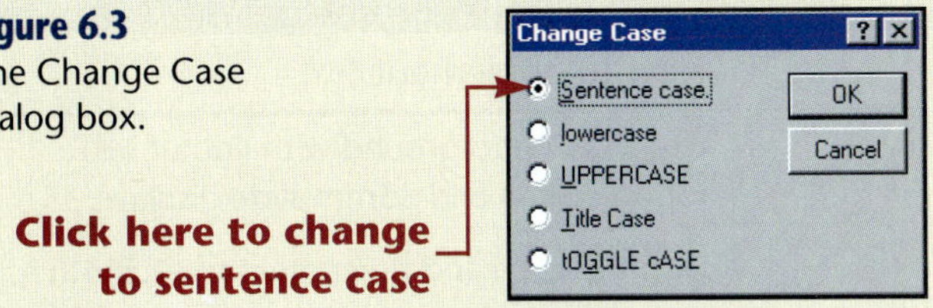

9 Choose OK.

The selected text changes to sentence case. Your slide should now appear similar to the one shown in Figure 6.4.

Figure 6.4
The completed slide.

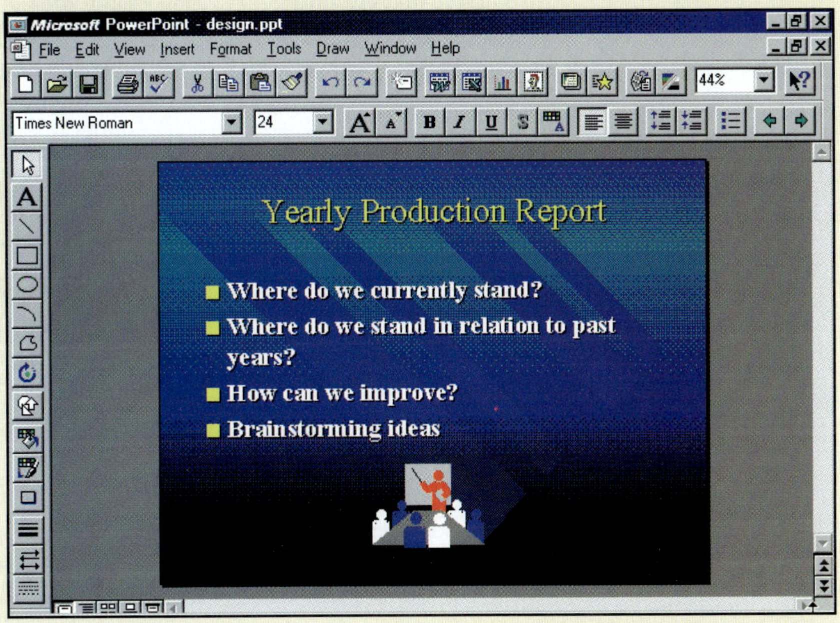

Save your presentation before closing it.

Table 6.1 can be used as a reference guide for designing slides.

Table 6.1 Design Guidelines

Main Guideline	How to Implement
Simplify	Use the minimum number of elements on a slide that will effectively convey your message.
	Use five or fewer data series per graph.
	Avoid too many drawn objects.
Emphasize your main point	Emphasizing draws attention to one element.
	Explode a pie slide or change data series colors on a chart to emphasize the most important data.

continues

Table 6.1 Continued

Main Guideline	How to Implement
Choose patterns and shades correctly	Use a dark background with lighter text for on-screen and 35mm slide displays.
	Don't use red and green next to each other, especially in chart series. Approximately 4 percent of men are red/green color blind and have some difficulty seeing the difference.
	If you are not artistically inclined, rely on PowerPoint's templates.
Choose text attributes carefully	Limit the number of typeface styles to two or less in a slide (for example, Times New Roman and Arial) to avoid a cluttered look. Use bold, italic and size differences to add emphasis rather than adding new typefaces.
	Text should be at least 18 points or larger if you are doing an on-screen presentation. Smaller text is hard for the audience to see.
Use sentence case lettering	Using sentence case (upper- and lowercase lettering) is significantly easier to read than all caps. Avoid using all capital letters except for an occasional title.
Limit the number of lines of text	Don't include more than six lines of body text on a slide.
Use phrases, not sentences	Use short, to the point phrases in body text rather than complete sentences.

Lesson 2: Choosing the Output Type

Once you create a PowerPoint slide, you can produce output in various ways. Each method has a specific purpose as well as some layout considerations. While many people create the presentations solely for on-screen display, you can also print the presentation and make it into 35mm slides.

Table 6.2 summarizes the main methods of producing output using PowerPoint.

Table 6.2 Output Methods for Your Presentation

Type of Output	Purpose	Design and Printing Considerations
On-screen presentations	Slides are developed that represent pages of a presentation. They can contain graphs, pictures, text, and media clips. On-screen presentations are	Use dark backgrounds with lighter text.

Type of Output	Purpose	Design and Printing Considerations
	generally shown directly on-screen displayed to a large screen with an LCD panel.	
Overhead trans-parencies	Black-and-white or color transparencies are printed on laser printers to use with an overhead projector.	Use a light background with darker text and graphics.
Paper printouts	You can print paper copies of your present-ation in order to include them as part of a manual.	Use a light background with darker text and graphics. Also consider using the Black and White view; then right-clicking to have access to a variety of grayscale print options.
Handouts and Notes Pages	Handouts are 2, 3, or 6 per page miniature versions of your slides that you can print out as support material for your audience.	Use the black-and-white options.
Outlines	Printing the Outline View produces a general over-view of your presentation.	Choose the Outline View, then print as usual.
35mm slides	35mm slides can be created from PowerPoint's slides by a service bureau such as Genigraphics.	Choose **F**ile, Slide Set**u**p if you know that you will be using 35mm slides for the presentation. To use Geni-graphics, follow the instruc-tions in the Genigraphics Wizard.

Try using some of these methods now.

To Choose an Output Type

1 Open Proj0602 and save it as Output.

2 While displaying Slide 1, choose File, Slide Setup from the menu.

The Slide Setup dialog box results (see Figure 6.5).

continues

To Choose an Output Type (continued)

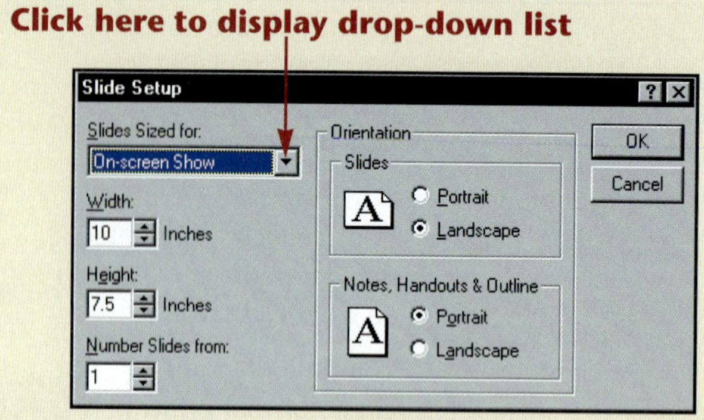

Figure 6.5 The Slide Setup dialog box.

3 Click the Slides Sized for drop-down list arrow, select 35mm Slides, and then choose OK.

The formatting for the slides is set for 35mm slides. Now you want to print the slides in black and white to save on expenses.

4 Click the B&W View button on the Standard toolbar.

The slide is shown in black and white, with a miniaturized color version in the upper right corner (see Figure 6.6).

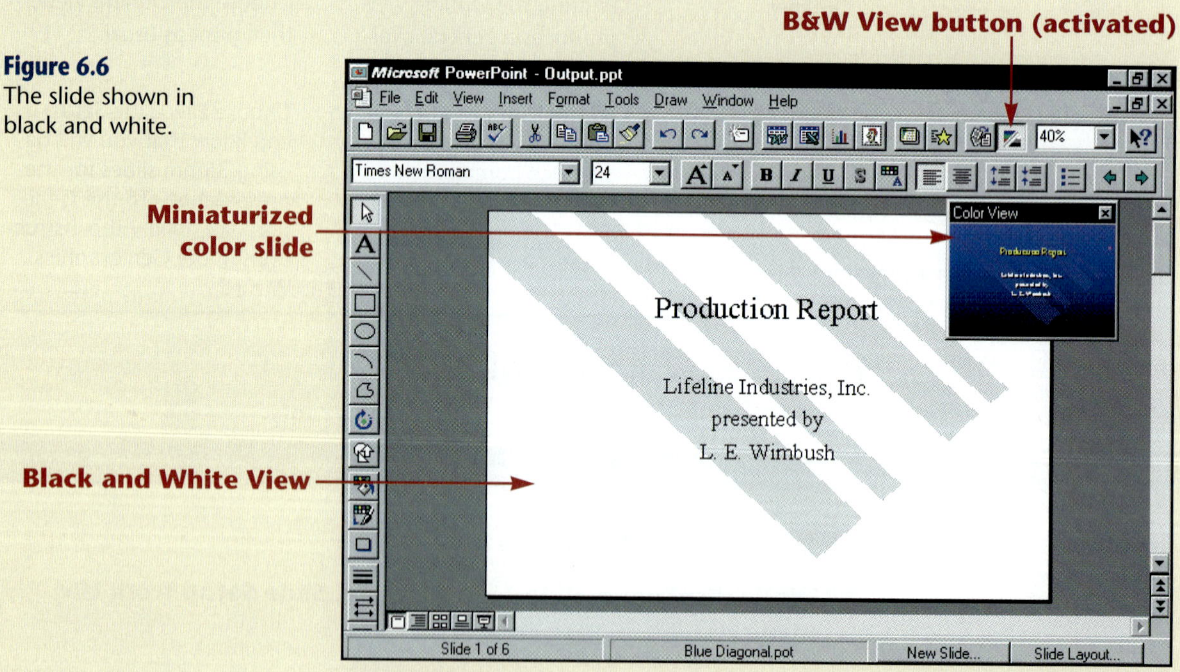

Figure 6.6 The slide shown in black and white.

5 Right-click the slide to activate the shortcut menu and choose Black and White, Automatic.

The black-and-white slide is redrawn in shades of gray and white for printing purposes.

6 Choose File, Print, Current Slide.

This prints the black-and-white version of the slide. Save the file before closing the presentation.

You can show a PowerPoint presentation on a business trip without installing the entire PowerPoint program. Choose **F**ile, Pac**k** and Go to copy the PowerPoint Viewer program on the same disk(s) as your presentation to take with you. A few PowerPoint features (such as animated builds) are not supported in the Viewer program, so try out your show before the actual presentation to avoid suprises!

This feature only works with Windows 95 or Windows NT. If you give your presentation on a computer with Windows 3.1, you need to use the viewer disk included with PowerPoint to view the presentation.

Lesson 3: Preparing Notes Pages and Handouts

You can prepare speaker notes pages as you create your presentation. Speaker notes pages include a smaller version of the slide with accompanying notes. The notes are a handy feature to help you remember key points while you give your presentation.

You can also print handout pages for your group so that they have a hard copy of the presentation and can follow it. Handout pages are printed two, three, or six slides to a page.

Try adding some notes to your presentation now.

To Prepare Notes Pages and Handouts

1 Open Proj0603 and save it as Notes.

2 Move to Slide 3, Where We Stand Currently, and click the Notes Pages View button.

Slide 3 is shown in Notes Pages View, as shown in Figure 6.7. A miniaturized view of the slide is accompanied by a text area for your notes. Because it is hard to read text in this view, you can enlarge the notes section.

continues

To Prepare Notes Pages and Handouts (continued)

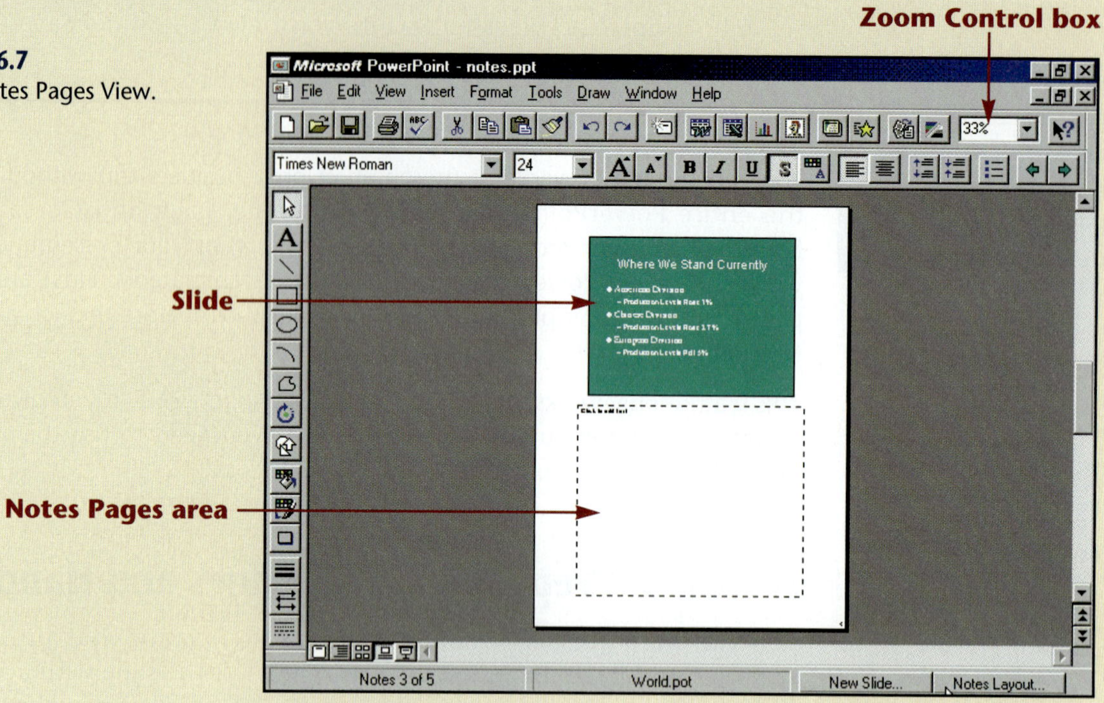

Figure 6.7
The Notes Pages View.

3 Click the Zoom Control drop-down list arrow on the Standard toolbar (refer to Figure 6.7).

The Zoom Control dictates how large or small a presentation appears on the screen. In this case, you want to see more of the notes area.

4 From the drop-down list, select 75%.

The display of the slide and notes areas enlarges so that you see a portion of each. Now you want to add some notes.

5 Click in the notes area and type the following:

American Division—Team-oriented approach pays off!

Chinese Division—Replaced outdated equipment at two plants.

European Division—Persistent supply problems plagued the Eastern European Plant.

You are now ready to print the notes as well as some handouts.

6 Choose File, Print.

The print dialog box appears.

7 In the Print what section, select Notes Pages and click the Current Slide option button.

The dialog box should look like Figure 6.8.

Figure 6.8
The completed Print Dialog Box.

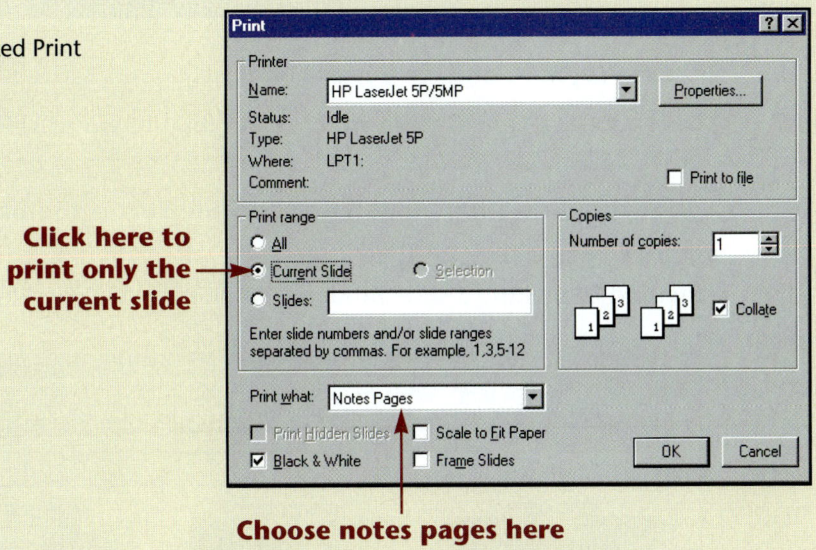

8 Click OK.

The notes page for the current slide is printed, consisting of the slide and accompanying notes. Next, you want to print handouts for your audience.

9 Open the Print dialog box, select Handouts (6 slides per page) in the Print what drop-down list, and select All for the Print range.

10 For a better printed appearance, make sure that the Frame Slides and Black & White check boxes are selected (at the bottom of the dialog box); then click OK.

The audience handouts are printed. Save, then close the file.

Lesson 4: Using Hidden Slides

You can include hidden slides as support material for your presentation. Experienced presenters anticipate potential questions and prepare related information in advance. For example, you may have a short sales presentation developed, but include more detailed slides designed to answer any objections that may come up.

You can specify a hidden slide with the **T**ools, **H**ide Slide command, or use the Hide Slide button on the Slide Sorter toolbar. When running the slide show, you can reveal the hidden slide by pressing H or using the Go To command. The H shortcut key command is active only if the next slide is the hidden one. Try your hand at using hidden slides now.

To Use Hidden Slides

❶ **Open Proj0604 and save it as Hidden.**

❷ **Display the presentation in Slide Sorter View and select Slide 5.**

❸ **Click the Hide Slide button on the Slide Sorter toolbar.**

Slide 5 is designated as a hidden slide (see Figure 6.9). Another method of making a slide hidden is to choose **T**ools, **H**ide Slide.

Figure 6.9
The hidden slide.

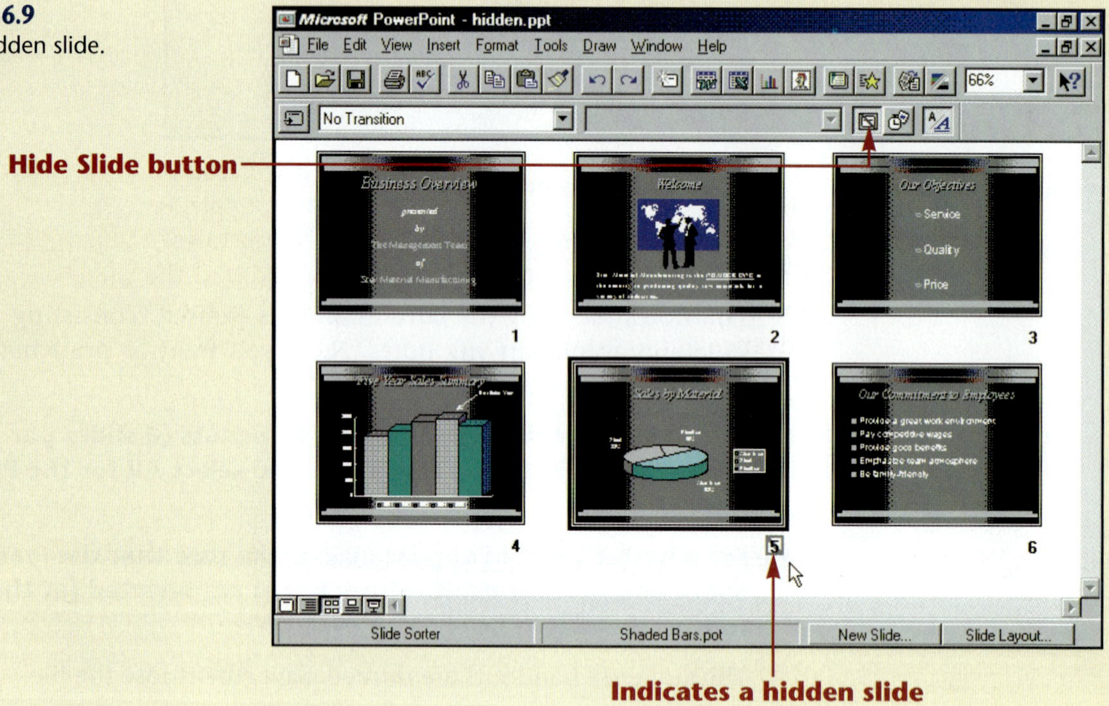

❹ **Choose View, Slide Show, Show.**

The slide show begins, starting with Slide 1.

❺ **Click through the slide show.**

Notice that Slide 5 is not displayed.

❻ **Choose View, Slide Show, Show again and move through the presentation until you view Slide 4, Five Year Sales Summary.**

The special shortcut Hidden Slide command is active because this is the slide preceding the hidden one.

❼ **Press H.**

The hidden slide is shown.

❽ **Finish viewing the remainder of the presentation, then save and close the file.**

Even if you are not at the slide just before the hidden one, you can still show it. Right-click to activate the shortcut menu, then choose Go To, Slide Navigator and select the hidden slide.

Lesson 5: Timing the Slide Show Presentation

Because no one has unlimited time to give to a presentation, timing the slide show for the greatest impact is important. When developing your final presentation, you can dictate if PowerPoint should advance to a new slide automatically after a certain number of seconds, or if it should change only when the mouse is clicked. If you are presenting the show to a live audience, you will certainly want control by using the manual advance. The general rule when using manual advancement is to allow 2–3 minutes per slide.

In contrast, automatic advancement is great if you have an on-screen slide show that you want to run continually (for example, at a trade show exhibit). When using automatic advancement you need to spend only as much time on a slide as the average person needs to read it. If the slide stays on-screen too long, people lose interest. PowerPoint has the capability to not only advance automatically, but also to time the show for you. The easiest way to work with the timings is to rehearse them as you run the slide show, then give PowerPoint the command to use the slide timings. Try setting some timings now.

To Time the Slide Show Presentation

1. **Open Proj0605 in the Slide Sorter View and save it as Timings.**

2. **On the Slide Sorter toolbar, click the Rehearse Timings button.**

   The slide show begins—but with a difference. A Rehearsal dialog box appears that keeps track of how many seconds each slide is viewed, as well as the overall length of the presentation (see Figure 6.10).

continues

To Time the Slide Show Presentation (continued)

Figure 6.10
The Rehearsal dialog box in the Slide Show View.

3 After 5 seconds, click the mouse to advance to Slide 2.

In future slide shows, the first slide will be advanced after 5 seconds. Notice that the Rehearsal dialog box keeps track of the total length of the presentation as well as the time for each individual slide.

4 In Slides 2–6, set timings of your choice (ranging from 3–10 seconds per slide).

When you are finished going through the entire show, PowerPoint displays a message box, as shown in Figure 6.11.

Figure 6.11
PowerPoint message box.

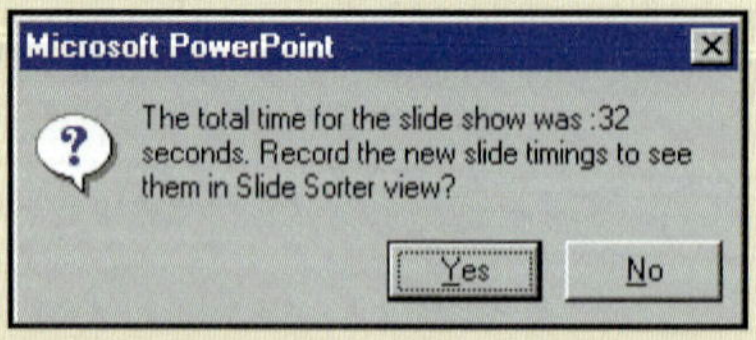

5 Choose Yes.

The slides are displayed in the Slide Sorter View, including the number of seconds after which each slide will advance (see Figure 6.12). You have now told PowerPoint how long to show each slide, but to make the presentation fully automated you need to add one more step.

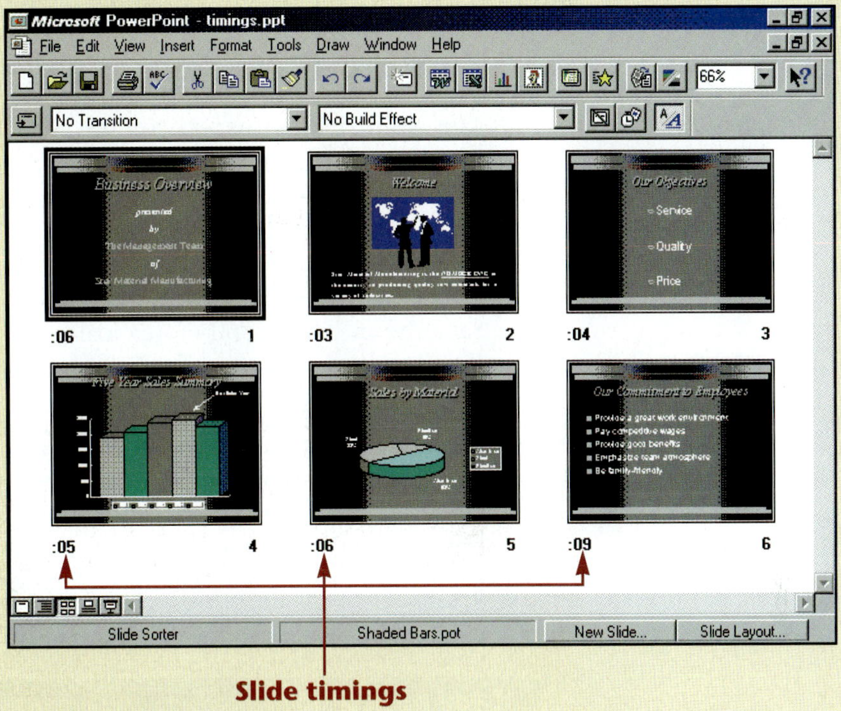

Figure 6.12
The Slide Sorter View, including the number of seconds until the next slide will advance.

❻ **Choose View, Slide Show.**

The Slide Show dialog box is displayed (see Figure 6.13).

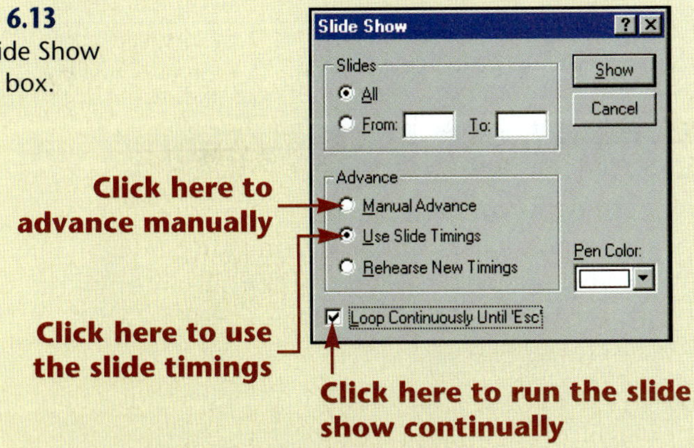

Figure 6.13
The Slide Show dialog box.

❼ **Click the Use Slide Timings option button and the Loop Continually Until 'Esc' check box.**

The designated options are set so that your slide show will automatically advance according to the timing you set earlier. The slide show will also continue to loop back to Slide 1 and run the entire show again until you press Esc. Try running the show to see these options in action.

continues

To Time the Slide Show Presentation (continued)

8 In the Slide Show dialog box, click the Show button.

The slide show runs, advancing automatically to each new slide. Notice that the entire presentation starts again after it reaches the last slide.

9 Press Esc.

This ends the slide show and returns you to the Slide Sorter View. Save the presentation before closing it.

INSIDE Stuff

Even if you are planning on using manual advance, the slide timings are a good way of measuring the overall length of the presentation. To use them to practice and time your presentation, simply click the Rehearse Timings button. Talk as you would to the audience for the first slide, then click to move to the next. When you are finished, you will have a good idea of the overall length of the presentation, as well as for each individual slide.

If you have problems...

If you have rehearsed the slide timings but the slide show still requires a mouse click to advance, chances are that you haven't chosen Use Slide Timings in the Slide Show dialog box. Choose View, Slide Show, Use Slide Timings to automate the show.

Lesson 6: Using the Slide Show Shortcut Keys

When you are presenting your slide show to a live audience, it's useful to know as many ways as possible to move among the slides. In Lesson 6 of Project 1, you learned some basic ways of moving among slides in your slide show. You can advance manually to the next slide by clicking the left mouse button or pressing ↵Enter. You can also right-click the mouse and choose Next, Previous or Goto. In this lesson, you expand that knowledge to include additional shortcut keys.

The shortcut keys have other functions as well. For example, you can use special shortcut keys to blank out a current slide so that the audience's attention is redirected to you. Try using some keyboard shortcuts now.

To Use the Slide Show Shortcut Keys

1 Open Proj0606 and save it as Moving.

2 Choose View, Slide Show, Show.

The presentation starts and the first slide is shown.

3 Right-click the mouse and choose Go To, Slide Navigator from the shortcut menu.

A listing of available slides is displayed in the Slide Navigator dialog box. Any hidden slides are listed in parentheses (see Figure 6.14).

Figure 6.14
The Slide Navigator dialog box.

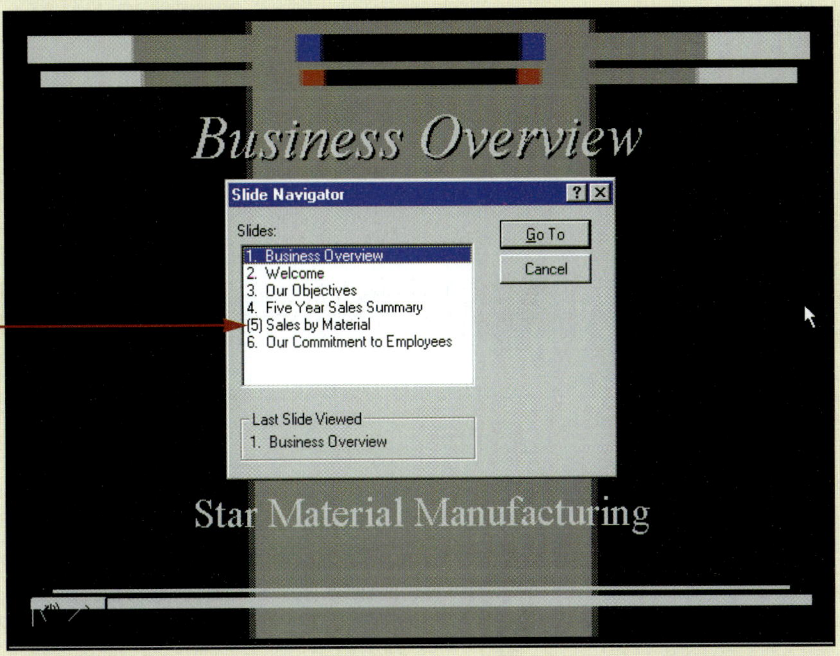

4 Select the hidden slide (Slide 5) and click Go To.

The presentation jumps to Slide 5.

5 Press F1.

The Slide Show Help screen results, with a listing of available shortcut keys to help you get around the slide show (see Figure 6.15). Try out some of the keys on the current presentation.

continues

To Use the Slide Show Shortcut Keys (continued)

Figure 6.15
The Slide Show Help dialog box.

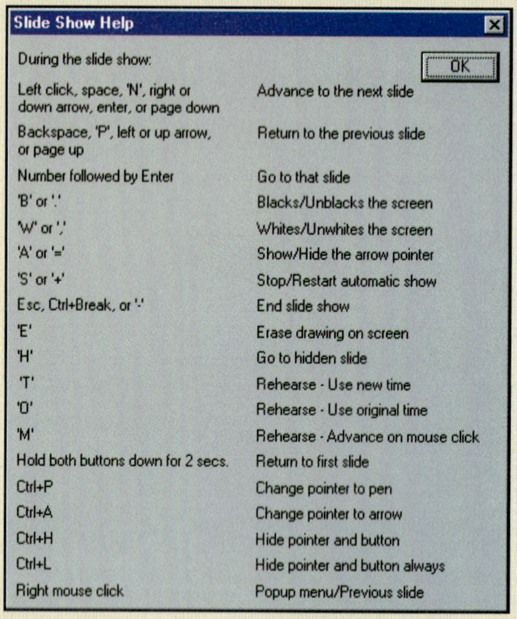

6 Click OK to close the dialog box, then press P.

PowerPoint moves back one slide.

7 Press B.

The screen blacks out. The presentation is still on the current slide, but the screen stays black until you press B again. This is a helpful feature when you want the audience to turn their attention to you, the presenter, rather than to the screen.

8 Press B again.

The slide reappears. You can also press W to white out and remove whitening from the screen.

9 Press 2, followed by ↵Enter.

The presentation moves to Slide 2. Not only is this method quicker than using the Slide Navigator, but your audience doesn't see the command on-screen.

10 Press Esc.

This ends the slide show. Save your presentation before closing it.

Table 6.3 lists the shortcut keys for getting around a slide show.

Table 6.3 Moving around a Slide Show

To	Use
Show a list of shortcut keys	Press F1.
Activate the shortcut menu	Right-click the mouse.
Go to the next slide	Left-click the mouse.
	Press ↵Enter.
	Press N.
Go to the previous slide	Press ←Backspace.
	Press P.
Go to a specific slide	Type the slide number, then press ↵Enter.
	Choose Go To, Slide Navigator from the shortcut menu.
Go to a hidden slide	Press H (if the hidden slide is immediately after the current slide).
	Choose Go To, Slide Navigator, Hidden Slide from the shortcut menu.
Go to the first slide	Hold down both mouse buttons for 2 seconds.
Black or unblack the screen	Press B.
White or unwhite the screen	Press W.
Erase a screen drawing	Press E.
End the slide show	Press Esc.
	Choose End Show from the shortcut menu.

Lesson 7: Using the Annotation Pen

Many times when you're giving a presentation, you may want to add additional comments to a slide to draw attention to an item or reference it. In PowerPoint, adding comments to a slide, or *annotating*, is done using the mouse—directly on the slide—during the slide show. You'll know when you can write on a slide by the appearance of the mouse pointer—it looks like a pen. For more impact, you can also change annotation pen colors. Try using the pen in a presentation now.

To Use the Annotation Pen

1. **Open Proj0607 and save it as Pen.**
2. **Move to Slide 3, then click the Slide Show View button.**

   The slide show begins.
3. **Right-click to activate the shortcut menu, then choose Pen.**

   The pointer changes into an annotation pen that you can use by holding down the mouse button and dragging. You can also activate the annotation pen by pressing Ctrl+P.
4. **Drag to draw a line emphasizing the salary progression from Programmer to Sr. Programmer to Systems Analyst (see Figure 6.16).**

   You can draw freehand or press and hold down Shift before dragging the annotation pen to draw straight lines.

Figure 6.16
Using the annotation pen.

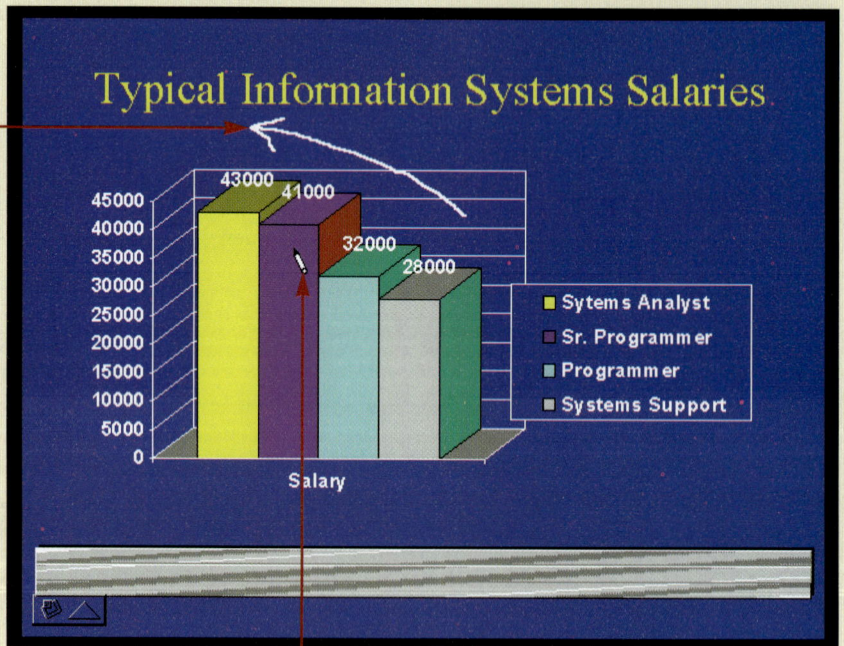

5. **Press E.**

   The drawing is erased. Drawings are also erased as soon as you move to another slide.
6. **Right-click to activate the shortcut menu, then choose Pointer Options, Pen Color, Yellow.**

   The annotation pen changes to the new color.
7. **Press and hold down Shift, then drag to draw a line.**

   A straight, yellow line results.

8 Press Esc.

This ends the show. Save, then close the presentation.

If you have problems...

When the annotation pen is active, clicking the left mouse button doesn't advance the slide show to the next screen, but instead produces a dot on-screen. Press Ctrl+A to change the annotation pen back to an arrow and then click or press N (next slide shortcut key).

Lesson 8: Using the Meeting Minder

The Meeting Minder is a feature that helps you take or use notes during a presentation. You can take meeting minutes and export them to Word. Information you develop on the Notes Pages can be viewed on-screen during the slide show. Finally, you can also record "action items" from your discussion that PowerPoint then includes as the last slide in your show.

Using the Meeting Minder is especially useful during an informal presentation, such as a staff meeting or brainstorming session. Try using the Meeting Minder now.

To Use the Meeting Minder

1 Open Proj0608 and save it as Minder.

2 Display Slide 4 in Notes Pages View.

Notice the slide contains notes for this slide. You can view these same notes with the Meeting Minder.

3 Click the Slide Show View button.

This starts the presentation from the current slide.

4 Right-click the mouse to display the shortcut menu, then choose Meeting Minder.

The Meeting Minder dialog box results, with three tabs: Notes Pages, Meeting Minutes, and Action Items (see Figure 6.17).

continues

To Use the Meeting Minder (continued)

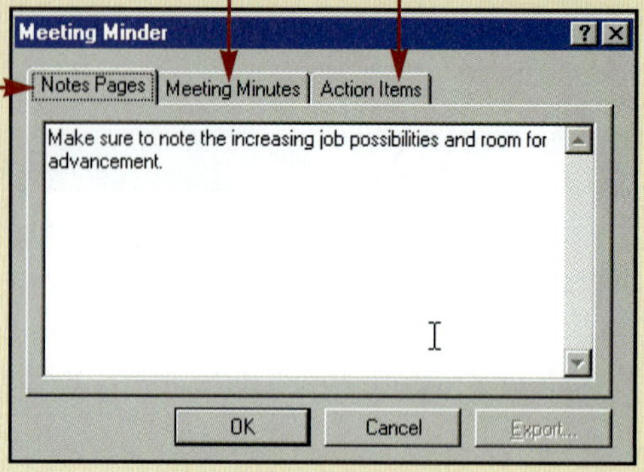

Figure 6.17
The Meeting Minder dialog box.

5 Click the Notes Pages tab.

The information that you saw previously in Notes Pages View is displayed.

6 Click the Action Items tab; then click to set the insertion point in its typing area.

7 Type the following:

Job fairs at top colleges and universities

Advertise in national computer magazines

Network with past employees and client businesses

8 Choose OK.

The Meeting Minder dialog box closes.

9 Move through the remainder of the presentation until you get to the slide entitled Action Items.

PowerPoint creates a slide containing the action items you entered in the Meeting Minder and places it at the end of the slide show.

10 Press Esc.

The slide show ends. Before closing the presentation, save your changes.

Jargon Watch

Designing a slide so that it is effective involves paying attention to how text appears. The **typeface**, or font, refers to the way text characters appear on-screen. **Case** refers to whether the letters are shown in upper- or lowercase. **Sentence case** capitalizes the first letter of each selected sentence, and is usually the easiest to read.

Annotation means to write or draw. In PowerPoint, it refers to using the annotation pen to add freehand drawings with the mouse to a slide during a slide show.

Project Summary

To	Use
Change text case	Choose F**o**rmat, Change Cas**e.**
Set output for 35mm slides	Choose **F**ile, Slide Set**u**p, **S**lides Sized for.
Print in black and white	Click the B&W button, right-click, then choose Black and White, Automatic.
Copy PowerPoint viewer	Choose **F**ile, Pac**k** and Go.
View or edit notes	Click the Notes Pages View button.
Hide a slide	Choose **T**ools, **H**ide Slide
Rehearse slide timings	Click Rehearse Slide Timings button (the Slide Sorter View).
Use slide timings	Choose **V**iew, Slide Sho**w**, **U**se Slide Timings.
Run a slide show continually	Choose **V**iew, Slide Sho**w**, **L**oop Continually Until 'Esc'.
Display slide shortcut keys	Press F1.
Activate the shortcut menu	Right-click the mouse.
Go to the next slide in the Slide Show View	Left-click the mouse.
Go to the previous slide in the Slide Show View	Press ←Backspace.
Go to a specific slide	Type the slide number, then press ↵Enter.
Go to a hidden slide	Press H (if the hidden slide is immediately after the current slide).
Go to the first slide	Hold down both mouse buttons for 2 seconds.
Black or unblack the screen	Press B.
White or unwhite the screen	Press W.
Erase a screen drawing	Press E.
End the slide show	Press Esc.
Use the annotation pen in a slide show	Press Ctrl+P.
Change pen color	Right-click; then choose Pointer Options, Pen Color.
Use the Meeting Minder	Right-click in the slide show; then choose Meeting Minder.

Applying Your Skills

Take a few minutes to practice the skills you have learned in this project by completing the following exercises.

Using Slide Show Commands Effectively

You are part of the management team for Technical Services, Inc., an organization that finds computer-oriented staff for various companies. You are giving a promotional presentation at several colleges to recruit graduating seniors. You want to create a notes page and hidden slide as support material for the presentation.

To Use Slide Show Commands Effectively

1. Open Proj0609 and save it as **Skills**.
2. Create a notes page for Slide 4 that says, **We have immediate openings for programmers and programmer analysts in five states. Salaries range from $32,000 to $45,000/year**.
3. Make Slide 5 a hidden slide.
4. Run the slide show, using the keyboard shortcuts listed in Table 6.3.
5. Use the Meeting Minder to add several action items; then display the newly created slide with a list of the items.
6. Save, then close the presentation.

Using Slide Show Timings

As part of the management team for Technical Services, Inc., you are again giving a promotional presentation at several colleges to recruit graduating seniors. To time your presentation properly, you decide to use PowerPoint's slide timing feature.

To Use Slide Show Timings

1. Open Proj0610 and save it as **Computer Programmmers**.
2. Display the presentation in the Slide Sorter View.
3. Use the Rehearse New Timing button to set slide timings as follows:

   Slide 1: 3 seconds

   Slide 2: 5 seconds

   Slide 3: 4 seconds

   Slide 4: 2 seconds

   Slide 5: 8 seconds

4. Choose **V**iew, Slide Sho**w**, **U**se Slide Timings for your show.

5. Run the slide show.
6. Change the slide timings.
7. Run the slide show again; then save and close the presentation.

Using Slide Show Commands

You are presenting information on your company, Bell Manufacturing, to a group of shareholders. Because you don't want them to see the shortcut menu on-screen while you are doing the presentation, you decide to learn the keyboard shortcut commands for moving around a slide show.

To Use Slide Show Commands

1. Open Proj0611 and save it as **Commands**.
2. Start the slide show.
3. Press F1 to display the list of keyboard shortcut commands, then clear the commands by pressing ↵Enter.
4. Press N to advance to Slide 2.
5. Press 6 followed by ↵Enter to go to Slide 6.
6. Press B to blacken the slide; then B to re-display it.
7. Press Ctrl+P to show the annotation pen. Use the pen to draw a line from the legend for Bell Manufacturing to the bar on the graph that represents the company.
8. Press Ctrl+A to show the arrow.
9. Press Esc to return to the Slide View. Save and close the presentation.

Using Notes and the Meeting Minder

You are meeting with the product development team at ABC Ergonomic Products to brainstorm the release of some new products. You want to use PowerPoint's Notes Pages and Meeting Minder to help with your presentation.

To Use Notes and the Meeting Minder

1. Open Proj0612 and save it as **Ergonomic Products**.
2. Display Slide 3 in Notes Pages View.
3. Use the Zoom Control button to change the display to 75% so that you can see the notes area more easily.
4. Type the following speaker note:

    Use the statistics provided by OSHA.

5. Display the presentation in the Slide Show View starting with Slide 3. Right-click the mouse and choose Meeting Minder from the shortcut menu.
6. Click the Notes Pages tab to see the speaker notes.

7. Click the Action Items tab, then enter the following information:

   Conduct Market Survey

   Research Competition

   Check Supplier Status

   Do Cost Analysis

   Produce Marketing Materials

8. Choose OK to return to your slide show, then advance to the final slide.
9. View the Action Item slide, then end the slide show.
10. Save, then close the presentation.

Checking Your Skills

True/False

For each of the following, check *T* or *F* to indicate whether the statement is true or false.

__T __F **1.** You can use the Meeting Minder to view speaker notes.

__T __F **2.** You can blacken out slides in your slide show.

__T __F **3.** The only way to erase an annotation pen drawing is to advance to the next slide.

__T __F **4.** An effective slide layout includes several typefaces.

__T __F **5.** Use all uppercase lettering throughout a slide's text to really grab the attention of the audience.

Multiple Choice

In the blank provided, write the letter of the correct answer for each of the following.

1. One way to take meeting notes during a presentation is to use the ______.

   a. Minute Taker

   b. Meeting Minder

   c. Notes Pages View

   d. annotation pen

2. Which one of the following is a good principle to use when designing slides? ______

   a. Use several clip art graphics on your slide.

   b. Emphasize several ideas on each slide.

c. Include two or fewer typefaces per slide.

d. Include as many colors as possible because people like colorful slides.

3. When the Action Items tab of the Meeting Minder is used, ______.

a. a printed list of action items results

b. the speaker's notes are updated

c. a final slide of action items is produced

d. the Action Items are placed in the Slide Minder for future reference

4. Hidden slides are ______.

a. used to provide supporting data in a presentation

b. used to hide speaker notes

c. shown by pressing Ctrl+H during a slide show

d. only available if the presentation is showing the slide after the hidden slide

5. The annotation pen ______.

a. is only available in the Slide Sorter View

b. is used to blacken the screen

c. is used to emphasize information on a slide

d. is used to recolor clip art graphics

Completion

In the blank provided, write the correct answer for each of the following statements.

1. Notes that you type in Notes Pages View to use as part of a presentation are called ____________.

2. You can use the Meeting Minder to create a list of ____________ that appear as the last slide of your presentation.

3. The shortcut keyboard command to activate the annotation pen during a slide show is ____________.

4. To add automatic slide timings to your presentation, click the ____________ button on the Slide Sorter toolbar.

5. To see a black-and-white version of a slide, click the ____________ button.

Appendix A

Working with Windows 95

In this project, you learn how to

- Start Windows
- Use the mouse
- Understand the Start Menu
- Identify the Elements of a Window
- Manipulate Windows
- Exit the Windows Program

Why Would I Do This?

Graphical user interface (GUI)
A computer application that uses pictures, graphics, menus, and commands to help users communicate with their computers.

Microsoft Windows 95 is a powerful operating environment that enables you to access the power of DOS without memorizing DOS commands and syntax. Windows 95 uses a *graphical user interface* (GUI) so that you can easily see on-screen the tools that you need to complete specific file and program management tasks.

This appendix, an overview of the Windows 95 environment, is designed to help you learn the basics of Windows 95.

Lesson 1: Starting Windows

Desktop
The background of the Windows screen, on which windows, icons, and dialog boxes appear.

The first thing you need to know about Windows is how to start the software. In this lesson, you learn how to start Windows; however, before you can start Windows, it must be installed on your computer. If you need to install Windows, refer to your Windows manual or ask your instructor for assistance.

Icon
A picture that represents an application, a file, or a system resource.

In most cases, Windows starts automatically when you turn on your computer. If your system is set up differently, you must start Windows from the DOS prompt (such as `C:\>`). Try starting the Windows program now.

To Start Windows

Shortcut
A shortcut gives you quick access to frequently used objects so you don't have to look through menus each time you need to use that object.

1. Turn on your computer and monitor.

   Most computers display technical information about the computer and the operating software installed on it.

   If Windows starts, you can skip step 2. Otherwise, you will see the DOS prompt `C:\>`.

2. At the DOS prompt, type **win** and then press ↵Enter.

   When you start the Windows program, a Microsoft Windows 95 banner displays for a few seconds; then the *desktop* appears (see Figure A.1).

Taskbar
Contains the Start button, buttons for each open window and the current time.

Start button
A click of the Start button opens the Start menu.

Program *icons* that were created during installation (such as My Computer, Recycle Bin, and Network Neighborhood) are displayed on the desktop. Other icons may also appear, depending on how your system is set up. *Shortcuts* to frequently used objects (such as documents, printers, and network drives) can be placed on the desktop. The *taskbar* appears along the bottom edge of the desktop. The *Start button* appears at the left end of the taskbar.

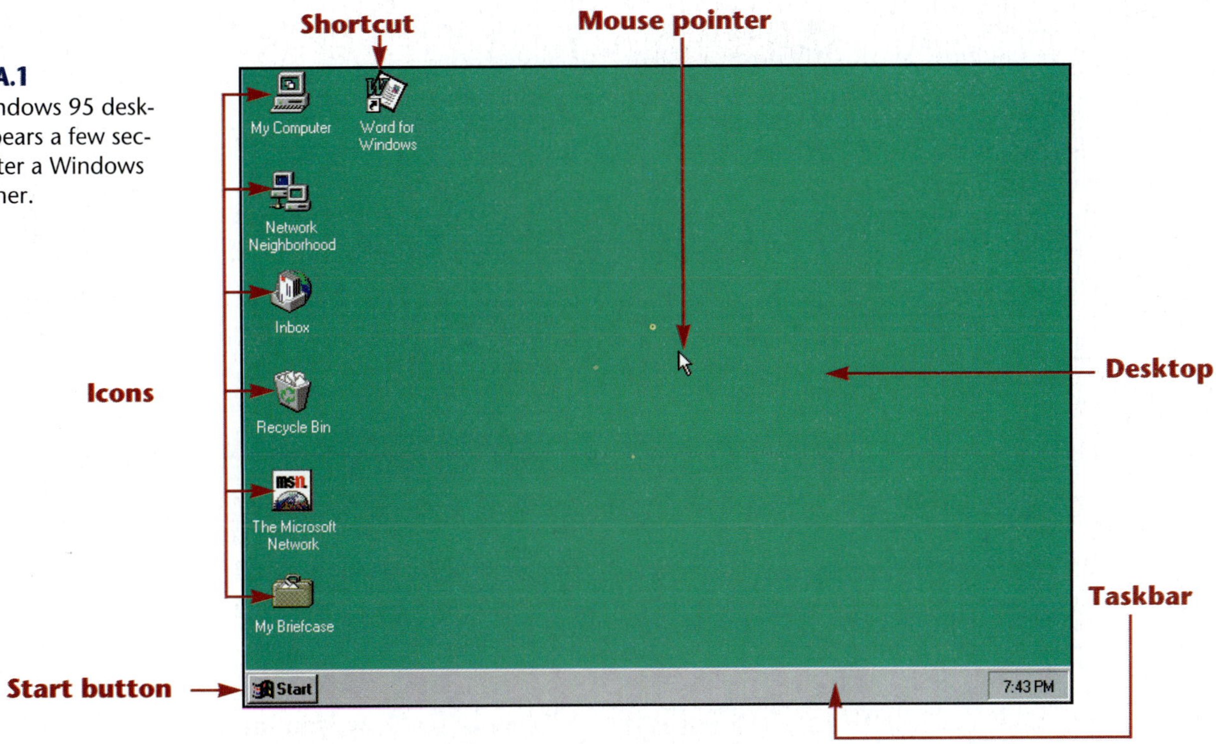

Figure A.1
The Windows 95 desktop appears a few seconds after a Windows 95 banner.

Lesson 2: Using the Mouse

Pull-down menus
Menus that cascade downward into the screen whenever you select a command from the menu bar.

Dialog box
A window that opens on-screen to provide information about the current action or to ask the user to provide additional information to complete the action.

Mouse
A pointing device used in many programs to make choices, select data, and otherwise communicate with the computer.

Mouse pointer
A symbol that appears on-screen to indicate the current location of the mouse.

Mouse pad
A pad that provides a uniform surface for the mouse to slide on.

Windows is designed to be used with a *mouse*, so it's important that you learn how to use a mouse correctly. With a little practice, using a mouse is as easy as pointing to something with your finger. You can use the mouse to select icons, to make selections from *pull-down menus* and *dialog boxes*, and to select objects that you want to move or resize.

In the Windows desktop, you can use a mouse to

- Open windows
- Close windows
- Open menus
- Choose menu commands
- Rearrange on-screen items, such as icons and windows

The position of the mouse is indicated on-screen by a *mouse pointer*. Usually, the mouse pointer is an arrow, but it sometimes changes shape depending on the current action.

On-screen, the mouse pointer moves according to the movements of the mouse on your desk or on a *mouse pad*. To move the mouse pointer, simply move the mouse.

There are four basic mouse actions:

- *Click*. To point to an item, and then press and quickly release the left mouse button. You click to select an item, such as an option on a menu. To cancel a selection, click an empty area of the desktop. Unless otherwise specified, you use the left mouse button for all mouse actions.

- *Double-click*. To point to an item, and then press and release the left mouse button twice, as quickly as possible. You double-click to open or close windows and to start applications from icons.
- *Right-click*. To point to an item, and then press and release the right mouse button. This opens a Context menu, which gives you a shortcut to frequently used commands. To cancel a Context menu, click the left mouse button outside the menu.
- *Drag*. To point to an item, then press and hold down the left mouse button as you move the pointer to another location, and then release the mouse button. You drag to resize windows, move icons, and scroll.

If you have problems...

If you try to double-click but nothing happens, you may not be clicking fast enough. Try again.

Lesson 3: Understanding the Start Menu

Program folder
Represented by an icon of a file folder with an application window in front of it, program folders contain shortcut icons and other program folders.

The Start button on the taskbar gives you access to your applications, settings, recently opened documents, the Find utility, the **R**un command, the Help system, and the Sh**u**t Down command. Clicking the Start button opens the Start menu. Choosing the **P**rograms option at the top of the Start menu displays the **P**rograms menu, which lists the *program folders* on your system. Program folders are listed first, followed by shortcuts (see Figure A.2).

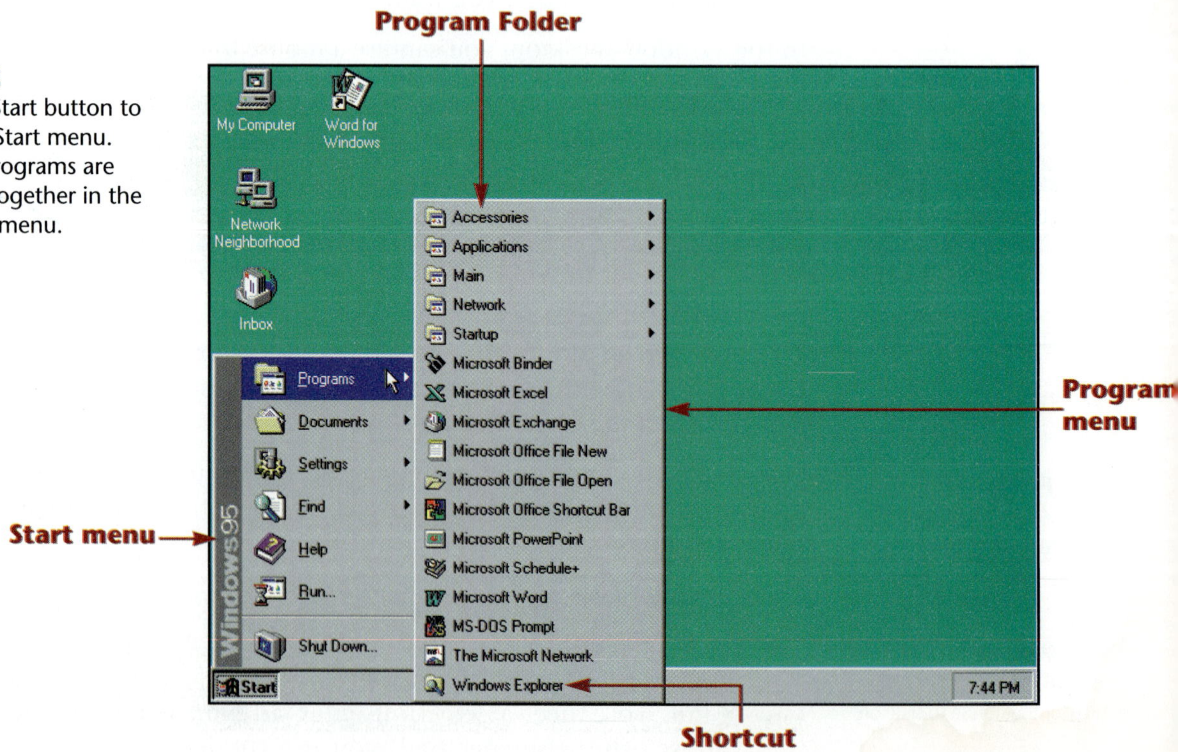

Figure A.2
Click the Start button to open the Start menu. All your programs are grouped together in the Programs menu.

When the Start menu is open, moving the mouse pointer moves a selection bar through the menu options. When the selection bar highlights a menu command with a right-facing triangle, a submenu opens. Click the shortcut icon to start an application. If a menu command is followed by an ellipsis (...), clicking that command opens a dialog box.

Lesson 4: Identifying the Elements of a Window

In the Windows program, everything opens in a window. Applications, documents, and dialog boxes all open in windows. For example, double-clicking the My Computer icon opens the My Computer application into a window. Because window elements stay the same for all Windows applications, this section uses the My Computer window for illustration.

Title Bar

Across the top of each window is its title bar. A title bar contains the name of the open window as well as three buttons to manipulate windows. The Minimize button reduces windows to a button on the taskbar. The Maximize button expands windows to fill the desktop. The Close button closes the window.

Menu Bar

The menu bar gives you access to the application's menus. Menus enable you to select options that perform functions or carry out commands (see Figure A.3). The **F**ile menu in My Computer, for example, enables you to open, save, and print files.

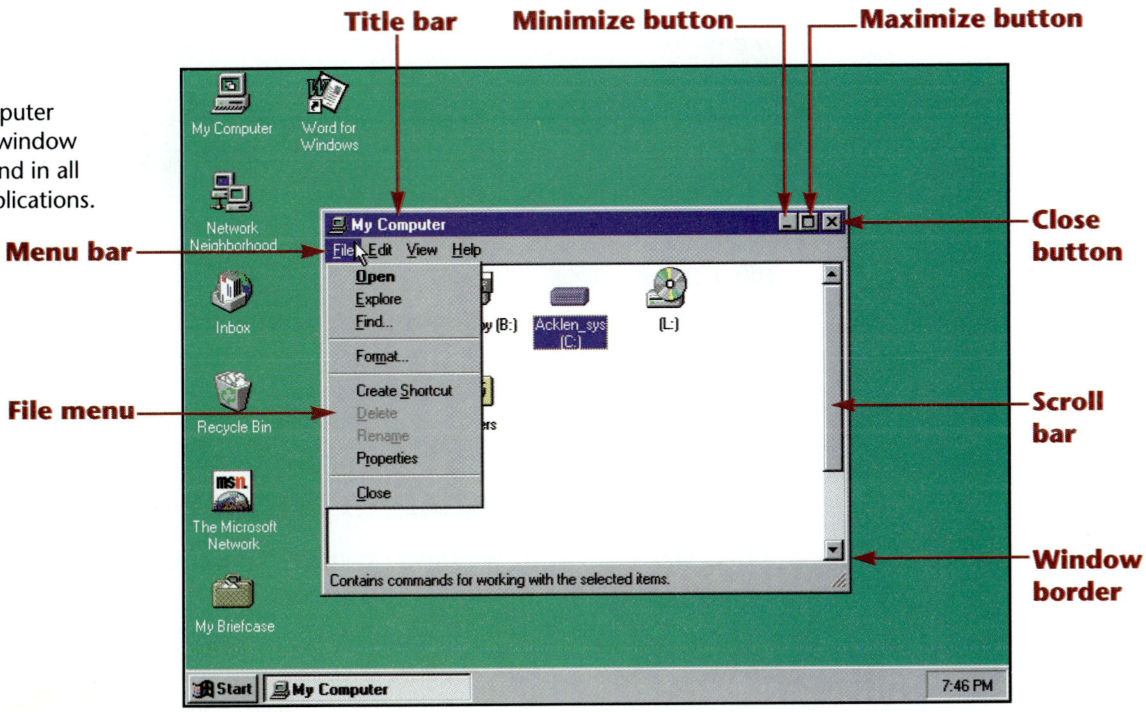

Figure A.3
The My Computer window has window elements found in all Windows applications.

Some menu options require you to enter additional information. When you select one of these options, a dialog box opens (see Figure A.4). You type the additional information, select from a list of options, or select a button. Most dialog boxes have a Cancel button, which closes the dialog box without saving the changes; an OK button, which closes the dialog box and saves the changes; and a Help button, which opens a Help window.

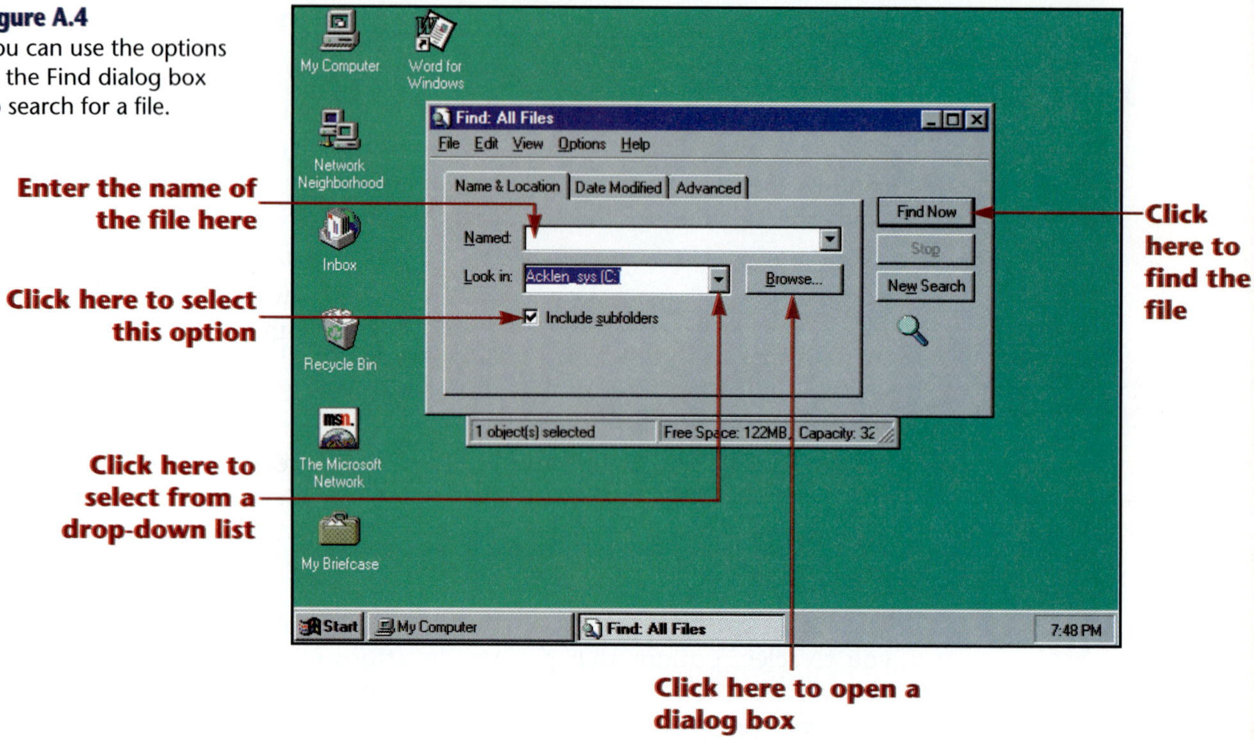

Figure A.4
You can use the options in the Find dialog box to search for a file.

Scroll Bar

Scroll bars appear when you have more information in a window than is currently displayed on-screen. A horizontal scroll bar appears along the bottom of a window and a vertical scroll bar appears along the right side of a window.

Window Border

The window border identifies the edge of the window. In most windows, it can be used to change the size of a window. The window corner is used to resize a window on two sides at the same time.

Lesson 5: Manipulating Windows

When you work with windows, you need to know how to arrange them. You can shrink the window into an icon or enlarge the window to fill the desktop. You can stack windows together or give them each an equal slice of the desktop.

Maximizing a Window

Maximize
To increase the size of a window so that it fills the entire screen.

You can *maximize* a window so that it fills the desktop. Maximizing a window gives you more space to work in. To maximize a window, click the Maximize button on the title bar.

Minimizing a Window

Minimize
To reduce a window to an icon.

When you *minimize* a window, it shrinks the window to an icon on the taskbar. Even though you can't see the window anymore, the application stays loaded in the computer's memory. To minimize a window, click the Minimize button on the title bar.

Restoring a Window

When a window is maximized, the Maximize button changes into a Restore button. Clicking the Restore button restores the window back to the original size and position before the window was maximized.

Closing a Window

When you are finished working in a window, you can close the window by clicking the Close button. Closing an application window exits the program, removing it from memory. When you click the Close button, the window (on the desktop) and the window button (on the taskbar) disappear.

Arranging Windows

Changing the size and position of a window enables you to see more than one application window, which makes copying and pasting data between programs much easier. You can also move a window to any location on the desktop. By moving application windows, you can arrange your work on the Windows desktop just as you arrange papers on your desk.

Tile
To arrange open windows on the desktop so that they do not overlap.

Cascade
To arrange open windows on the desktop so that they overlap, with only the title bar of each window (behind the top window) is displayed.

Use one of the following options to arrange windows:

- Right-click the taskbar, and choose Tile **H**orizontally.
- Right-click the taskbar, and choose Tile **V**ertically. See Figure A.5 for an example.
- Right-click the taskbar, and choose **C**ascade. See Figure A.6 for an example.
- Click and drag the window's title bar to move the window around on the desktop.
- Click and drag a window border (or corner) to increase or decrease the size of the window.

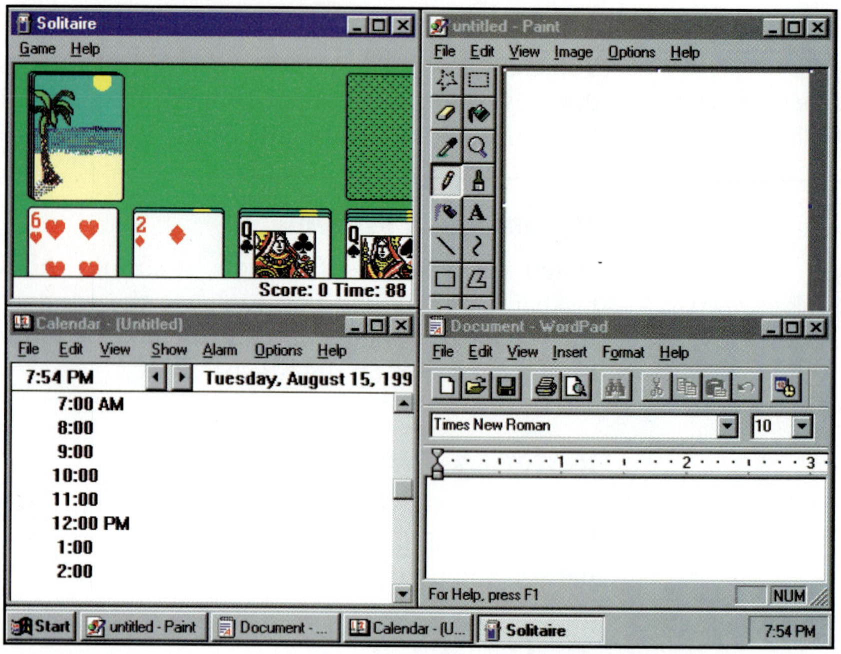

Figure A.5
The windows are tiled vertically across the desktop.

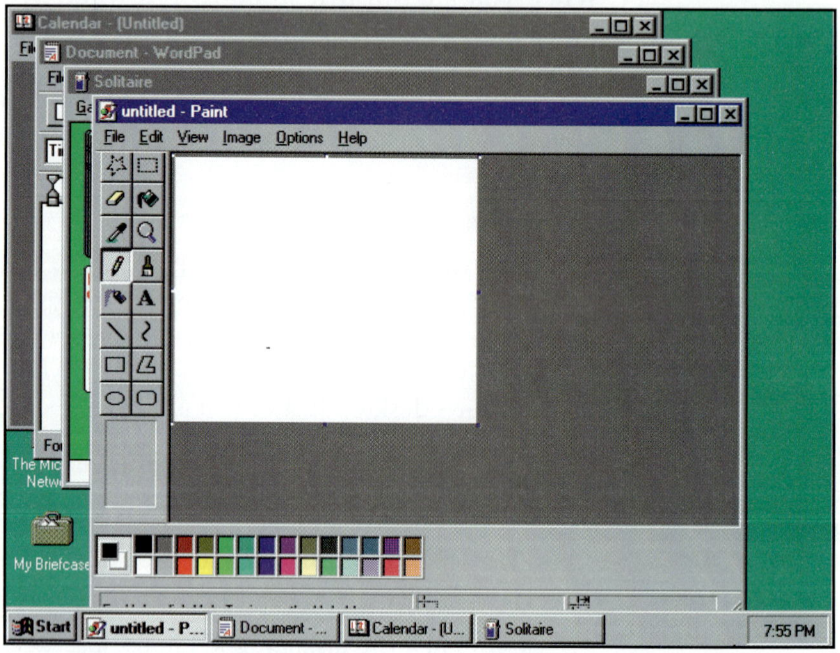

Figure A.6
The windows are cascaded on the desktop.

Lesson 6: Exiting the Windows Program

In Windows 95, you use the Shut Down command to exit the Windows program. You should always use this command, which closes all open applications and files, before you turn off the computer. If you haven't saved your work in an application when you choose this command, you'll be prompted to save your changes before Windows shuts down.

To Exit Windows

1. Click the Start button on the taskbar.
2. Choose Sh**u**t Down.
3. Choose **S**hut down the computer.
4. Choose **Y**es.

Windows displays a message asking you to wait while the computer is shutting down. When this process is complete, a message appears telling you that you can safely turn off your computer now.

INDEX

D

E

F

G–H

I–J

K–L

M

N

O

P

Q–R

S

W–Z